Three Little Girls

Murder in Rochester, New York

ALSO BY JUANITA TISCHENDORF

Circle of Seven
Fiction – Thriller

Love Will Find A Way
Fiction – Romance

Playground In My Mind
Fiction - Thriller/Suspense

All The Missing Pieces
Fiction – Thriller/Suspense

Body Of Evidence
Fiction - Thriller/Suspense

Don't Look Back
Fiction – Thriller/Suspense

The Selfie
Nonfiction – How To

Mastering Childhood To Womanhood
Five book series
Nonfiction – How To

Over My Head
Nonfiction - Biography

An Unfair Advantage
Nonfiction – Biography

The Madman The Marathoner
Nonfiction – Biography

Three Little Girls

Juanita Tischendorf

Copyright Page

First Edition

Library of Congress Cataloguing-in-Publication Data has been applied for.

ISBN: 978-1-928613-90-9 Three Little Girls (Hardcover)
ISBN: 978-1-928613-91-6 Three Little Girls (Paperback)
ISBN: 978-1-928613-99-2 Three Little Girls (eBook)

DEDICATION

This book is dedicated to the families of children who have been murdered. Losing a child is something we never get over, no matter how old or how young the child may be. My son was murdered in 2010 and he was an adult, living on his own. Yet still 10 years later I miss him and wish I had been able to at least say goodbye. For me it was different. His murderer was captured and is now in prison serving her sentence. I can't imagine the pain of knowing the murderer was still scot free. My heart and soul go out to you.

Preface

You can feel the chill at the mention of Upstate New York and can't help but wonder why anyone would want to live there. It must be bleak to live in a place like Rochester, New York, you say, wondering how one deals with facing bitter cold wintry days, as you view the stark grayness of the sky and lake.

Only it's not all bad. This unknown 'flour city' soon found its niche, so that the mention of 'New York' would no longer mean only New York City and the Burbs.

Rochester could even compete with Albany and Buffalo as a city with big-city culture and small-city charm, nestled on the Genesee River, a few miles south of Lake Ontario. In its early days, Rochester banked on success when the Erie Canal was built and routed through Rochester, creating America's first boomtown. But that was then, and this is now.

Rochester knew how to keep itself in the cultural forefront, as it became a center for social progressivism, attracting history-making individuals to settle in the area, such as Frederick Douglass who lived on Alexander Street and is buried in Rochester's historic Mount Hope Cemetery. The suffragist Susan B. Anthony settled on Madison Street in downtown Rochester, which was also the site of her famous arrest for voting in 1872. She too is buried in Mount Hope Cemetery.

Many people saw beyond the cold and misery and settled here, putting Rochester into the limelight as they reached success. With the financial backing of Rochester businessman Henry Strong, George Eastman formed the Eastman Dry Plate Company which would become the

Eastman Kodak Company. Not far from his heels, John Jacob Bausch and Henry Lomb opened a retail optical shop in Rochester which would later become The Bausch and Lomb Company.

The boom in industry continued to direct the eyes of the world toward Rochester. Founded by Chester Carlson, who had the foresight to visualize photographic imaging, the Haloid Photographic company eventually grew to become Xerox Corporation.

It was by bits and pieces that Rochester made its uphill climb to fame. As it became financially a great place to do business, dealing with fluffy white snow, blizzards, and cold damp drizzle became unimportant.

However, as the saying goes, 'be careful what you wish for.' In the following years, Rochester would also experience the underbelly of success. Problems began with widespread crime rings and the notorious mobster, Salvatore "Sammy G" Gingello. He was killed, and four decades later his murderer was still at large. However, the unsolved murder of one gangster would be over-shadowed when a number of serial killers grew up in Rochester or were drawn to live there as adults.

Francis Tumblety, suspected by many to be the notorious Jack the Ripper, was raised in Rochester and was buried in Holy Sepulchre Cemetery. Joel Rifkin, a serial killer who attended SUNY Brockport, would murder as many as seventeen women. Arthur Shawcross, also known as the Genesee River Killer, found his way to Rochester. Joseph Naso, a former photographer who had been accused of several similar, once lived in Rochester, and Kenneth Bianchi, known to most as 'The Hillside Strangler,' grew up there.

Murder, whether of one person or many, is horrific, but a serial killer who commits a series of murders, often with no apparent motive, is beyond horrendous.

People were dying, and the worst of it was not knowing for a long time who committed the crimes.

When it comes to serial killers, the criminal becomes notorious and the victims are often forgotten. Yet to their family and friends, the pain focuses on the victim, and when the killer is not found, that pain festers and grows.

One of the unsolved serial crimes that will never be forgotten was the murder of three victims: Carmen Colón, ten, Wanda Walkowicz, eleven, and Michelle Maenza, also eleven. The murders started in 1971 and ended in 1973. All the girls were abducted during the day, sexually assaulted, strangled, and dumped outside the city of Rochester. Carmen Colón was found in Riga/Chili, Wanda Walkowicz in Webster, and Michelle Maenza in Macedon, Wayne County.

This is their story.

CARMEN COLÓN

Chapter 1

Wednesday, February 1, 1961, emerged cold and dreary with clouds covering the arrival of dawn and the temperature at eight degrees. If she had a choice, Guillermina would have waited for a better day in Rochester to be driven to the hospital, but what she wanted didn't matter now. Listening to the car radio as she looked out the window, she couldn't help thinking about her homeland. While the rest of the northern hemisphere is bundling up, February in Puerto Rico is warm and usually sunny. Basically, you can expect almost perfect weather there. Although the weather is warm, it can get humid on the island, and rain isn't uncommon, but right now Guillermina would welcome the warm rain with open arms.

Her mind continued to wander. Right now, in Puerto Rico, she would be rushing to get ready for school instead of leaving a chilly apartment to climb into a freezing cold car. She wouldn't complain now at how hard it was in school. No, compared with what she was going through it had been heaven. All she had to worry about then was her grades, which she managed to do well at, especially the classes such as English that meant the most to her. She had to study hard in English, since all classes were taught in that language, apart from Spanish class, foreign language classes and Puerto Rican history class.

But she had been stupid and gullible and look where that had landed her at fourteen years old.

In her condition, everything was an effort and she used most of her energy just getting into her heavy fleece winter coat that struggled to cover her growing belly. She had been petite and beautiful. She had possessed a nice body and a captivating smile...

Now, when he had to help her just to put on her boots, Justiniano looked at her differently. It was not fun, not fun at all. A tear rolled down her cheek as she thought about her situation. All she wanted was for people to like her, nothing more. But she had learned, much too early, that in some cases the only way to get someone to like you was to give them something in return.

"Come on Girl, stop daydreaming."

Guillermina wiped the tears from her face and put on her gloves. "Don't yell at me. I'm going as fast as I can."

Soon she was walking across the threshold, holding on tightly to the wall until she could reach the railing. With a firm grasp she slowly descended the steps, careful not to slip. She paused as a contraction took control of her body. It was like a wave as it began in her abdomen, moved to her back, and built pressure in her pelvis. It took her breath away, and at that moment the idea of giving birth brought on a sense of panic, making the pain worse. She tried to breathe deeply and slowly, waiting for it to abate before taking her next step.

"Come on. It's snowing out here. Get in the car!"

Guillermina ignored him as she stretched up, trying to relieve the dull ache in her back. The only thing that kept her going was that soon it would be over. Soon she would be herself again. With that thought, she mastered the balance of the steps and slowly dragged her feet along the snow-covered sidewalk as she testily made her way to the car door. Under her breath she whispered, "Asshole!"

Justiniano impatiently waited for her to get to the car. As soon as she was there, he opened the passenger door, holding back an urge to push her in.

"Woman, get a move on or you will drop the baby right here."

"Shut up, shut up!"

Guillermina turned her body backwards to the door, then, grabbing the roof of the car, she slowly lowered her body down to the seat. There she sat getting her breath, before finally swinging her legs into the car.

She had barely put her boot-clad feet on the floor when the door slammed shut.

The pain came again, floating through her until she wanted to scream out, but knowing that wouldn't help at all, she breathed hard, counting as she did and praying that this would soon be over.

She looked over at Justiniano, frowning as he drove cautiously down the street. If the circumstances had been different, she would have been happy, but she was not. She was only fourteen years old, and her biggest worries should be doing homework and washing dishes, not how to behave when she had a contraction.

"We're here," Justiniano said triumphantly. Instead of parking the car, he pulled up at the emergency entrance. After turning off the engine, he climbed out of the car. Guillermina concentrated on his bulk from the heavy winter coat as he hurried up to the glass doors as they automatically swung open. She could see him standing stiffly in the entranceway, but didn't hear his voice as he made the announcement, "My wife is having a baby."

Guillermina saw the animated motion as attendants rushed about, locating a wheelchair and pushing it through the entrance. Justiniano was right behind them, watching as they helped Guillermina out of the car and asked her questions about her contractions and how often they were coming. Frightened, Guillermina responded as best she could before another contraction took her breath away.

In minutes she was out of the car and helped into a wheelchair. Two attendants held onto the chair as they wheeled Gullermina into the welcome warmth.

"Sir?" Someone behind the reception desk called out. "I need you to fill out some information for us."

Justiniano looked over at them and then back at the wheelchair hurrying up the hallway. "Can it wait?"

"She'll be fine. Everything will be fine."

Justiniano shrugged his shoulders and walked slowly to the reception desk. A form was placed in front of him and he was handed a pen. Realizing that he spoke little English, the receptionist gave instructions in Spanish and helped him write the information in the proper location on the form. When asked, Justiniano pulled out his ID and his Medicaid card and passed them over the desk. Then he waited, walking toward the hall and peeking down it. "Okay, Mr. Colón. Everything is in order. Here's your license and insurance card back."

"Where did they take my wife?"

"She's in the labor room. You can have a seat in the waiting area, and someone will come for you."

Hesitantly, not sure exactly what to do, Justiniano stood looking around him.

"Mr. Colón have a seat. It will be just a moment. Someone is already on their way to get you."

Justiniano nodded, and started to sit, but before his butt reached the seat, he heard his name and was ushered to the elevators. Soon he was on his way up to the fourth floor where they stopped, and he was taken to the waiting area.

Justiniano was nervously pacing, unsure of what to do. He regretted how he had yelled at Guillermina and rushed her, but he had been scared that they wouldn't make it to the hospital in time. Now he wished he had a chance to explain himself to her. Finally, he found something to read and sat down. He stared blankly at the pictures in the magazine, his mind elsewhere. He was proud of himself. It had gone smoothly, and he was now able to relax. He didn't have long to wait before he heard his name called and was told they had taken his wife into the delivery room.

He gave the nurse a half smile and said, "Thank you." Justiniano wondered if he had time to get a cup of coffee. He stood, looked around the room and spied a coffee machine. He went over and put his coins in the slot, then watched as the cup came down and settled snugly on the platform before the brown liquid began to stream out, filling the cup. He was fascinated, wondering how the cup seemed to always settle itself properly on the base, then how the coffee knew when to stop before the cup overflowed. When the stream of coffee ceased, he leaned over and removed the cup, taking a sip as he walked back to his seat. Once he sat back down reality hit him.

This was all going too fast. He had a wife, and he had Guillermina. That started memories rushing to the surface.

He could potentially develop fantasies or feelings of lust towards any woman who crossed his path. That was his nature. However, in this case, he had developed a sexual fantasy about his sister-in-law. He had tried to nip that fantasy in the bud as that could have serious negative consequences, but he could not. They were living in Puerto Rico where he and Guillermina were born and raised, making them rightfully US citizens. He had been happy there and had married Guillermina's older sister. All was right with the world until Guillermina came to live with them. At first, he tried to ignore her, but then he couldn't, and they began a sexual relationship. Fool that he was, he never expected that she would get pregnant. She was but a little kid. But, just his luck, she did. What made it worse was that he was a married 32-year-old man, with his wife and his wife's fourteen-year-old sister, both pregnant at the same time.

It wasn't long before he was forced to decide. There was no way the two women could remain in Puerto Rico together, so he gathered up this fourteen-year-old child, left his wife and hightailed it to Rochester, New York, a place where there were relatives and good jobs.

"Sir? Mr. Colón," a voice interrupted his thoughts.

"Yes," he said groggily.

"Come with me. Your wife is being settled in her room. I can take you to see your new baby girl."

In a daze, Justiniano followed the man in the white coat who led him down the hallway and stopped. Justiniano looked through the massive window facing out to the hospital corridor. Here he could peer into a newborn nursery with rows of bassinets holding sleeping and some crying, tiny babies. He heard his companion say, "This is where your newborn baby girl will be cared for when she is apart from her mother."

Justiniano scanned the bassinets until he saw the sign that read, "Baby Colón." He was speechless. Several minutes passed before the man walked him down the hall and into a room. There was Guillermina, propped up on pillows, her face flushed, looking as if she had just finished running in a race.

8

"I'll leave you two," the man said.

"Ah, Guillermina, are you all right?"

"Did you see her? She's perfect. I'm naming her Carmen, Carmen Colón."

He tried to smile, but it was hard. Justiniano was like most people who don't see themselves as poor until the rug is pulled out from under them. As he looked at Guillermina and his baby girl, he felt a lurch in his stomach. It was like standing on a swing, holding on tightly so he wouldn't fall. He barely made enough for the two of them to survive, and now there was this baby and another in Puerto Rico. He experienced a head-spinning fear as he realized that the expense of having a baby might put them over the edge. He didn't know what to say to her smiling face.

"So, when can you get out of here?"

It didn't matter. Guillermina didn't know what to say either, as she kept smoothing the blanket, glad she could see her feet again. She didn't want to think past this moment. She didn't want to think about taking home a baby whose care she would be responsible for. She barely knew how to take care of herself, let alone a helpless baby.

Carmen Colón arrived on Wednesday, February 1, 1961, into a world that was unprepared for her. At the moment of Carmen's birth, her mother, Guillermina, was no longer simply a 14-year-old girl; she was a mother. Guillermina's life had changed drastically. She would be a carefree child no more. She now had grown-up responsibilities to face, and she wasn't ready. Playing house with Justiniano was one thing, but being a mother was a whole different world.

She had always been tiny, so soon she had her figure back, and with that came her energy. She now felt like her old self as she got into the swing of taking care of baby Carmen. But as much as she tried, she did not feel at home anymore. She missed Puerto Rico and her family there.

She was lonely as she stared out the window at the snow, wishing she could feel the sun on her face instead of the cold snowflakes falling everywhere. The fact that she couldn't speak English didn't help either. There were many different nationalities in the neighborhood, but she didn't know who she could trust, so she just minded her own business.

She could tell that Justiniano wasn't happy either, so it didn't surprise her much when he told her they were moving back to Puerto Rico. She was so happy that she didn't care that she would have to face her sister. She was sure her sister would forgive her. After all, Guillermina was just a kid, and if her sister was to be mad at anyone, her anger should be directed at her husband, Justiniano. So Guillermina eagerly packed up her things and those of baby Carmen. Just days after his announcement, Justiniano came home with their plane tickets and hurried Guillermina along with the preparations. Soon they climbed into his raggedy car with baby Carmen, not yet a year old, and headed for the airport.

Not even the crying of her baby girl could bring Guillermina down. She was going home, back to her hometown of Guayama, Puerto Rico

Guayama is quite the opposite of Rochester, being just a little inland off Puerto Rico's southern coastline, but it is a beautiful city. Guillermina remembered her mother telling her that Guayama was known as "La Ciudad Bruja" (witch city) or "Pueblo de los Brujos" (city of witches), and the region around Guayama still honors African legends of sorcery and witchcraft. That didn't scare Guillermina. She loved seeing the Caribbean sea and the mountains. She loved the forests and all the different types of birds that she could spy on any given day. Sure, the people were poor, but she understood poverty. The difference there was that people were friendly and accepted the fact they were poor. Most of all they spoke Spanish.

Carmen was not even a year old the day they left Rochester, and she was miserable during the four-hour flight, but nothing could dampen the new mother's spirits. Guillermina was looking forward to having help with taking care of her baby girl. She even imagined she would have time to do things for herself while someone else cared for baby Carmen.

The minds of the young are optimistic, so they are often surprised by reality. This was the case for Guillermina. Once they were back in Guayama, she saw less of Justiniano, and no one stepped up to give her a hand. She could feel the anger that her sister held against her, and that made it hard to ask for any help.

The only things that didn't disappoint were the weather and the ease of communicating with the people around her. She was adjusting, and eventually the thought that she was missing out on her childhood evaporated. She faced her responsibilities, and, as best she could, she made a home and took care of baby Carmen.

Carmen, being just a baby, saw none of the struggles of her mother. For Carmen, life in Puerto Rico was good. With the early years, especially the first three years of life, being the time when everything a child sees, touches, tastes, smells or hears shapes her brain for thinking, feeling, moving and learning, Carmen became embedded in the culture and the language. And she was loved.

As the years had marched by, the fourteen-year-old girl who had arrived in Guayama had grown up. It was a journey of twists and turns, but Guillermina had mastered her time well. Through the good and bad, the happy and sad, Guillermina continued to move forward, accepting the life she had started for herself at such an early age. She had been a wide-eyed child, struggling to get her own way, and now she knew that there were those who showed interest in her, and even some who tried to support her, but at the end of the day, nobody cared about her dream as much as she did. It was time she figured out what she wanted to do with the rest of her life.

It was clear to her now that life for her and Carmen was not better in Puerto Rico. The island is distinguished by its poverty and joblessness, which are far worse than in any of the 50 states.

Guillermina couldn't make a decent living and what she was used to enjoying in Rochester was not part of her life here. She was struggling as she tried to care of herself and baby Carmen, and she knew she had to make a change.

Chapter 2

The family in Guayama was not blind to her struggle and could see how she suffered, but the way they offered to help was not something that Guillermina could accept.

Felix and Candida, Justiniano's parents, and the grandparents of Carmen, suggested that it would be easier if they took Carmen and raised her. Guillermina didn't even have to give it a thought as she told them, "No!" Carmen was her child, and she was not going to give her up to anybody. The dark-haired little imp, with her broad smile, had won her mother's heart.

After taking her and baby Carmen back to Guayama, Justiniano had soon left her. He didn't provide her support, and she struggled bravely to take care of herself and baby Carmen. However, not having a high school education and with little skill, she could see no light at the end of the tunnel. Yet, stubbornly she would not give up Carmen.

A solution occurred when Felix and Candida announced they were moving to Rochester and asked if she wanted to come with them. Guillermina was leery at first, thinking this might be a trick to take Carmen from her. She knew that they loved Carmen and had her best interests at heart, but be it selfish or not, she laid claim to her daughter.

"I don't know," she responded.

Knowing the reason for her hesitation, Candida replied in Spanish.

"Guillermina, we would like you to come with us. We are not asking you to give Carmen to us, but we can help you. There is nothing here for you."

They were right. She was eighteen years old. She could get a good job in Rochester and a good place to live, and she believed Felix and Candida were willing to help her with no strings attached. "Okay, yes," she said as she hugged them. "Yes."

It didn't take long to pack up their things as she didn't have much more than she had before. Carmen was now four years old, and besides their scant wardrobes, there was little else.

On that day, Guillermina smiled as she made her way over to Felix and Candida's home. She was still smiling as they helped her get herself and little Carmen into the car before settling in themselves. Guillermina took one last look at her homeland and thought she was as happy to leave as she had been to return almost four years earlier. Baby Carmen would have a chance at a better life, and that made Guillermina happy.

And so, the family climbed into the car and drove to the Luis Muñoz Marín International Airport, thirty-two miles away. When they arrived, they went through the lines and had little time to spare before climbing on board the plane. For Carmen, just being on a plane was an adventure, since she was only an infant when she flew last and living so far from the airports on the island, she hadn't seen a plane up close. She asked all kinds of questions as they boarded, entertaining the people around them.

Once on board, Guillermina gave Carmen a toy to play with to keep her occupied during the six-hour flight. She hoped Carmen would get tired and fall asleep. That hope came true. Guillermina peered out the window at the Caribbean Sea below. It was so blue, and at some points the reflection of the sun on the water made her eyes blur. When she looked again, she saw the island of Cuba below, floating in the sea, until finally the plane was over Florida where the view from the window changed dramatically. Guillermina took it all in, feeling increasingly confident that her life was changing for the better.

Having her roots in Puerto Rico, Guillermina spoke Spanish fluently; it had always been the language spoken in the household. Guillermina hadn't learned much English when she had lived in Rochester, because she had spent her time at home, so she would not be much help to the grandparents who were settling here for the first time. They would be living in Rochester where the language was predominantly English, but in the neighborhood, there were several families who spoke Spanish.

It wasn't easy, but they managed, with Guillermina stumbling through communications to help herself and the grandparents, Felix and Candida. The first step was to file for public assistance, and once that was handled, it was on to setting up residence. The grandparents found a place at 746 Brown Street, and Guillermina set up residence nearby at 72 Romeyn Street in Rochester, New York.

With the housing and financial assistance in place, Guillermina gave a sigh of relief. They were settled in by the time Miguel Colón, Justiniano's nephew, began coming around. Guillermina had met Miguel and liked him. He was much closer in age to her than Justiniano, and she welcomed his attention. When he asked if he could move in, Guillermina said yes.

In the beginning Carmen lived with her mother and Miguel in the home located in the Charles house settlement area in northwest Rochester. The house was a two-story structure with white siding and brown trim around large windows. It was much larger than the place they had stayed in Puerto Rico, but the neighborhood wasn't much better.

That was fine with Guillermina. She knew how to handle herself, and she would teach Carmen how to be careful too.

Admittedly, Guillermina fit into the environment of this inner-city neighborhood. Most people in the area were on welfare, struggling to make ends meet, and there were many families with language barriers like hers. She recognized that desire to have the basic essentials could lead to robberies, burglaries and other crimes, so she took extra precautions to protect herself and Carmen. Who knew how far a person would go to provide for their family? They might even go as far as to commit a violent act to strike back at misfortune, and not necessarily at the right person.

Guillermina was still young enough that she could look on the bright side. Financially she was lucky to be living here. The apartment was affordable and spacious with a little over 1600 sq. ft of living space, quite adequate for a family of three.

Guillermina didn't have time for romantic notions, but having Miguel move in offered another layer of protection for the family. She had met him in Puerto Rico but didn't like him then. When she came to Rochester, he came too. She hoped he would also help her with the expenses, and no one passed judgment on her decision.

So it was that little Carmen lived in an atmosphere of handicaps and deprivations from the start of her life, so she knew no differently.

Chapter 3

Carmen came to the US as a four-year-old Spanish-speaking Puerto Rican who had been born in Rochester, New York. She came with her mother and her grandparents on her father's side. The year was 1965. Her father, Justiniano, remained in Puerto Rico and wasn't involved with them, while her mother, Guillermina, struggled to assimilate to the culture and the climate.

Life had been simple before then. Carmen was active and energetic. She moved at a fast and frenetic pace, running and jumping more than she walked. She was well coordinated and laughed and played all day. But once they were back in Rochester and settled, Carmen was enrolled in school, and when school began, she experienced her first slam against the language barrier. At the John Williams School No. 5, she attended, there was a class for children whose native language was not English, but there were not enough staff to go around.

This put Carmen at a disadvantage from the start, plus the fact that she lived in a household of Spanish speaking people. Her mother's inability to speak English added to her frustration, and during her entire adolescence Carmen was her mother's translator. She actually didn't know any more English than her mother, but Guillermina figured that, because Carmen was young, she could learn the language faster.

Nevertheless, Carmen somehow managed to remain a happy child who had a smile for everyone. Even though her mother wanted to live in Rochester, she gave up trying to master the English language, which put Carmen in a household that spoke only Spanish. She was surrounded by

Spanish-speaking relatives as well as friends in the neighborhood who also spoke Spanish. Her grandparents, the Colóns, did not know any English, and she spent a lot of time with them.

Thus, it was not surprising that from the start Carmen was placed in special education classes at the John Williams School No. 5 which housed the Pre-K through Grade 8 classes. But as with countless other students who spoke Spanish as a first language, she was one among many, and the school was unable to increase its resources to accommodate them. As she struggled, seeing her diligence toward learning, the school staff figured she would eventually be able to master the English language.

As upsetting as this could be, Carmen was not one to let life bring her down, even though she struggled to learn. Carmen managed to look at the bright side. Because her playmates were her cousins, and sometimes neighbor kids who also spoke Spanish, her lack of good English wasn't a barrier. Besides, it was important to Carmen to fit in with family and neighborhood friends.

As the years progressed, Carmen grew into a very pretty little girl. She wore her thick brown hair long, with bangs covering her forehead. Her smile was contagious as it lit up her entire face, and Carmen smiled often.

Through it all, Carmen was happy and well adjusted, never complaining about school, where she still struggled to keep up with her classmates. Not fully grasping the English language put her behind in her other schoolwork, since it required a good grasp of the English language. If she had learned English along with Spanish as a child, it would have been easier for her now. But that hadn't happened, so now, with those around her speaking only Spanish, she was at a loss to keep up with her classmates.

It was a problem, but now she had something more going for her. She knew that people thought she was educationally challenged, but they liked her. She was the girl with the effervescent smile and was constantly told how pretty she was. Hearing this gave her confidence and boosted her ego.

From a family of three, the Colón household was growing. After returning to Rochester, Carmen's mother gave birth to another girl and named her Maria. Then in 1970 her mother had a baby boy and named him Luz. After the birth of their son, Miguel and Guillermina married.

With three children, the walls seemed to close in, and space was at a premium. Carmen loved her half-sister and brother, but she liked her own space. Consequently, Carmen began spending more time at her grandparents' home.

PaPa Felix Colón and her Mama Candida lived at 746 Brown Street, just a short distance from Guillermina, and they enjoyed having Carmen around. During one of her many visits, they took her to a room, saying that since she spent so much time there, she could decorate the room and make it her own.

This made her happy. She would have a room of her own, and it would be just as she wanted it to be. So Carmen spent her time putting her treasures in her room, which for most little girls would be dolls and things, but for Carmen it meant displaying her many religious items on her walls and any flat surface she could find.

Carmen started out as a cradle Catholic, but at a very young age she chose to make this faith her own. She loved the Catholic faith for many reasons, but mostly because the Catholic Church recognized saints in heaven who could pray for her. That she could appeal to saints as well as to God was the reason, she had so many religious objects in her room. Carmen was happy with the neighborhood church because it offered masses in Spanish as well as in English.

Eventually, Carmen found it more inviting to be at her grandparents' home and asked her mother if she could move in with them. Guillermina's first instinct was to tell Carmen, no, but the more she thought about it, the better the idea seemed. Carmen was ten years old, a very pretty and friendly girl. She was also naive and required more supervision than her mother could spare, as her hands were full with the two younger siblings. Guillermina finally gave her approval to the move.

Carmen packed up her belongings and soon was settled in at her grandparents' house, where she became the center of attention. She did not miss the noise at home or companionship since she had relatives right next door to her grandparents. As for her mother, she could see her often, as she was only a ten-minute walk away from home.

Carmen was happy. Guillermina was happy too, but if she had known that baby Carmen, her firstborn, would only be a part of her life for ten years, would she have felt differently?

Chapter 4

A change came over Carmen when she turned ten. She was still sweet and considerate, but she wanted to be given more freedom. This was a problem for those around her since she still remained child-like, both physically and emotionally.

But, being ten years old is all about change. It is a period of transition that can offer challenges and delights as a child starts to embrace the approach of adolescence. Carmen began questioning everything, especially why her mother moved back to Rochester. When she asked, her mother would say it was because she wanted to be near the grandparents. That response worked for a while; it even seemed logical when she thought of the other relatives who had also moved to Rochester.

But later Carmen had problems accepting this, since her father had left her mother when Guillermina left Puerto Rico. Carmen thought, just maybe, her father would live with them again if they returned to Puerto Rico. When she was younger, his absence didn't faze her, but now it did, because she was able to understand much more about life, what was accepted and what wasn't. Her faith taught her about mortal sins, which must be grave, committed in full knowledge of the sinful action, and committed with deliberate and complete consent.

Carmen saw herself as grown up, but her age and the fact that she was only four feet tall and weighed around sixty-five pounds affirmed otherwise. Still, she wanted more freedom. This put her at odds with not only her grandparents, but her mother as well. She listened as other children her age said they were able to go to the store by themselves or to their friends' homes to play. She wanted that freedom.

Not one to disobey, Carmen needed their approval. On many occasions she would be invited to parties or to join the other kids on their way to the store or the playground, but unless her grandparents or her mother could accompany her, she was not allowed to go. This frustrated Carmen. She had worked hard to gain friends and 'fit in' and saw this as an affront against her. As it was, because of her language problem, Carmen had to work hard on friendships while still facing a lot of peer pressure.

Over and over Carmen would tell her grandparents that she understood the challenges that she could face in the neighborhood, but unless they allowed her more freedom, she would never be able to take care of herself. She continued the pressure on her mother and her grandparents until they relented, knowing that they wouldn't always be around to protect her, so she did need to know how to take care of herself.

Eventually Carmen wore them down, a little. It may have been that they were tired of the constant arguing, more so than recognizing any ability to take care of herself, but the reason why didn't matter as far as Carmen was concerned.

On several occasions, Carmen could be seen walking to Morrell's Cigar Store on Brown Street where she usually made the trip to purchase penny candy. She knew, but didn't let it bother her, that when she went on these outings, her grandparents kept a watchful eye on her. Sometimes it was from the front porch, other times it was by following her at a distance.

Carmen was smart enough to know it wasn't that her family didn't trust her. Their reluctance to allow her to walk down the streets alone or to visit strange households, had to do with the fact that the neighborhood wasn't safe.

It was hard for Guillermina too since she was dealing with a 'tween for the first time, and she, at twenty-four, was barely older than her daughter. In addition, she had two other babies to deal with, which left little attention for the expectations of Carmen. When she did give thought to it, it was frightening. She had few friends she could turn to, so each time Carmen asked if she could do something new, her mother wondered if it was one of the ways she should help her achieve independence, or if it was one of the ways she would put her child in danger. All she was sure of was that she didn't want to smother her.

In some ways it felt good to be ten years old, but in other ways it was scary, because there was a lot more of importance to Carmen than before, and a lot that she found disturbing. Her mother would tell her in Spanish not to worry what other people said and to just be herself. She appreciated the advice but felt a little resentment as she heard these words in Spanish. Heck, most of her problems stemmed from not getting enough English spoken around her.

Carmen sat on her bed thinking and wondering. She stood up and stared at herself in the mirror. She looked smart and capable, and she was. Hadn't she learned how to clean her room by herself and get herself ready for school? She sat back down and smiled. Well, there had been that time when she had a massive knot in her hair, and she had to call for help. But most times she could take care of herself.

Again, she stood, this time to walk over to her dresser where she picked up the baby Jesus from his crib. She smiled lovingly at the image and placed it gently back in its cradle. She took her now empty hand and began counting with her fingers as she said out loud, "I can fix my own breakfast. I can pick out my own clothes. I can use a knife and scissors without cutting myself. Ah, that is unless someone calls my attention away from what I am doing. I know how to call for help, cross streets with caution and be aware of strangers…"

At that point her voice trailed off as she frowned. If there was one thing that was hard for her, it was trying not to be too friendly. She liked talking to people, all people, no matter their age. Her frown grew deeper. "I know, Jesus, I know. I need to stop being so friendly with strangers, but people are only strangers until we speak to them. Isn't that right?"

So, as far as her mother was concerned, she was to be herself, but there was another problem with being told to be herself. That was she wasn't sure who she was. She was ten years old and still not sure of what she liked or didn't like, because most of the time a grown-up made those choices for her. She had moments when her eyes danced happily because she figured out something on her own, but that was becoming less often now.

She liked that feeling of success and tried to do everything in her power to feel that way, but there were a lot of new expectations and a lot of new limitations.

Carmen frowned, feeling less capable, and that was her uneasy state when she was brought out of her reverie by her grandmother calling her.

"Guisa, su madre viene por encima de." She always called her Guisa. For some time now Carmen had been trying to teach her grandparents English by answering their questions with English. She thought it was smart of her to think of doing it this way. She would put this into practice when they said or asked her something to which they already knew the answer. This was one of those times, so she replied, "Yes, I know mother is coming over."

The first time she did it, her grandmother got a quizzical expression on her face, forcing Carmen to reply

"Sí, sé que mamá viene." She would then repeat it again in English, "Yes, I know mother is coming over."

That effort continued for a while, and it also helped Carmen with her own English. Eventually there were several common retorts that her grandmother was able to translate on her own. In fact, it became a game that they both enjoyed.

Chapter 5

It was November and getting colder outdoors, but that didn't stop Carmen from wanting to go outside. She was used to the cold now and she liked the snow. Rochester's first snowfall of winter usually arrives in November, although a rare snowstorm can show up in October. For about two-thirds of winter days, Rochester has at least an inch of snow on the ground, which was the case then. The snow begins to pile up during January and February, but the last snowfall typically happens in April.

There was a chill in the air, so Carmen put on her long red wool coat, mittens, her knit hat and boots before going out to play. Once outside, she stood on the porch looking out at the yard. It had snowed a little and there still remained snow on the lawn, not quite enough, but she didn't care as she lay down and made a snow angel. When she got up, she admired what she had done. It never snowed in Puerto Rico, and Carmen had to admit she would miss being subjected to snow. The cold, well that was another thing.

Inside, her grandmother and her mother, Guillermina, were busy planning Thanksgiving dinner. It would take them time to hunt down the all-American ingredients for the family's traditional Thanksgiving recipes. Instead of the traditional roasted, stuffed turkey, they would have stuffed fish. It would be sea bass, hake, bream or cod, which most of the stores in the neighborhood would carry. She heard the women talking about hoping to find a good sea bass that they could stuff with lemon, shrimp and leeks,

Just like the American Thanksgiving turkey stuffing she heard some of her peers talking about, the Spanish version was made from day-old bread ripped into small pieces and fried in pork fat and paprika-spiced chorizo sausage. It was one of her favorite parts of the meal.

There would be fresh flat Spanish green beans with plenty of garlic and olive oil, and potatoes with slices of garlic, sweet poached onions and, of course, plenty of olive oil and mojo picón packed with smoky peppers. Carmen could take or leave that spicy red sauce, but her mother would always say she would grow to love it.

Carmen loved Thanksgiving, especially the meal. She couldn't wait until she was old enough to join the adults as they sipped warm, spiced sangria. And there were the desserts. Everyone would be so full that dessert would be held off until later. When it was finally served, no one would turn down a piece of pumpkin flan with whipped cream, and ice cream for those who wanted it.

It was a big day for them. There were so many items to prepare, and so many ingredients needed, that she understood why they started planning the meal a week ahead of time.

Carmen had another reason for liking the celebration. The work would keep them busy and therefore less attention would be on her. There was also the possibility that she would be needed to go to the store to get some of the grocery items.

On Tuesday, November 16, 1971, Thanksgiving recess was a week away and Carmen couldn't wait. She had so much going on in her life, and she wasn't able to share it all with family or friends. She tried to be happy and smile all the time, but there were demons in the shadows when she went to bed. That was another reason Carmen had chosen so many religious icons to decorate her room at her grandparents'. She spent a lot of time praying, her crucifix clutched tightly in her hand, asking to have a good sleep. Sometimes it worked, but lots of times the night terrors would return, waking everyone in the house.

She couldn't remember when or how long she had night terrors, but she wished they would stop. When she moved into her room at her grandparents' house, she prayed for them to stop but they didn't, and she had them just as frequently as before.

In the beginning, her grandparents would hear her and come to her bedroom to find that she had fallen out of bed. They would stay a while and tuck her in. She had liked that very much. Only that attention stopped. As usual, Carmen understood why they had stopped coming to soothe her night terrors. It was because the disturbances were so frequent, and her grandparents needed their sleep. Besides, she was old enough to get herself back into bed, and she had her crucifix and other religious icons to soothe her.

Thinking about it now, Carmen wondered if that was a sign, she was becoming more responsible. But she wasn't sure it counted. On one hand it showed her independence, but she still missed the attention, so she was conflicted.

On that Monday night, Carmen had one of her nightmares, making it hard for her to be cheerful at school that Tuesday. She could remember only bits and pieces of the nightmare, but they were enough to scare her, and she was restless the remainder of the night, unable to get back to sleep. The next morning, she was up and dressed early and headed for the kitchen. If she were to stay awake, she needed help, so she fixed herself a cup of coffee with lots of cream and sugar in it and grabbed a handful of crackers. When she finished what she called breakfast, she was still sleepy, so she fixed a second cup of coffee and drank it standing at the counter, while she waited for her grandparents to get up.

It was hard on her grandparents to get up and dress early each morning to walk her to St. Peter and Paul's Church where the school bus would pick her up and take her to school, but they didn't complain and always managed to be ready in time for her to catch the bus.

No matter how many times she told them she could go alone, they wouldn't hear of it, and all three of them made the trip to the bus stop together.

After saying her goodbyes, Carmen climbed on the bus and took a seat. She waved to them from the school bus window and then watched as they headed back toward home. She could see the effort in their steps as they sauntered away and told herself she would try again to make them understand they didn't have to continue walking her to the bus stop. She would convince them she was old enough to go by herself. That made her smile as she whispered, "Yeah, that's going to happen."

When the bus arrived at the school it was ten to nine and there stood her teacher, Mrs. Joyce DeMasi, who taught the class of special education students where Carmen had been placed. That was another item on her list to prove she was growing up. She wanted to advance beyond this class. Now, as her teacher stood waiting for the students to disembark, she scrambled off with the rest of them and began walking quickly in the group behind the teacher and into the school.

Though her relatives said she spoke little English, Carmen knew it was because they encouraged her to speak just Spanish with them. They knew different here at school because here Carmen was encouraged to speak English. She was doing so well that by the fall, Carmen was no longer in the special-class program for students who had English as their second language. As far as the school was concerned, Carmen no longer required special lessons in English.

When she was first told about the change, Carmen was a little hesitant because she wasn't sure she was ready. But as time passed, she was able to enjoy the fact that she had at least completed one course in her special education classes.

She had a way to go and she knew it. She was still in special education for her other subjects. Recently she had been tested and found to have an IQ of between 50 and 70 which labeled her in the range of mild to moderate retardation. She wasn't retarded; she knew that and so did the school. They told her that she was behind because of having such a hard time with the English language, not because she wasn't smart.

What made it worse was Carmen hated not being able to get passing grades in her classes. Sometimes she did, but most times she did not. That made her sad because she really tried. Her teacher was constantly telling her not to be so hard on herself and to give it time.

It helped that her teacher, Mrs. DeMasi, liked her, even though Carmen tended to disturb the class by chattering away about one thing or another and at times bouncing up and down in her seat. At first Carmen thought it was a sign that she did have a problem, but she later realized that it was because of the coffee she drank on a regular basis in the morning.

She didn't know why she didn't share this revelation with her teacher, because it would have helped Mrs. DeMasi understand why Carmen was so active in class. Instead she kept it to herself and continued to drink the coffee.

Carmen, being fond of Mrs. DeMasi, tried hard to be less interruptive. She would manage for a bit, but before she knew it, would be caught up in a burst of energy that needed to be let out. She promised her teacher she would work on her behavior, and she did, silently promising herself to find a way to sleep through the night.

If Carmen had known this Tuesday would be her last Tuesday on this earth, the day might have gone differently. When class attendance was called, she said, "Here!" When it was time to salute the flag, she stood with her hand over her heart as she recited from memory the 'Pledge of Allegiance.' Like most of us, Carmen lived every single day with regrets, depression and stress. She should have lived as if each day would be her last day on earth.

Carmen sometimes tried to focus and enjoy the little things, but not as often as she should. She wanted to prove to God that He did the right thing by sending her into this world.

Chapter 6

That day continued to be uneventful. After drinking her morning milk at school, Carmen tried hard to concentrate on her reading and spelling lessons before being dismissed to change into her gym clothes for a half-hour of physical education class. Carmen loved gym class because she was encouraged to run and let all that pent-up energy out.

After gym, Carmen showered and dressed with the rest of her classmates and returned to the classroom where it was a little easier to concentrate, especially since she had burned off a lot of her morning coffee. She became fidgety as the clock hands moved toward 11:50 a.m., and then it was time for lunch.

As Carmen stood in line waiting her turn, she looked around the cafeteria, searching for a place to sit. Then, because she was hungry, having no solid food in her stomach that day, Carmen turned her attention to the lunch line. She chose sloppy joes and potatoes. She continued down the line and decided on a vegetable, fruit, and milk.

With her tray laden with food, Carmen again glanced around the cafeteria hoping to catch someone's eye, an open invitation to join them, but no one looked her way that day, so she made her way back to the classroom to eat with Mrs. DeMasi.

Here she felt comfortable. She knew that most of the kids liked her, but there was a stigma against her because she was a special education student. This made her peers shy away from associating with her in school, even though they did enjoy her company.

Carmen did have friends, but it took an effort to fit in with them, so she liked a break from it all at times. Occasionally she had the feeling that any kid who acted as if she was her friend, was not really a friend at all. She hated feeling that way, but something they would say or do made her feel that way.

When lunch was over Carmen quickly walked back to the cafeteria to return her tray, and then hurried back to the classroom for her writing and arithmetic lessons. She had to concentrate and put in more effort whenever something new was presented. Even with extra help, Carmen had to admit that she could only count and write her numbers up to twenty, a fact that was holding her back.

Math did not come easy to her, and today it seemed even harder, so she made a mental note to work on her skills during the Thanksgiving recess.

Finally, it was time for her to go to her special speech class, where she was doing much better. This boosted her ego, and she was able to settle down.

As the day progressed, Carmen was more than ready to see an end to it. At last, the clock showed 3:00 p.m., and school was over. Following her usual pattern, Carmen waited for Mrs. DeMasi to walk her and her class to the bus. There the teacher stood, waiting for each of them to disappear through the door. She waited a moment longer to see the doors to the bus close before she departed.

Once they were all on board, the bus driver looked into the rearview mirror, waiting for everyone to be seated. To Carmen, it seemed like forever before the bus finally pulled away from the curb and they started the ride home.

The bus ride was a half hour, and Carmen spent most of that time staring out the window, only turning now and then to answer a question from the student next to her. When the bus was at her stop, Carmen gathered up her belongings and climbed off the bus to join her PaPa, who waited at the bus stop to walk her back home.

That marked the end of this school day. It had been the same as all the days before.

The first person Carmen saw when she entered her MaMa's home was her mother. She started toward her, but stopped when her MaMa said, "Tranquilo. Quítate el abrigo y las botas." Carmen smiled and replied in English. "I will take it easy. Look, I'm taking off my coat and boots."

Her MaMa nodded her approval as Carmen quickly removed her coat and boots. With her outerwear off, Carmen moved quickly across the room to where her mother was seated and, leaning over, she gave her a big hug, before moving back so that she could see her face as she asked, "¿Mamá quiere ver lo que aprendí hoy?" She knew it made her mother happy to hear her speak in Spanish and knew she did this to please her. Carmen wanted to show her what she learned today and that pleased her immensely.

Guillermina gave her daughter a smile and nodded. Carmen giggled as she moved back toward the center of the room and began dancing. She twirled around, telling her mother in Spanish that these were new dancing moves she had learned in gym class. As she twirled around, ending facing her mother, she searched Guillermina's face to see if she liked what she had shown her. Although Guillermina was watching her, Carmen could tell her mind was on something else.

Carmen danced faster, adding some of her own inventions to the movements, but she still couldn't get her mother's full attention. The more she danced, the more upset she got. Why wasn't her mother impressed with what she had learned? Letting it get the best of her, she finally stopped dancing, waited, and when there was no reaction forthcoming, commented, "You should do them too if you want to be skinny like me." Then, realizing her mother didn't understand what she had said, with frustration apparent in her voice, Carmen repeated in Spanish, "Deberías hacerlos también si quieres ser flaco como yo."

All she wanted was a minute of her mother's time, but she couldn't get it no matter what she did. Why was it so hard for her to pay attention to her, Carmen wondered? She knew that she shouldn't have retorted with such harsh criticism, but she couldn't help herself. Not waiting to hear what her mother was saying, she turned and stomped up the stairs. She made sure to slam her bedroom door hard as she entered her room.

Being the oldest child in the family had been fun at first. She could pretend her siblings were her babies and take care of them, but then they grew up. Instead of wanting to care for them, now she wanted her life to be as it had been before she had half-sisters. Before they were born she had every bit of attention from her mother. She was doted on, obsessed over, and smothered with love. Then her younger siblings came along, and, well, she felt as if she had been pushed aside. It was clear that they were her mother's and Miguel's natural children, while she was not.

"It doesn't matter. I couldn't care less," Carmen tried to reassure herself, as she sat on her bed pouting. But she knew it did matter. Finally, she got up from her bed and started changing out of her school clothes. She went to her dresser and took out a pair of jeans, a sweatshirt and heavy socks. She laid everything on her bed and looked at them, making sure they went well together. She may be just going out to play, but she still wanted her clothes to match properly.

Satisfied that they did, she put on her socks, stepped into her jeans and jumped up and down until they were situated properly on her thin frame. Next, she laid her sweatshirt on the bed so that the back was up, and the waist was toward her. Once the shirt was positioned, she leaned over, putting her arms in the sleeves and her head in through the bottom. With that done, she stood up straight, shifting her upper body until the sweatshirt fell down over her head, chest and finally down to her waist.

Carmen moved across the room with her head just poking through the neckline. In front of the mirror she made funny faces before taking her hands and pulling her head all the way through the neckline.

Again, she inspected herself. Her hair was going every which way, so she picked up her brush and ran it through her hair. She made a final check and smiled her approval before walking to the window in her bedroom.

Carmen opened the curtains and looked down. She could see her cousins next door playing in the front yard. From here, looking down at the fenced yard she thought it looked like a prison, even though the fence was low enough for them to climb over. Even that wasn't necessary, as to get out they just had to open the gate.

She knew the fence made her family think they were keeping the children safe, so she accepted that as being okay. It was important for them to think that, and it didn't impede their fun. She stood there watching, until one of her cousins saw her face in the window and waved her down. Carmen nodded, closed her curtain and ran down the stairs.

The front room was empty now, but she could hear voices in the kitchen, so she paused just long enough to put on her coat and boots before yelling over her shoulder in Spanish that she was going out to play.

She loved her cousins, and after struggling all day with English, being able to just speak Spanish relaxed her. It might upset her when she was with her mother and grandparents, but that was because she needed them to learn English if she ever wanted to be fluent in the language. But not her cousins. She wasn't sure how much English they knew, but it didn't matter.

She saw her aunt and uncle at the window as she entered the yard, and she waved. They waved back. She loved them, even though she once heard them tell her mother that they thought she might be retarded. It was during a game of hide and seek, and they could speak English well enough to recognize that Carmen not being able to count beyond twenty was not normal for a child of her age. Her mother had laughed it off, disagreed, and that was that.

Carmen had brooded over it for a day or two, but it didn't change the fact that she loved playing with her cousins, so she let it go.

As she played with her cousins, the time slipped joyously away, so it wasn't until she heard her aunt calling them in for dinner that she realized how late it had grown. Carmen said "Adiós," opened the gate, and returned home.

Once inside, she stopped in the front hallway to take off her coat, her hat and her boots, and was in the midst of putting everything away when she heard her mother talking to MaMa in the kitchen.

She paused what she was doing so she could listen. She could tell by the tone of her mother's voice that she was worried as she told her MaMa that she needed medicine for baby Luz.

Carmen headed toward the kitchen worriedly as she could hear her baby sister crying loudly. When she stepped into the kitchen, she heard her mother tell MaMa that she couldn't wait until Miguel got home. She needed the medicine now.

At that moment flashes of her day ran through her head. She had not had any opportunity to demonstrate how grown up and responsible she had become. Here was her chance. She could show her mother and MaMa that she could take care of herself and could be depended on when they needed help.

Carmen wanted more than anything for them to see her as dependable. She wanted to show that at home, as well as at school. She knew she could be counted on to do what she promised. She wanted to be respected and allowed to show selflessness.

Carmen waited for a break in the conversation and then said in Spanish, "Mommy, I'll go! I'll go!"

Before the words were out, she knew she had spoken too fast and too childishly for them to agree.

Her mother spoke first, "No!" Her grandparents chimed in, telling her it was late and would be dark soon. It was not safe for her to be running to the store at this hour.

"I can do this for you. You said Luz needs the medicine. Trust me. I will go to the drugstore, pick up the medicine and come right back."

"Make no mistake," Guillermina said, "I trust you will do just that. If you think that is my reason for not letting you go, you are wrong. It's that I don't want to have to worry about you."

The arguing continued with three against one, but Carmen was a serious adversary. The words flew back and forth, with Carmen eventually forgetting to reply with respect and saying whatever entered her mind.

Her grandmother grew weary first and turned around to attend to the food. Her grandfather gave his granddaughter a frown before he left the room. That left Guillermina holding her ground and holding her sick baby.

She had to admit Carmen was raising some good points as to why she was their only chance of getting the prescription filled right away. Before Carmen got too upset and started crying, she had said that she could do this and wanted to do this for her mother. That was so thoughtful it made Guillermina weep.

Then, when Carmen added that there was no one else who could go for them, it gave her mother pause. Against her better judgement, Guillermina finally gave in.

"Puedes irte, hija mía, puedes irte." ("You can go, my daughter, you can go.")

Carmen was victorious. She had achieved her goal, won the fight, and defeated the other side. It felt good because this would give her a chance to prove herself. They would soon see that she could be treated like a grownup, and that gave her a feeling of pride.

Carmen went over and hugged her mother, whispering that she need not worry. She would be all right, and she would bring her baby sister's medicine back as quickly as she could.

Guillermina was being as cautious as possible. She knew the drugstore owner would recognize Carmen, but she wanted to be sure they didn't just send her back. Carmen watched as her mother put her ID card in an envelope. She next wrote a note with all the information needed for filling the prescription and signed it. She put that in the envelope also, telling Carmen this would verify her signature.

Her mother asked, "Carmen, tráeme mi bolso, por favor." Carmen turned and went to get her mother her purse.

39

She went across the room and returned with the purse. She handed it to her mother and then waited.

Guillermina reached in her purse and took out her wallet. She removed several dollars and some change and put it all into the envelope. As she did so, she explained to Carmen that this money would cover the cost for the prescription, plus a little more for her to buy herself a treat.

Carmen smiled. She watched as her mother held up a card and told her that this was her Medicaid card. It would allow her daughter to purchase the medication.

Guillermina was trying to be brave as she moved closer to Carmen and said, "Gracias mi hija." (Thank you, my daughter.) She hugged Carmen, stood back and asked her to be careful. She then told her to be sure they gave her back the Medicaid card and her ID. She told her to just put them in the bag with the filled prescription.

Carmen did not take offense at all the instructions. She was so happy to be able to do this errand for her mother. It was a whole different feeling, a great feeling for her, as she waited while her mother gathered what she'd need to take with her and explained each piece of information. As anxious as she was to be on her way, Carmen stood listening carefully to her mother, not wanting to make a mistake and never to be trusted again. When she had all the instructions and that final hug, Carmen hurried to the foyer, afraid her mother might still change her mind.

Chapter 7

It had rained earlier in the day and the temperature had been a chilly 46 degrees that morning as she made her way to the bus stop before school. No one had to warn her that it would be even colder now, because she had felt it when she was outside playing with her cousins.

Carmen realized her pants were wet from rolling on the ground, so she ran upstairs to her room. She pushed down her slacks and put them in the hamper before digging in her drawer and coming up with her green pants. She jumped into them. She yanked off her top and put on her red sweater, then ran fingers through her hair until it was presentable again. Quickly, she hurried back down the stairs.

She didn't have to worry about how cold it was, because her grandmother came over to help her get ready, telling her that it was only 39 degrees outside, so she needed to wear her long, red wool coat. Carmen smiled and opened the closet to get her coat. She saw the satisfied smile on her grandmother's face as she helped her put it on.

Lastly, she sat down on the step and took off her sneakers to replace them with her boots. Carmen was ready.

She stood at the front door when her mother called out to her. "Please don't let her change her mind," Carmen whispered to herself as she turned to face her mother.

Guillermina stood there, her arms around baby Luz who was grabbing at her own ears and crying loudly. Carmen didn't wait to hear what her mother had to say, but instead soothed her by telling her not to worry, that she would be all right and would hurry back with the medicine.

Carmen let out a sigh of relief. She had been worried, but it seemed it was okay again. As she looked around the front room, putting on her mittens and hat, she didn't see her grandfather anywhere. She watched as her mother bounced up and down, trying to soothe baby Luz, as she headed toward the kitchen where her grandmother was preparing dinner.

Carmen now stood alone in the front room. She hesitated, remembering there was a rule in the house and she always followed it. She could hear her heart pounding as she tried to decide what to do. She didn't want her mother to have time to change her mind, but the rule was that Carmen's grandfather, Felix, was to walk behind her when she left the house on an errand. Everyone knew that her grandfather was always there watching as she crossed Essex Street and Kensington Street. When she was sent to Morrell's Cigar Store on Brown Street she was able to walk alone without Felix trailing behind only because he could see her from the front of the house, but the pharmacy was on Main Street, and she would have to turn the corner to get to Main Street

All of this went through her head as she wondered what she should do. Finally, she reminded herself that this was the start of her independence, so this time she broke the rule, opened the door and headed out on her own.

Unbeknownst to her, back at the house, Guillermina told PaPa Felix that Carmen was running the errand to the drugstore for her, and that she had given her a bag with some money, her Medicaid card and form along with the prescription. She added in Spanish, "She wanted to go, so can you watch her?"

He responded, likewise. "Don't worry, Guillermina, I will."

From the moment she stepped out on the sidewalk, Carmen felt empowered. She was really doing it on her own with no one watching. This was the day she had hoped for and wanted for so long, the day she was treated like a responsible adult. She smiled, thinking that she would remember this as the best day of her life.

Carmen knew where she was going. Jax Drugstore wasn't far from home, but it was around the corner. She would not have to cross any dangerous streets, so there was nothing to worry about. She moved confidently down the street, walking quickly as she had promised her mother she would. She had left the house at 4:25 p.m. She knew that to be a fact as she had checked the clock in the living room. This was important as she wanted to report back and tell her mother just how long it had taken her.

Carmen shivered. It was quite chilly and growing darker out as she headed down Brown Street toward Essex Street. At Essex Street she turned left onto West Main Street and, in less than four minutes from the time she had left home, she arrived at Jax Drugstore in Bull's Head Plaza. It had been the famous Bull's Head Tavern that had marked the historic Bull's Head section of Rochester, giving the Plaza its name.

Back at the house on Brown Street, Felix Colón put on his coat, gloves and hat. He opened the front door, and the blast of cold air made him hesitate a moment before he stepped outside. He moved to the farthest side of the porch so he could see his granddaughter as she made her way to the drugstore. His eyes teared, making his vision blurry and he squeezed them shut to clear them.

Carmen was moving quickly and was almost to the corner before Felix's eyes adjusted enough to see her. It was cold, so very cold out, and Felix shivered as he made his way to the porch steps and started to descend. He stopped and looked around. There was no one out walking at this hour, and few cars passed. He stepped back up onto the porch, stood there a moment, and then, shaking his head, went back inside.

He could hear the baby still crying in the kitchen and his daughter-in-law, Guillermina, doing her best to calm her. He could catch the sounds of his wife, Candida, getting out pans and utensils. The commotion was almost too much for him as he stood in the front room, warming up.

It felt so good inside that he lingered to enjoy the warmth before he forced himself to go back outside to stand on the porch and wait for Carmen to return home.

He knew how long it should take her to get to the drugstore and back, and he knew what time she had left. Of course, she would need time to give the pharmacist the prescription and have him do whatever he did to fill it. He figured that could take maybe an extra fifteen to twenty minutes.

He was getting cold again. "What's taking her so long?" he asked himself in Spanish. He walked stiffly across the porch and stepped back inside to check the time.

At first, he was irritated with his granddaughter. She should have been back by now, but he told himself that maybe the pharmacy was busy, and she had to wait in line. But even if she had had to wait, she should have been back by now.

Then he remembered that Guillermina had said she gave Carmen extra money to buy something for herself. He had been with her on other occasions and knew how indecisive she could be when she was making a purchase, so that was probably what was holding her up now.

But his mind would not accept that. He knew his granddaughter. Carmen understood how important the medicine was for her baby sister, and she would be hurrying as fast as she could. He started to feel uneasy as he stepped back inside again.

Just like Felix, Guillermina was watching the clock, and hearing the door, she rushed into the front room. "¿Es que tú Carmen?" (Is that you Carmen?) she asked as she rushed into the front room carrying baby Luz. Instead of Carmen, she came face to face with her father-in-law. She tried to look behind him to see if Carmen was with him.

"¿Dónde está Carmen?" (Where's Carmen) she asked.

With a worried expression on his face, Felix told her he had seen Carmen as she made her way down Brown Street on her way to Jax's. He had walked out to the sidewalk and looked up and down the street to check if there was any traffic or anyone following her. There was no one out at that time, probably because everyone was keeping warm indoors.

He continued, telling her that he had stood out there and watched Carmen until she turned the corner. Once she was out of sight, he had come back in to warm up, and then when he went back out, decided just to wait on the porch.

Guillermina was less worried now since the drugstore was only a block and a half away from home, and Felix had watched her most of the way. Carmen had made it safely to the drugstore, she was sure of that. True, she had turned the corner and was out of their view, but she was confident her daughter was at the drugstore.

They were right, of course. While this discussion was going on at home, Carmen hummed to herself as she

45

walked along the sidewalk, feeling as though she was on an adventure. When she reached Jax Drugstore, she opened the door and quickly stepped over the threshold and into the warmth that greeted her. She was cold, but nothing could get her down as she looked at the clock and saw that it was 4:30 p.m. She had made good time.

Carmen smiled as she walked confidently down the aisle to the back of the store and the prescription counter. There were few employees working there, so it was the store owner who greeted her.

The prescription counter was almost level with the top of her head, so she had to look up to see him.

"Hi. I have a prescription to fill."

She had been here so many times that they knew who she was, so she didn't have to identify herself.

"You do?"

"Yes, I do." Carmen smiled before looking down and reaching into the bag her mother had given her. She pulled out the prescription and handed it to him.

She waited patiently as the pharmacist looked over the prescription and then looked up at Carmen. He did know her and had seen Carmen many times before in his store, both alone and with her mother, so he had no problem with filling the prescription.

He was staring at the paper so long that at first Carmen started worrying that something was wrong, and he wasn't going to let her fill the prescription. When he finally looked down at her and said, "I need to see your mother's Medicaid card," Carmen let out her breath and smiled.

Wasting no time, she reached back into the bag and pulled out the card. She started to hand it to him but paused to reach back in the bag and pull out the other sheet of paper that her mother had tucked inside.

She gave him both at the same time. Then she stood patiently as he looked over the information.

"This will take a few minutes. I must fill out some forms and prepare the prescription. You are welcome to wait, but it will take at least twenty minutes."

Carmen was confused, and it must have shown on her face, because he looked at her and said, "Go home and come back at around 5 o'clock when it will be ready for you."

"Okay."

Carmen turned and walked slowly back down the aisle to the front of the store. She patted the envelope that she had put back in her pocket and thought about buying some candy, but she didn't know how much the prescription would cost so she decided to wait. Instead, she stepped back outside.

She stood there in deep thought. She knew that once she returned home, her family would absolutely not allow her to leave by herself a second time. Was she okay with that?

It was getting colder and darker out as she stood there shivering, pondering what seemed to be a dilemma. In the next instant came her reaction, a feeling of happiness because she knew what to do.

It didn't matter that they would not allow her out later to get the prescription. What mattered was that she had run the errand and reported back home. That was what responsible people did. She pondered the matter no more, as she realized she had only one choice and that was to go home. Carmen was smiling as she slowly turned toward her house.

The cold hurried her steps as it penetrated her coat, and she felt it through her clothing underneath. But that didn't bother her, nor did the fact that her fingers were growing stiff from the cold. Instead she just balled her hands into fists inside her mittens, and that made them feel better.

"Geez," she said aloud as she tried to bend her toes within her boots, noticing a burning, tingling sensation in her feet. This was her special moment, and she was determined to enjoy it as long as she could. But even as the desire ran through her mind, she could feel her feet moving faster and faster. The cold was in control now as she hurried down the sidewalk, knowing that the longer she was out there, the colder she would get.

She became aware of the darkness and felt the silence all around her. The chill in the air added an eeriness to the night, and Carmen found she was shivering, not only from the cold, but at the realization that she was alone. There were people inside the houses she passed, inviting light flickering inside, but they were not aware of her while they were enjoying their dinner or watching television.

Carmen knew she was to pay attention to what was happening around her when she was outside, but she was not paying attention now. Her mind was busy dealing with the cold and the darkness as she picked up the pace toward home. She was so busy coping with the cold that her mind traveled to her nightmares which always had her fighting something in the dark.

She could feel it overcoming her, that extreme fear of night or darkness that caused her nightmares, and sometimes an intense anxiety and depression the next day. It was easy to believe there was nothing in the darkness to hurt her when she was in her bedroom, but all alone out here it was different. Her body froze and she had trouble breathing as her heart raced in her chest.

She couldn't move if she had wanted to, and any sound she heard increased her fear. The only sound she wanted to hear was her PaPa calling her, but his voice didn't come.

Carmen didn't see the car that had been following slowly behind her since she left the drugstore. The driver was deliberately keeping just behind the walking figure and paused when she stopped.

It took a few minutes for Carmen to compose herself. She prayed to God to help her make it home, saying she would be ever so grateful if He helped her finish the walk home so that she could see her family.

Her prayer was answered, and her feet began to move again. Carmen had walked past the vacant lot right before the turn back on to her street, when she heard someone call out to her.

Normally this would be a welcome signal, but for some reason it put dread in her body as her head lifted high on her neck and her feet again froze in place. She didn't know what to do.

"Carmen!" The voice came again, and this time it shook her free, allowing her to turn in the direction of the voice that had called her by name.

Unsure of what to do, Carmen stared hard at the car, but she couldn't recognize it. She moved forward a step knowing she wasn't going to figure out who it was by their car. She didn't know one car from another.

She watched as the car moved over to the side of the road and stopped, the engine still running. She could see the driver was a man as he leaned across the front seat and pushed the passenger side door open, saying, "Get in. I'll take you home."

Carmen was hesitant at first, but she was cold and besides that, the person must know her. He had called her by name. Nevertheless, Carmen walked suspiciously toward the vehicle until she stood right beside the open door. She leaned down so that she could see the driver better, but she couldn't place the face that smiled back at her. She dawdled, trying to make up her mind what she should do.

"Come on Carmen, it's cold out there. Are you getting in or what?"

She scrambled in. Not forgetting her manners, she said, "Thank you."

"Put your seatbelt on and close the door."

Carmen obeyed, ignoring the change in tone that the man was using now. She figured he was irritated by her taking her time making up her mind to get in the car.

The car started moving. They probably only had a few minutes' drive until they would be at her grandparents' house, but she still appreciated the warmth inside. She was relaxed, staring around the interior, when she realized they had passed her grandparents' house.

"You've passed the house," she said. "I live at 746 Brown Street. You've gone too far."

The man didn't seem to be listening to her as he continued driving. Carmen leaned forward, trying to see his face better, but she couldn't. From where she sat, she couldn't identify him except for his silhouette and his tight knit cap. He continued to stare straight ahead, and she felt her first tinge of apprehension.

"Sir, you are going the wrong way."

Still he didn't respond. Carmen could feel her body stiffening and her jaw clenching as she tried not to scream. She was overcome by an uncontrollable outburst of fear, as she wept silently. Now she knew that he had passed her grandparents' house on purpose. She had a feeling that he really didn't know her, but just had heard her name from people around the neighborhood.

Carmen tried to plan what to do as she looked out the window, seeing the street signs and already unaware of where they were or where they were going. When she saw the sign pointing the way to the expressway, she sat up straighter. Until now the area had been barren of traffic, but if they were headed to the expressway, there would be lots of cars and people. She allowed herself to feel hopeful.

But hope didn't last long as she felt the car slowing down and then turning off the road. She stared out the window and, in the darkness, all she could make out was a railing. Then as the car jogged further down the unpaved road, she could see a small cement building amongst some trees. Panic surged up her spine as she moved as close as she could to the passenger door when the car stopped.

She stared mesmerized at the driver's hand as it turned the key; then she was paralyzed by the car's reaction to this motion, feeling her body quiver as the car shook and vibrated as if wanting to take off again. Then it stilled.

That was when Carmen came to life. With one hand she reached down and grabbed the door handle while her other hand tried to release her seatbelt. But before she could master the feat, strong hands grabbed her and pulled her across the seat.

The motion rendered Carmen powerless. She couldn't move, nor could she speak, as terror filled every fiber of her being. She didn't feel like a big girl anymore as she wildly kicked and screamed to no avail.

She knew she was fighting a losing battle as she beat the man's chest and even managed to kick him in the shin when he turned slightly to open the car door on his side.

As petrified as she was being in the car, she was more scared of leaving it. Carmen felt herself being hauled across the car seat until they both were outside.

"Please, oh please, let me go."

Tears blinded her, making it harder to see in the darkness, as he walked briskly along the gravel path, dragging her further away from the car.

Even at her young age and not having experienced this type of situation before, she knew that this man was going to hurt her if she didn't get away from him. But how, she asked herself. How could she make him let her go?

All of this was running through her head when she finally saw where he was headed. In the distance was a cement structure. Carmen wasn't sure exactly what it was, but she thought it might be a public bathroom.

"No, please, let me go. I won't tell anyone. I promise."

As soon as the door opened, a smell so strong and unpleasant filled her nostrils and throat. The odor of urine and sewage made her want to gag, as she fought harder and harder to free herself.

"Oh, God, I am sorry for any way I have offended you. I am so, so, sorry…"

"Shut up!"

The man had finally spoken. If she had managed to make him speak, maybe, she thought, she still had a chance. She carefully chose her words.

"I only want to know why God is punishing me," she said through choking sobs.

He stopped in the middle of the room and lowered her to the floor. And for one-minute Carmen thought he was going to let her go. But instead, he reached under her coat and grabbed the side of the waist of her slacks and pulled, ripping them off her. He did the same to her panties, throwing the clothing off to the side before tearing her coat and shirt away from her body.

Somewhere deep inside, Carmen found the strength to renew her struggle to get away. She didn't feel the coldness of the room or the penetrating chill of the cement floor on her back and buttocks. What she did sense and know was she was alone. There was no one there to save her.

Tears filled her big brown eyes and rolled down the sides of her face as she sobbed uncontrollably. Her fear intensified as she watched the man struggle to get his belt loose, and when he accomplished that, to undo the button and lower the zipper on his pants. She heard him grunt before lowering himself upon her.

The man forcibly penetrated her while Carmen screamed out in agony. To stop her screams, the man reached up and put his hand over her mouth. Then he began pumping into her until she thought he would rip her apart. The pain was excruciating as she stared at the fluorescent light above him and fought to breathe in the foul air around her. Thankfully, she finally passed out.

Carmen didn't know how long she was unconscious, but when she opened her eyes, she was aware she was still lying on her back on the floor. She could feel the coldness on her naked lower body. She tried but couldn't seem to move her arms or legs.

She felt a wetness under her and tried to get up, but the man held her firmly as he again inserted his penis in her. Waves of pain pulsed through her body as he raped her again. And once more the world around her slid away into darkness.

When Carmen regained consciousness for the second time, she found herself lying on the back seat of the moving car. She scrunched her body up against the passenger door, her eyes watching through the driver's side back window. She prayed silently that he would stop and let her out, but the car kept going. "Please God, please." But the man kept on driving.

Her whole body ached, but she knew that if she wanted to live, she had to get out of the car. And she wanted to live. He had taken her innocence, but she still had her life.

Finally, she felt the car slowing. She tried to see what was happening, as she turned her head to stare out the other side window. There were other cars. This was her chance.

Carmen grabbed her pants that lay on the floor beside her and moved her hand down the side of the door to grab the handle. She said a prayer. "Please let it be unlocked." It was. The door swung open and she jumped.

Carmen hit the ground brutally and rolled for several feet beyond the hard shoulder of the road. She could feel pain in her shoulders and legs, but she ignored it.

Carmen, naked from her waist down, her top in tatters, began climbing up to the road. When she reached it, she ran with her pants in one hand, crying hysterically. She didn't know where the man was, nor did she care. This was the expressway and there were lots of cars passing by her now. She was sure someone would stop and help her.

Carmen started waving her arms, trying to get someone's attention. Even though the traffic sounds made it impossible to hear her, she screamed loudly, "Help me," repeatedly.

Cars kept speeding by Carmen, dozens of them making their way down the busy expressway. She didn't know where they were going, only that she wanted them to stop and help her.

Carmen was sure the people in the cars could tell she was in danger, as she ran facing traffic on the busy expressway. She was in pain, cold and afraid, but she kept running as fast as she could.

Then she heard someone yell, "Stop!" and she slowed enough to turn and see where the voice was coming from. She sucked in her breath as she saw the car she had escaped, backing up on the shoulder. It was almost even with her now.

Frantically she ran, moving dangerously close to the edge of the road, wondering why no one was stopping to help her. Surely, they had a full view of her from the light of the headlights, so why didn't they stop? Did they think she was just a bad girl running away from someone she knew? Couldn't they see she had no pants on? Why wouldn't they stop? Tears blinded her as she tried to outrun the car and then the man who had got out to chase her.

Then it was too late. He had caught up with her and parked on the shoulder. She cried hysterically, and tried to run even faster, but she was in such pain and so tired now, it was easy for the man to catch up with her.

Giving one last chance for someone to help, she screamed as loudly as she could, just before she felt his hands grab her. She continued screaming as he forcefully hauled her back to the car.

Several drivers did see a young girl, almost naked, with a car backing along the shoulder toward her the afternoon of her disappearance, but they were driving upward of 70 miles per hour when they passed her and couldn't stop. Others who passed were unsure of what they'd seen. The sight seemed too bizarre, and they had only caught a flash as they drove the speed limit on the expressway. Later, when the facts came out, they would realize that they had missed a chance to save Carmen, and would probably feel guilty that they didn't stop to help.

That was the way the nightmare ended. Carmen could no longer hope because soon she would be dead. She fought with all the strength left in her body, making it hard for her captive to control her, but he managed. He carried her back to the car and restrained her so that she couldn't get out again.

Carmen was choking on her sobs now as she stared out the window, still hoping someone was going to stop and save her. She saw a sign that said "Riga" as she watched and struggled to free herself. It was useless.

She glared out the side window, mad at everyone and everything. She was wrathful at all those people who she knew had seen her desperate sprint along the shoulder of the road, and at this man who had injured her body and her soul. She had never felt so helpless or alone. She stared out the car window and her fear grew. Outside the window she saw nothing but woods and open fields. There were no houses, just trees and brush. When she felt the car slowing, she screamed. She didn't stop screaming as he dragged her out of the car and into the field.

As shocked as she had been before, what he did next shocked her even more. It wasn't that she had thought he was letting her go, but even so she wasn't prepared for him to take his hands and wrap them tightly around her neck.

The man's hands were squeezing so hard she couldn't take a breath. She felt the pressure in her throat, and her eyes began to water. She struggled to get free as her chest was on fire as she strained to breathe into lungs that refused to function. She was like a rag doll as she went cold. Behind her eyes she saw stars and then darkness. Her last thought was that her innocence was the first to die, and now her body was joining it.

Chapter *8*

While Carmen was breathing her last, that evening at her grandparents' home they were frantically wondering where she could be. Carmen should have been home by now.

At first, they tried to keep each other calm. "¿Dónde está esa chica?" (Where is that girl?)

"Tal vez tuvo problemas para conseguir la receta." (Maybe she had problems getting the prescription.)

"No, le di todo lo que necesitaba.." (No, I gave her everything she needed.)

"Bueno, también le diste dinero para conseguir un regalo. ¿Sabes cómo se toma su tiempo tomando una decisión, ¿no? (Well, you also gave her money to get a treat. You know how she takes her time making a choice, don't you?")

They nodded. Guillermina turned her attention to trying to make the baby more comfortable, while the Grandmother went to fix them coffee and tea.

Several minutes passed and their worry grew. It just wasn't like Carmen not to follow instructions. She knew the baby needed the medicine, so why would she dilly dally?

"Creo que algo anda mal," (I think something is wrong,) Guillermina said worriedly.

There was no pretending nothing had happened. It had been almost an hour since Carmen went to the store, and even if she had dragged her feet or had to wait for the prescription longer than expected, she should have been home by now.

"Deberíamos revisar en mi casa y ver si se detuvo allí para ver a sus hermanos y hermanas." (We should check at my house and see if she stopped there to see her brothers and sisters), Guillermina said.

"Buena idea. Llama a la casa y yo iré a la farmacia y veré si ella está por ahí." (That's a good idea. You call the house, and I'll go to the drugstore and see if she's just hanging around there), replied Felix.

Guillermina handed the crying baby to her grandmother and went to the phone. Candida Colón tried to hush the baby, bouncing her up and down and smiling at her, but her heart wasn't in that smile. Where could Carmen be?

Candida could hear parts of the conversation as Guillermina spoke. By the time her daughter hung up, Candida knew that Carmen was not at her mother's house.

Candida was beside herself and could see that Guillermina was having trouble holding herself together. Carmen was nowhere to be seen. In a panic, Guillermina rushed out the door and knocked on the neighbor's door. When it opened, her nephew stood before her. Without explaining herself she said, "Antonio, puedes buscar en el vecindario. Necesitamos que encuentres a Carmen." (Antonio, can you search the neighborhood? We need you to find Carmen,)

"Sure," Carmen's Uncle Antonio said. I'll contact the rest of the family to help.

So, on a raw, drizzly evening, they turned out to sweep the neighborhood, asking questions and going up and down the streets, determined and confident they would find Carmen. It was a relief to Guillermina that something was being done to find her daughter. It helped alleviate some of the guilt she felt at giving in and letting her go alone to the drugstore.

Felix Colón kept his eyes peeled as he began the walk to Jax Drugstore, which probably had taken Carmen four minutes, but at his pace would take longer. The cold seeped into his bones, as he made his way out the door of his home on Brown Street, carefully going down the steps onto the sidewalk. He paused and looked around, hoping to see his granddaughter, but when he did not, he moved forward.

When he came to the side street of Silver, he paused again and stared down the street. He saw nothing, so he continued walking, looking both left and right, even peering into yards. Usually when Carmen ventured out, she was going to Morrell's Cigar Store for a candy bar or a bottle of pop, so, on the off chance she had stopped in on her way back, Felix entered the store and walked around the interior. She was not there.

When he reached the corner where Brown Street crossed West Main to become Genesee Street, Felix stopped again. This was a main thoroughfare, so he took his time, especially since there was the Bar at this location which he ventured into, waiting for his eyes to adjust to take a look around.

"Can I help you, old man?" the bartender asked.

"My granddaughter." He replied, unable to say much in English so he kept it short.

"No, no little girl here."

Felix nodded and left. He then turned the corner and arrived at Jax Drugstore.

The druggist spoke Spanish, so Felix was able to communicate with him. He told him he was looking for Carmen, his granddaughter, and the druggist said he knew who she was. The druggist told him that Carmen had been there and dropped off the prescription. Since he had to fill out some paperwork for the insurance before filling the prescription, he had told her to go home and come back in a half hour.

"She left?"

"Yes. I told her to go home and come back later."

"She no home."

The druggist shook his head and told Felix he assumed she had. He then walked over to a rack of files, and in a few minutes, he turned to Felix. "I have the prescription here," he said. "Do you want to take it with you?"

Felix nodded. The druggist reached across the counter and handed the prescription to Felix. "I hope you find your granddaughter."

Felix thanked him and turned around, opened the door and stepped out into the cold. Just that few minutes of warmth made it seem even colder outside as he walked slowly back the way he had come. He peered into each yard again as he passed, hoping to see Carmen coming toward him or to hear her laughter. By the time he reached his home, he admittedly was shaking and not just from the cold.

"Aquí está la receta," (Here's the prescription) he said, handing it to Guillermina.

"Gracias. ¿Hubo suerte? (Thank you. Any luck?")" she replied, worry apparent in her voice.

"No, y miré por todas partes." (No, and I looked everywhere)

Guillermina tried to smile as she told him that family and friends were now out looking, in their cars and on foot. She hugged her father-in-law and tried to reassure him, saying that she was sure they would find her. But there was no conviction in her words.

They both knew that Carmen was a very friendly little girl and would not hesitate to go with someone whether or not she thought she knew them. That knowledge they could not think about.

It was close to 7 o'clock, dark, wet and cold outside when everyone reported in. Even with duplicate efforts on the side streets off Brown and over and beyond Romeyn Street where Guillermina lived, there was no sign of Carmen. Others who had canvassed the area of West Main could find no one who had seen Carmen. There were some friends who went all the way up to Brown Square Park with nothing to report.

This southwest area of Rochester, known as the Bull's Head area, was one of the city's oldest neighborhoods. It ran down West Main Street to Chili Avenue, West Avenue, Genesee Street, and Brown Street. Eventually all the streets would converge within a few hundred feet of each other. Each had been checked. It wasn't the safest area of the city, though there were others that were worse, but for a little girl, alone on the streets at night, it was very scary to think what could have happened.

Guillermina was scared for her little girl, but this being an area where one does not call the police unless it is absolutely necessary, she hesitated to make the call. So many of the people in the neighborhood were undocumented and didn't want any trouble, but if they were to help Carmen, it was beginning to look as if it was necessary.

They had done everything they could think of and looked everywhere that they could. They couldn't just knock on doors of people who didn't know them. Beyond their immediate neighborhood it wasn't that kind of area. What Guillermina knew was that Carmen was out there somewhere, cold and scared, and of that she was now sure.

So, Guillermina thanked the friends and family members who had gathered, and then she peered at her father-in-law.

"Creo que tenemos que llamar a la policía." (I think we need to call the police.)   He nodded.

After seeing the others out, only family members remained. Everyone agreed that this was what they had to do, and a cousin who spoke English well offered to make the call.

Chapter 9

"Nine-one-one operator. What is your emergency?"

"We need help. My cousin is missing."

"Where are you calling from?"

"I am calling from my grandparents' home at 746 Brown Street."

"What is your name."

"My name is Antonio and I live next door. "

"What is your cousin's name?"

"Carmen. Carmen Colón."

"How old is she?"

"She's ten years old."

The dispatcher sat up straighter in her chair. Her body went on instant alert when the caller said the missing girl was only ten years old. She hadn't been an operator long, but she knew what was expected of her. She had to remain calm, or she might overlook critical information. She took a deep breath.

"When did she go missing?"

"It's been a while now. She went to the drugstore down the street and we can't find her. Please can you send the police to my grandparents?"

"Yes, they are on their way now. Can I speak to your grandparents?"

"My cousin's mother and my grandparents don't speak English well."

"Oh, I see. Then, can I ask you questions?"

"Sure."

The call was made at 7:50 p.m. The operator wrote the time down before continuing.

"What is the parent's name?"

"Guillermina, Guillermina Colón."

"Where does the mother live?"

"Ah, she lives at 72 Romeyn Street, but Carmen spends most of the time with her grandparents, Felix and Candida Colón. That is where I am calling from."

"Okay, what is that address?"

"It's 746 Brown Street."

"How long has she been missing?"

There was silence and more whispers... "I think about three hours, almost four. Listen, she is just a little girl. We have been checking the neighborhood and talking with people all around the area and even beyond. No one has seen anything or knows where she might be." There was a pause. "I think she was taken."

"Can you think of anyone or any reason she would have been taken?"

"No, but that is the only logical conclusion."

"Okay, what was Carmen wearing?"

There was another pause and the dispatcher could hear people whispering in the background. When the cousin spoke again, he said, "She had on her boots, a long red wool coat and green pants." More talking in the background. "And a red sweater with a black collar."

"Thank you. Is it Mr. Colón?"

"Yes, but call me Antonio."

"Is there anything else I should know?"

"Yes, Carmen is ah, a little slow, if you know what I mean. I do not think she is retarded, but she is a little slow. She is also very friendly."

"Good to know. Thank you, Antonio. That helps. I will give the officer assigned to the case this information so that he can pass it on to his detectives. He should be at your address shortly."

It was Detective Alexander Ford who was dispatched promptly to take the initial report and to conduct the preliminary investigation. He could feel the tension in the room as he walked over to sit at the table where he could take notes.

"My name is Detective Alexander Ford, and I have been assigned to help you find your daughter." He paused to pull out a sheet of paper.

"This is the report from the nine-one-one call. I want to read it to you for verification of its contents. Is that okay?"

They nodded and he read the information that had been given to the dispatcher.

"Is that accurate?" Antonio was translating everything he said. The detective watched as they nodded in agreement.

"How tall is Carmen?"

Angel Colón, who spoke English, replied, "She is tiny, probably four feet tall, and weighs about 65 pounds."

"Good. Hair color?"

"She has long brown hair down to her shoulders and a light complexion. Her eyes are dark brown, and she has a somewhat large nose. Don't get me wrong, she's cute, extremely cute."

"When was she born?"

"February 1, 1961."

"She's ten?"

"Yes."

When the officer finished writing he asked, "Do you have a picture of her?"

The words were barely out of his mouth before the grandmother headed across the room and came back with a picture of Carmen Colón.

She handed the picture to the detective and he took it, looked at the photo and said, "She is cute. Can I keep this?"

"Yes."

"Here's my card." He reached into his pocket and pulled out a couple of his cards to hand to Angel.

"I am going to head this investigation, and you can call me anytime. I will keep you informed of what is going on. Right now, there are officers out canvassing the neighborhood as well as at your home, Guillermina," he added, looking in her direction.

"I want you to know we will do everything possible to find Carmen. It's good that you called."

At that moment there was a knock at the door and Antonio went to answer it.

"Is Detective Ford here?"

"Yes, he is."

"My name is Officer Paul Rodríguez. They sent me over to continue the interview as I speak Spanish."

Antonio stepped aside and the officer entered the room. Antonio and Angel stood by as Officer Rodriguez interviewed Guillermina and the relatives, asking them personal questions about the family.

"Who does Carmen live with?"

"She lives with her grandparents, here, Felix and Candida Colón."

"Where is her father?"

"Her father, Justiniano, left some time ago, and her uncle, Miguel, now lives at the home at 72 Romeyn Street."

"Could her father have taken Carmen?"

"No. He would not. He didn't want anything to do with us or the family."

"I think that is all for now." With that the officer rose and Guillermina walked him to the door. He went down the sidewalk and climbed into his car where he placed a call to the officers, giving them the additional details, he had collected. He then turned to Detective Ford, who gave instructions on the search pattern.

He also called in a "Be on the Lookout" Bulletin, announcing that this was the case of a minor child being missing.

Back at the house, friends and relatives again hit the streets in search of Carmen. The police, having more power than the family, began a methodical door-to-door search of the entire Bull's Head neighborhood, forty officers strong. They went to vacant houses and other possible hiding places; on the off chance she had ducked into some place and was too scared to come out. Three other police officers searched along the east-west railroad tracks that crossed Brown Street several blocks north of her home. They even checked in the thick underbrush along the tracks off Taylor Street, but they found nothing.

This was not an area where residents were anxious to contact the police, but the sheriff begged eyewitnesses to come forward. Only a few did. There were many households that did not speak English, so the police had to make a note to return with another interpreter when they couldn't reach Officer Rodriguez. They knew there had to be witnesses to whatever had happened to Carmen, but most residents were either too embarrassed that they had not helped her, or too suspicious of the police, to say anything.

Detective Ford returned to the office to act as the initial contact person. He reviewed his notes to be sure he had followed protocol. He had coordinated the search, and would follow up on any leads as they came in. He reviewed the initial description. He had the clothing and physical appearance of the child, and, from interviewing the parents, he knew a little about her personality. They had said she was a little slow, friendly, and cute. He checked the spelling of her name and noted that she was born February 1, 1971, making her ten, but almost eleven years old. In addition, the family had told him her nickname was "Guisa," and that she was in the custody of her mother, Guillermina, but lived with her grandparents. He pulled out the photo and noted that it was a good quality picture.

The detective leaned against the back of his chair, then leaned forward, and wrote down a reminder to check on who Carmen's friends were and where they lived.

He wanted each step documented, so they could review it later. After writing this down, Detective Ford picked up the phone and made a call. He asked the officer to stop by the Colón home and get a list of the little girl's friends and their addresses. He then inquired if they had checked the home thoroughly and was told they had.

"We even checked under beds and in closets, but nothing."

"Detective Ford, we ran into some girls who mentioned that they had seen men in the area. They seemed to think the men were stalking them."

"So, did they give you a description?"

"What do you think? If they had, we would have called it in. They could not even tell us if they were black, white or Hispanic. They said it was too dark."

"Okay, keep checking."

Detective Ford sat staring down at his pad. If anyone had passed by his office, they would have thought he was sleeping, but that would be furthest from the truth. He was reviewing the case and thinking about what they had learned during the interview with the family.

He had been told that PaPa Felix went out to look for Carmen. He went with Carmen's Uncle, Antonio Colón, to speak to the man at the pharmacy who said he neither knew nor saw anything after Carmen left his store. After that, the two men had talked to several other people in the area and had come up with nothing. That was the moment they decided to call the police.

The detective paused, rubbed his eyes, and then peered at the notes again. He had been told that Carmen's father, Justiniano, and her Uncle, Miguel, had been working, and that they worked at the Gerber Plant. He picked up the telephone book and flipped through the pages until he found what he was looking for.

The Gerber complex was at 460 Buffalo Road, just west of Mount Read Boulevard. He stared into the distance, thinking. That was maybe six minutes, or a mere one and half mile drive, away from the Brown Street residence.

When he had interviewed Guillermina he could see she had an inkling what he was thinking, because she had quickly added that even though they got off at four or four-thirty that evening, Carmen's father wouldn't have taken her. She was sure of that.

Seeing the quizzical look on Detective Ford's face, she had quickly explained that her current husband, Miguel, was Carmen's uncle, and he loved her like his own daughter.

Detective Ford had tried not to allow his face to show his surprise when she had said this. Then, when she added that Miguel had grown up with Carmen, well, that was a little disturbing, but who was he to judge the dynamics of a family.

In retrospect he thought about one piece of information relayed from the police who had been to the Romeyn Street house. They had said that Miguel was not there, and they were unable to find him. It was normal to suspect the husband, after all, so they needed to interview him, but he was nowhere to be found. Ford needed clarification on this and dialed the phone.

"Sí?" Guillermina answered.

Using his best Spanish, he asked if Miguel was there. He could hear Guillermina speaking to someone in the background before she came back on the phone and said, "No está aquí, pero no es culpable." (He is not here, but he is not guilty.)

Someone took the phone from Guillermina and said, "Miguel hasn't contacted the police because her brother-in-law told him that she would get into trouble if he did."

"Who am I speaking to?" he asked.

"This is a friend of the family."

"Can you tell me why she was told that?"

Hesitantly she said, "Guillermina is on welfare, and his living with her is not allowed by law.

"You're not going to say anything, are you?"

"No, don't worry. We will need to talk to Miguel, but tell her she is not in any trouble. We just need to speak with him."

He heard whispers and then the friend asked, "Can she go to jail?"

"What? Oh, no. As a single parent receiving assistance, with a spouse having moved into her home, the state would review both incomes to reevaluate her monthly eligibility."

"They will take money away?"

"They may reduce her funds, but that would be the extent of it. That is a matter to take up later. Not now.

"One more question. Does she still have family in Puerto Rico?"

Again, there were whispers. "She says she has a sister and two nieces."

At first, he was going to ask Guillermina to call them, but decided it would be better if he called. He did not know this family well and hadn't had contact with the distant relatives. It could be that little Carmen had already called them, and, if so, they might try to protect her by not telling her mother. So instead, he asked for their number, and Guillermina willingly gave it to him. Not able to think of anything else to ask or say, he ended the call.

"I want to thank you for taking the time to answer my questions. I feel sure that we will find Carmen. As soon as we do, we'll call you."

Detective Ford had written it all down, and then added that, when they found Miguel and had a chance to talk with him, to make sure they first told him he was not in trouble, and that no one was going to turn Guillermina in because he lived with her.

Ford paused and bit his lip, thinking. Slowly, his face softened, and his eyes opened wide. There was something he could do right now. At his desk he picked up his phone and began dialing. Luckily, in winter the time in Puerto Rico is only one hour ahead of the time in Rochester, so he was confident he could make contact.

As he waited, he started trying to think like a ten-year-old girl. The conditions of her life here were not that great, and maybe she missed her life in Puerto Rico. Maybe she had called a relative there, and perhaps told them she was homesick.

Anyway, they were running out of alternatives. Although the call sounded like a long shot, at least it was worth a try.

What else could they do? Not a single witness in the neighborhood could be found who had seen Carmen after she left Jax Drugstore.

It was frustrating to say the least. What was even more frustrating, no one was answering the phone in Puerto Rico. He held the receiver a while longer, listening to it ring a long time before finally hanging up.

He gave the matter more thought. From what the family had told him, Carmen didn't have much money with her so she couldn't make a call from a pay phone, and he didn't think she would ask a neighbor to use their phone to make the call, so it was looking less as if this was a possibility.

He made another note, then leaned back in his chair contemplating the matter. Even if she had called Puerto Rico, she would still be here, somewhere, but where?

What the searchers would not know until it was far too late was that, two hours before they were even notified of Carmen being missing, she was attempting a horrifying escape on Interstate 490 West. Even as he was dialing the phone, hundreds of cars were speeding past Carmen, and nobody was stopping to help.

Chapter *10*

Thursday, November 18, 1971, there was no snow, no wind to speak of, and the temperature was a chilly 38 degrees to start the day, but with a prediction of it going to reach upwards of 69 degrees.

On that day, close to the Riga/Chili border south of the village of Chili, two teenage boys were out riding a motorcycle, taking advantage of the mild, sunny weather that would soon be replaced by the unpredictable wintry storms of snow, freezing temperatures and more snow. After being cooped up in school all day, Evan, who had a Suzuki motorcycle, called his friend to see if he wanted to go riding. He did, and it did not take him long to get ready and head out the door.

Evan could not wait to go out on his motorcycle, so he asked his mother if it was okay. She had heard all too often the dangers of riding a motorcycle, and as a result had made Evan take a class for motorcyclists. For that reason, she felt comfortable allowing him to take his bike out. She nodded her approval.

Evan went into the garage and checked the handlebars, seating position and foot pegs. Satisfied, he put on his driving gear. He was starting to put on his helmet when his friend entered the garage, and together they walked the bike out to the driveway. "Ready?"

"Ready."

They were off. Evan was thankful for the company, but not because he wanted someone to talk to. The bike was too loud to hear what anyone was saying, even if they were riding behind him. Once he started the engine, he was fully engaged. His mind was like a blank slate, soaking up the pure joy of the ride and only paying attention to the terrain around him.

The area was perfect for bike riding as they headed down Griffin, starting at the beginning of the road near Palmer. They turned and headed west until they reached Stearns and stayed on the road all the way to the Mill Creek Golf Club. That was only a five-mile stint. Evan adjusted for a turn of the bike and, checking the traffic, they returned the way they had come to complete another circle. They turned back onto Stearns Road. There was practically no traffic and the area was mostly flat, so the visibility was great. Every now and then they would see groves of trees, then nothing but the flat farmland of the area.

They were heading south on Stearns Road when Evan's friend felt the motorcycle slowing down. At first, he figured the driver was turning back, but looking around, he could see they were still a few miles before their usual turnaround. He leaned around Evan to see what was ahead, but he could see nothing.

"What's the matter, Evan?"

"I don't know. I think I saw something in the ditch. I am going to turn. Hang on."

"What did you see?"

"Not sure. May have been a doll, or something."

Evan turned the bike around, and they headed back the way they had come, going slowly until they reached the spot where he had spotted something. They were about 700 feet south of Griffin Road.

Evan moved the bike off the road and onto the shoulder, where he pressed down the kickstand. He slowly put his foot on the ground and swung his other leg over to join it. He did this in slow motion, as if he were in a daze.

His movements alone had his passenger feeling eerie as he climbed off the bike and stood beside Evan.

The side of the road went down into a ditch just beyond the shoulder and visible from where they stood.

"Look," Evan said, pointing down into the ditch.

His friend's eyes followed the direction that Evans was pointing. He stared down, then turned to look at Evan. "I think it's a doll." He touched Evan's arm. "What do you think?"

At first Evan did not say a word as he continued to stare at the area. Finally, he said, "That's no doll!"

There, in the ditch, was the figure of a little girl with no pants or underwear. Her head was toward the south and her eyes were closed. She lay there motionless, but as he looked at her, he felt that any moment she would open her eyes and stare back at them.

Neither boy moved. They were now sure this was not a doll, and after a few minutes, they were sure that what they were looking at was a body, a dead body of a little girl. It was as if they were in a trance, unable to form a coherent thought, let alone put it into words. Finally, they looked up at the same time, as if hoping the other would take the initiative. "What should we do?"

"I don't know."

A shrug of a shoulder showed their confusion, and they stayed frozen to the spot. Finally, Evan turned toward the road, as if waiting for a car to stop and give them assistance, or better yet, tell them what to do.

But no one came to their aid and probably no one would. So, Evan tried to get his mind working toward a solution. There was only one thought that entered his mind.

"We need to go back to my house."

"What?"

"You know, go back and tell my dad. He'll know what to do."

His friend agreed.

Stupefied, they climbed back on the bike and headed toward Evan's home. It felt as if they would never get there as they retraced their route, both wondering what might have happened to the little girl, yet at the same time, not wanting to think about it. Finally, they pulled into the driveway. Seeing his father's car in the driveway, Evan let out a sigh of relief. It was not that he didn't think his mother could handle the situation, but if he had to describe all of what they had seen, he would feel uncomfortable saying that to her.

"Want me to stay?"

"Sure," Evan said to his friend. As quickly as they could, they moved the bike up the driveway. Evan entered the garage door code and, while they waited for it to open, they took off their helmets. Then, together they pushed the bike to its spot in the garage. They went to the inside door of the garage and took off their boots. Evan touched his friend's shoulder. "Okay, let's do this." Slowly they entered the house.

Neither of them was aware of the expression on their faces as they walked into the kitchen to stand in front of Evan's dad. Evan's father looked up, started to smile, but suddenly stopped. He could see that the boys were either scared or hurt. Something was wrong, that was for sure.

"What is it, Son?"

Evan did not even pause before the words rushed out of his mouth. "Dad, we saw a body."

Not sure he had heard right, his father replied, "A what?"

"A body of a little girl in the ditch. We didn't climb down, but she was half naked and, and..." The words were flying out his mouth, and for the first time he realized how scared he was. Why should he be scared, he wondered?

"Where, Son?"

"About 700 feet south of Griffin Road."

It was as if a load had been lifted off his shoulders as he let the matter go. Evan watched while his father went to the phone and called the sheriff's office. When he hung up, he turned to Evan and asked, "Did you put the bike in the garage?"

"Yes, sir."

"Okay. Come with me." He turned to Evan's friend and said, "You can come too."

Evan gladly followed his dad's orders, along with his friend, and they all climbed into the car. Evan sat in the passenger seat so that he could let his dad know when to pull over. When they were just before the area where he had parked the bike he said, "We're close. Pull over."

He could feel the motion of the car slowing as his dad steered over to the shoulder. "This is it. Right over there," Evan said, pointing just in front of where they were parked.

His father opened his car door and got out, followed by the boys. They walked single file toward the area until all three of them stood looking down in the ditch.

The body was still there. No one spoke, as Evan and his friend stared, as though seeing the body for the first time. Evan's father was silent, trying to decipher in his head what he was seeing. He had never seen a body before either.

Evan let out a sigh. "Here she is, Dad. Here she is."

They just stood there, the father thinking how fragile life was, not sure what had happened to this child, but imagining that she had been hit by a car and rolled into the ditch. His hands trembled and his knees felt weak, but he controlled himself, not wanting to let his son see how disturbed he was. This body was someone's little girl, and he had an overwhelming desire to hug her and comfort her.

Evan and his friend did not know what to think as they stood paralyzed to the spot. They were still staring down into the ditch when they heard a car pulling over behind them. All three turned at the same time, their movements stiff as if they were soldiers about to salute. They watched intently as the police car pulled off the road and onto the shoulder. They continued their vigilance as the deputy climbed out and walked over to join them.

Should they say something, his father wondered, relieved to know that he was about to turn over the reins to someone else. As if connected, all three turned around to face the ditch again, Evan's father moved his head slightly to look at the officer, who just stood there, shock on his face. Evan's dad could tell he was just as disoriented, as if his brain had not yet caught up to what his eyes were seeing. Then, the officer suddenly snapped out of it.

"I've got to call an ambulance." He headed back to his cruiser, and, leaning in through the driver's side window, he picked up the mike to his radio dispatch.

First, he asked for an ambulance to come to the location that he gave them, and then he described the situation. When done, he returned to the trio by the side of the ditch.

"Who found the body?"

"We did," the boys said in unison.

"What were you doing here?"

"Nothing, Officer. We were just riding my bike and we saw her. We thought it was a doll at first."

"Did either of you go down there... Touch anything?"

"No, no Sir, we stayed right up here where we are standing. When we saw her...the body, we climbed back on the bike and headed home to tell my father," Evan said as he pointed at his dad.

"Good. Okay, can you wait here a bit? The investigators should be here soon and may have questions for you." They nodded.

The three of them started toward their car. "No, please," the officer said. "Get in the back seat of my car." Without questioning, they followed his instructions. Once seated, Evan started to ask his father a question, but before he could, the action outside halted him.

They had barely climbed in when several cruisers and an ambulance pulled up.

Two of the investigators immediately walked down the side of the road, one going north and the other south, carefully studying the area for any evidence. They took pictures of the tracks, even the tires on Evan's father's car, as they moved slowly up and down the area near the crime scene.

The three continued to stare out the windows of the cruiser, as one officer moved down the side of the ditch, a distance from where the body was, and started walking around, watching each step he took. In a few minutes, another officer followed behind him and followed the same path, keeping his eyes pinned to the ground on either side of him and in front. Soon they were standing by the body.

The first officer to the scene headed toward them, and this time they saw his name, Officer Peters. He stood by his cruiser and explained that the police were in the process of doing a walk through, to get a feel for the crime scene and hoping to find evidence to explain what had happened here.

"So, I have to ask you again, did you go near the body?"

"No, we swear we didn't," Evan said adamantly.

"I believe you, but I have to ask. Someone put her there, and we want to be sure of any evidence we find. If you had, they could rule out anything from you during the processing. They need to know about and identify everything."

"We thought that maybe a car had hit her, and she was thrown into the ditch."

"It doesn't seem to be the case right now."

Evan let out his breath and felt his dad's hand on his shoulders as the officer left, and they continued to watch.

By now, other cars had stopped and pulled off the road, the occupants trying to get a glimpse of what was happening. There was nothing the police could do about that, nor was it necessary since they had already scrutinized the roadside area. Now they made sure that no one went any further than the edge of the road.

The investigators were focused on what they were here to do. After that initial walk-through, they were busy taking notes and photographing the area. More investigators carefully made their way to the area that had been roped off with yellow tape. One stood back and drew sketches of the scene as it appeared, while another, who had stayed up top, came over to talk with the boys and Evan's father. When they were satisfied that the boys had not been involved, they told them that, but also said they should remain in the cruiser, so that Officer Peters could take them to the station and get their statements.

The police continued documenting the scene, and when they were done, they began gathering the evidence from the crime site. They systematically made their way through the area, collecting all potential evidence, tagging it, logging it, and packaging it, so it remained intact on its way to the lab. The job seemed to take forever.

Down in the ditch, the investigators carefully inspected the body and gathered evidence off the little girl. They made more sketches and took photographs of her body, carefully turning her to get every angle, and to gather any remote piece of evidence that clung to her.

When they were done, they motioned the ambulance men to come down, then waited while the little girl was placed carefully on the stretcher and just as carefully carried up the bank, before being loaded into the ambulance. Now it would be up to the medical examiner and others to inspect the body.

It was dark out by the time the boys and Evan's father were taken to the station. Once there, they called the house to let Evan's mother know where they were and asked that she call his friend's mother too. After they had answered the detective's questions, another officer drove them back to their car. They climbed in, exhausted by the events that had unfolded that day and anxious to put it all behind them.

Before the end of that day the investigators knew that this was a case of a strangulation and most likely a sexual assault of a little girl. Soon they would know more.

Chapter 11

It was Thursday, November 18, 1971, two days into the investigation of Carmen's disappearance, when a call came in to Detective Alexander Ford at the police station.

"They found the body of a young girl out in Riga, near the Chili border."

"Do you know who it is?"

"Well, we're not sure, but the girl is Hispanic and has black hair. She appears to be around ten years' old. We saw the missing person's report from your office and thought this might be your girl."

The caller filled in Detective Ford on all the details from the site and gave him the location where the body had been found. Detective Ford recorded the information and then asked to have a copy of the report sent to him, ASAP.

"No problem. We will keep you updated. When we learn something, you will too."

"Do we know how she died?"

"Strangulation…but that's preliminary. We don't want to say until we have the Medical Examiner's report."

"Fair enough."

"Is that it?"

"Ah, yes…"

"What is it?"

"Well, this is not confirmed, but I think this was a body dump and not where it happened."

"Good to know."

At that point he hung up.

Detective Ford stared off into the distance, then rummaged through his desk. He found what he was looking for and put it in his pocket.

This was not his first time having to tell a family their loved one was dead, but no matter how many times he delivered the news, it ripped his heart out to have to say it. This was the worst because the victim was an innocent child, and he knew that the family would ask the question, "Why?" and there was no answer.

How he wanted to turn this task over to someone else. Having to drive to the house and knock on the front door, clammy sweat breaking out all over him, was not what he wanted to do or how he wanted to feel. He knew how to tell the family the devastating news, but not how to keep his feelings from tearing him apart.

When the door opened and he was face to face with them, he had to swallow that lump in his throat and keep his pain hidden. They were about to hear the worst news a parent can hear, and he must keep his own emotions in check. Carmen had been only missing, so they still had hope. But he was about to shatter that hope. He had to tell them her body had been found.

He needed a moment before he made the call. Slowly he pushed his chair back from the desk and walked down the hall to the lavatory. He looked around the room and saw no one. He leaned over and peeked under the stall partitions. There were no feet. He turned and went over to the sink and looked down at the drain, adjusting his face before finally staring into the mirror.

"Okay. You got this!"

He raised his head and stalled a moment longer until his face was void of any feeling, and rehearsed, "I wanted to tell you straight away that they found a little girl's body in

Chili." He paused as he had learned to do. "She fits the description of Carmen." Another pause.

Yes, he knew the routine, and he would get through it. He had to be honest with them, but because the body had not yet been identified, he could not say for sure it was Carmen. This made it trickier to do.

One more check in the mirror, a splash of cold water on his face, and he was ready. The officer went back to his desk and took a deep breath. With a solemn expression, he picked up the receiver and dialed.

It was this part of the job that he hated most. It did not matter what the circumstances were, or who the person was, even their age didn't matter. It was always the same feeling he got when making the call.

"Hola!" It was Guillermina who answered. He could hear the urgency in her voice. He knew that tone, and it was not one that expected bad news.

"Guillermina," he said slowly. Then in his best Spanish, added. "I would like to come and see you." To the point and brief, just as it should be.

"Yes," she replied.

He was glad she could not speak English well, because she would have asked what was wrong, and even in English he would have had a hard time holding back. It felt as if he were lying, but he knew that was not true.

He hung up the phone. It was time to bring everyone up to date. He got up from his chair and turned to face the room of detectives.

"Men, they found the body of a little girl out in Chili. The description matches that of Carmen, our ten-year-old missing girl. I am on my way to her mother's house now to give her the news and have someone come down to identify the body."

"I'll go with you," Detective Ward offered.

"Thanks, Patrick. It's not going to be easy."

Patrick Ward knew that. He had done it enough times to know it was necessary to have another officer with you when you broke the bad news.

Being Detectives, Patrick and Alexander wore suits and ties. They grabbed their coats and gloves before walking down the hallway to the exit together.

The two detectives did not wait for the elevator but went over to the stairs and opened the door. "After you," Alex said, stepping aside. As they went down the stairwell, Alex told Patrick how he wanted to handle the encounter. He was quite sure that probably other family members had already been summoned to the house, so there would be someone to go with them to identify the body. Alex said that he was sure Guillermina might want to but would be in no shape to handle it herself.

They stepped out into the lobby of the building and made their way out the side door to the parking lot. "I'll drive," Patrick said. They climbed into Patrick's car and headed out.

It was a silent ride over to 72 Romeyn Street. They would have plenty to say once they arrived. The family would have questions, and at that moment they were going over in their minds the correct procedures. When they pulled up in front of the house, they had not even stepped out of the car before the door of the house was opened.

Alex turned to Patrick and said, "Okay, let's do this."

Slowly they got out of the car, and, after adjusting their ties, made their way up to the front door, careful to keep their faces from showing any emotion.

Guillermina stepped back to allow them to enter, and for an instant Alex's eyes met hers. He allowed himself to nod, before entering the front room.

As expected, there were several family members present, including several he had met earlier. He knew that they would be able to help translate his message. He had not given much thought to it, but maybe he should have brought along an officer who could speak Spanish. Alex looked over at Patrick and decided that he himself was best equipped to handle the sensitivity of the matter. That was more important now.

As if testing the situation, he looked at Guillermina. "Please, have a seat."

Immediately someone came forward, repeating his words and helping Guillermina to a chair. When she was seated, he nodded at Alex.

"Guillermina, I wanted to tell you straight away that they found a little girl's body in Chili."

He paused. The atmosphere in the room was so tense he wanted to continue, but knew he had to wait and give them time to absorb what he had said.

He saw the change in Guillermina's expression. Her eyes stared at him as if trying to see into his soul, while her mouth trembled. One of the other family members in the room said something in Spanish and gave Guillermina a handkerchief.

Clearing his throat, Detective Ford looked at Guillermina with respect and held her gaze as he continued.

"She fits the description of Carmen."

Another pause. He felt the heaviness of the words hanging in the air, and his pulse raced as he forced himself to maintain eye contact.

Someone in the room asked in English, "What are you saying? They found a body in Chili that fits the description of Carmen or that it is Carmen?"

While he spoke, someone was whispering to Guillermina. Through her sobs Guillermina spoke in Spanish, tugging at her cousin's arm to translate her question.

"Detective, she wants to know if Carmen is dead and what happened to Carmen."

Patrick stepped forward and surprised Alex by speaking to the mother in Spanish. This time Alex waited, and when Patrick was finished speaking, he told Alex that he had explained why, until a family member identified her, they could not know for sure that the body was Carmen.

That seemed to satisfy Guillermina, but the cousin had questions of his own. He wanted to know who did this and how she was killed. Detective Ford explained that they had no leads yet, and, until the coroner completed the autopsy, they wouldn't know exactly what had transpired.

The relatives translated each word, and he could watch Guillermina's reaction to each devastating announcement. At the proper moment, he moved next to his partner. They stood uncomfortably in front of the grieving family, giving them time to adjust to the news before saying another word. Before they could leave, they had to break her heart one more time.

From the moment they entered the house it was easy to see from the relatives' expressions they had not thought for a minute that Carmen was dead. They thought that she was out there somewhere. The night she went missing they figured she might have stopped to get some candy or gone to a friend's house. Even though it had been two days, they still held on to hope that she was out there somewhere. Never did they think she was dead.

After enough time had passed, Detective Ford said, "Mrs. Colón, we can't be positive this is Carmen until we have her identified by a member of the family." He then paused, looking around the room.

"Can someone accompany us downtown and identify the body?"

There were several small children in the household who could not be left alone. He hoped this would encourage someone other than Guillermina to come identify the body.

Guillermina was beside herself, unable to speak. He could see her trying to grab hold of what little hope he had just given her. She had not been identified yet. Maybe it was not Carmen at all.

He had not said those words to give hope, but because it was procedure. The body looked like Carmen, but there was no identification on her to support that.

Detective Ford reached into his pocket and pulled out what he had taken from his desk.

He moved over to Guillermina and touched her gently on the shoulder. She had been sobbing into the hanky and looked up, her eyes red and puffy, her face twisted in her grief. The detective reached over and took her wrist, bringing it towards him. He placed the picture in her hand.

Guillermina looked confused as her fingers wrapped around the edge of the picture. She looked down and sobbed openly as she stared at her daughter's face, smiling up at her.

"I want you to remember her this way." That is all he said.

The moment was interrupted when the detective heard someone in the group say, "I'll go."

Detective Ford gave Guillermina's shoulder a light squeeze and turned his attention back to the room, searching for who had spoken.

"Angel Colón, Detective, I'm Guillermina's nephew."

"Yes, I remember you. Thank you, Angel."

"I'll go with him," added Julio, another uncle of Carmen's. There was a pile of coats on a chair in the room, and while Angel searched through them to find his, Julio said something to the other family members present before gathering up his outerwear from the chair.

While Julio was putting on his coat, Alex turned to his companion with a puzzled expression. Patrick leaned toward him and whispered. "He told them not to mention any of this to the grandparents until they were sure it was Carmen."

"Okay, Angel, Julio. If you are ready, I think we should go." Before leaving the room, the detectives nodded at the group before heading out the door.

The four men went to the cruiser, and Alex opened the passenger door. "Watch your head." Angel lowered his head and once seated; Alex closed the door. On the other side of the cruiser, Patrick did the same as Julio climbed in. With the passengers set, Patrick climbed behind the wheel and Alex settled in the passenger seat.

While Patrick pulled the cruiser out onto the street, Alex picked up the two-way radio and made a call to the coroner's office to let them know they were on their way. While in the midst of making the call, he turned and looked out the passenger window and saw Guillermina with her rosary, watching from the front window of her home.

The detectives headed southwest on Romeyn Street toward Campbell Street and turned right. The streets were quiet when they reached Grape Street and made a quick left before heading toward Wilder Street and making another left-hand turn.

Inside the cruiser there was quiet, except for the static coming over the lines on the radio. Alex found the silence comforting, knowing where they were going and why. He stared out the window at the two story homes that seemed to be basically all the same as they turned right onto Brown Street before making another right onto West Main, where the street was wider and the view changed from homes to businesses. The silence continued as they made their way to NY-33A.

Patrick concentrated on his driving, while Alex stared out the window. Occasionally, during the three-mile drive, he chanced a glance at the back seat passengers who sat with their hands folded in their laps. He had been in this position before, but he could never get used to it. He could feel the strain in his neck as he barely turned his head during the drive. Finally, Patrick saw the sign for East Henrietta Rd and guided the cruiser over to the exit. They were almost there now.

Patrick turned right at the end of the exit and soon they were pulling up in front of the Medical Examiner's office. Once the car was parked, the passengers wasted no time in debarking. They walked together to the front of the building. Once inside they continued down hallways until arriving at the coroner's office.

"Wait here," Detective Ford said as he disappeared behind the doorway.

Several minutes passed. Patrick did not know what to say as he stood with the two men, working his neck back and forth to relieve the tension. He was relieved when Alex reappeared and announced, "Please, follow me."

The reality of the situation seemed to have slowed the feet of Angel and Julio as they moved into the room. In a few steps they would be close to the metal table that was draped with a white sheet. The Medical Examiner stood silently waiting for them, not rushing the moment. Finally, Angel spoke. "Let's do this."

They walked closer and, when the men stood near the table, the Medical Examiner slowly lowered the sheet.

She was white as chalk. Her eyes were closed as if she were sleeping. Angel's face showed stunned surprise, knowing that had her eyes opened, she would have been staring straight at him. But she did not see him.

Julio stood next to Angel, his reaction differing in that his shoulders hunched together as if he were trying to disappear inside himself. He reached over to hang onto the side of the table and, feeling his legs begin to buckle, leaned his weight against Angel.

Angel was shaken back to reality and supported Julio. At that moment, the Medical Examiner raised the sheet.

"Are you all right?" the detective asked.

"Yes, I'm fine." Angel took a deep breath. "That's her. That's our Carmen."

"Are you sure?" asked the Medical Examiner.

"Yes, I'm sure. That's Carmen Colón."

The detectives thanked the Medical Examiner and then walked the two men out. Stolidly they walked down the hallway, out the door and to the car. Patrick unlocked the front passenger door for Alex and then walked around to open the driver's side, while Alex unlocked the door and helped Angel into the back seat. Patrick did the same, waiting for Julio to be seated in the back behind him.

"So, what now?" Angel asked.

Alex cleared his throat and said, "That depends. Because she was murdered, they will need to do an autopsy first and gather any physical evidence to determine what caused her death."

"So, you've done this before. What amount of time are we talking? I need to tell her mother something."

Alex gave himself time to think and then added, "Even if a cause and manner of death are pending, her body will be released within 24 to 48 hours of examination and sent to the funeral home you choose.

"Thank you."

Julio had finally recovered and asked, "What will you do now?"

"Well, we have evidence that we gathered at the scene and will add what the coroner finds after the autopsy. That will help us to further our investigation."

"Will it help you get who killed our Carmen?"

"It should. But I can tell you that we will start right away and not stop until we catch him, or her."

That seemed to satisfy the passengers, and they were silent the rest of the way back to the residence. When they pulled up in front of Guillermina's home, the detectives started to get out, but were stopped.

"Thank you, detectives, but we would rather tell the family alone."

They nodded and waited until the men were inside before pulling away from the curb.

Chapter 12

On Monday, November 22 at 8:30 a.m. Carmen was laid to rest. In St Peter and Paul's Roman Catholic Church at 720 Main Street West, some two hundred family and friends gathered to celebrate a life cut all too short. Carmen Colón, just ten years old, had been murdered. Those who attended her funeral, given in Spanish, faced trying to remember the child while trying to forget what happened to her.

Who knew Carmen would die that day? They recalled the yelling and crying that filled their lives on hearing the news, and that stayed with them, that and the sleepless nights knowing she would never come home again.

The service may have helped give family and friends some much-needed closure, but the memories of what happened would stay with them a long time. It was so hard to let those memories leave because a child of 10-years-old had not had enough life to live.

The priest reminded them that God created each person for eternal life, and that they should be confident in their conviction that death is not the end, nor does it break the bonds of family, friendship and community that are forged in life.

Even with the knowledge of their Catholic beliefs over many years of being faithful Catholics, they found it hard to understand why Carmen had been taken from them.

The priest ended the services by emphasizing that funerals are a special time for God's grace and mercy, a time to open their hearts, receive His blessings and place their hope in the resurrection of His Son, Jesus Christ.

It was with solemn faces that they left the church to take Carmen to her final resting place, Holy Sepulchre Cemetery.

The mourners climbed into the waiting cars and headed east on West Main Street toward Willowbank Place. Not a word was spoken, as the car turned left onto Jefferson Avenue and then right onto Brown Street. Carmen's grandparents were beside themselves, unable to hold back their tears as the caravan continued and finally reached State Street that changes into Lake Avenue. The closer they got to their destination, the harder the journey became. When the car entered Holy Sepulchre Cemetery at 2461 Lake Ave a few minutes more would pass before they arrived at the gravesite, and the passengers disembarked. The five-mile drive had not been long enough to deal with its inevitable ending

The pain did not end for her grandparents. At their home on Brown Street the shadow of Carmen was everywhere, and it became too much for them to handle. So as not to forget her, but to be able to go on with their lives, Felix and Candida decided to move. They found a place on Grand Avenue just off Webster Avenue, four miles away from their current location.

Chapter 13

Carmen Colón, ten, disappeared November 16, 1971. She was found two days later in Riga, New York, near Chili, twelve miles from where she had last been seen.

Thursday, November 18, 1971, the body of Carmen Colón was found around 4:30 p.m., at which time the missing person investigation became a homicide case.

When the autopsy report was completed, the investigators had valuable information to aid in their search for the murderer.

The Medical Examiner reported that Carmen Colón had been dead for at least twenty-four hours by the time her body was discovered, which meant she had been murdered around 5:30 p.m. on November 16. It was observed that she had been raped, and there was food in her stomach. On her body, it was noted that she had bruising marks on the front of her neck, black eyes, and blood in her eyes, which led to the conclusion that Carmen had been strangled, and that it had been done from in front, face-to-face. She suffered a skull fracture from head trauma, and scratches which might have been made by fingernails were found over Carmen's entire body.

This final piece of information started the investigators wondering if the man had a female accomplice.

The department acted quickly, and within the first twenty-four hours of the murder investigation, eight men had been questioned. From the information gathered, they began to identify possible suspects among the prospects.

Prior to beginning each interview, they researched the suspect. They gathered information to set up a profile that included criminal records, if any, and any past investigations that they were included or involved in.

Detective Ford was at the head of the investigation, and he refreshed his knowledge of the Carmen Colón case, then sent out feelers to find out if there was anything new to add to the case. He spent hours trying to discover evidence to demonstrate motive, opportunity, and means.

The detective wrote down everything, knowing it would be important to have versions of events recorded. From experience, he knew that some of the information would prove useless, and some might include purposely untrue statements. Either way, the information would be useful in identifying suspects.

This was the way to proceed until more evidence was discovered; evidence that would give the investigators reasonable grounds to suspect that a specific person was involved in the rape and murder of Carmen.

At the end of the last interview, Detective Ford sat back and reviewed everything he knew, and though he had hoped for a more positive result, he believed none of the men interviewed was involved in or performed the murder of Carmen Colón. They had no motive and their alibis checked out.

With the police working overtime on the case, another suspect was identified. His name was James Barber, and in checking out his profile, they learned that he was a known sex-offender from Ohio. He was a suspect in the case of a 13-year-old girl child named Sandy Ann Wesolowski, who had last been seen in Glens Falls, New York on August 8, 1971. This was just a 3-hour 52-minute drive to Rochester; a total of 239.4 miles by way of the Thruway.

The report said that Sandy Ann had gone to Haviland Cove Beach to swim with her brother and a female friend earlier in the day, and she had last been seen walking away from her home on Broad Street in Glens Falls, New York at 3:00 p.m. on August 8. Sandy had been sent back to the beach by her mother and had disappeared near the intersection of Hudson Avenue and Spring Street. Authorities were still looking for her.

As the detective read the report, his confidence dwindled that this suspect could be the man who had raped and murdered Carmen Colón. But he read on.

Suddenly he leaned back in his chair with a surprised expression on his face. The last part of the report stated that James Barber was in Rochester now, and he worked in the Bull's Head area.

The police acted quickly. Several police officers were dispatched immediately to pick up James Barber. They were to tell him they would like him to come in for an interview and nothing more. As they drove to his place of work, they were going over what they would say to get him to come into the precinct, but they would find they need not have bothered.

When they arrived, the officers went into the building and checked in with his foreman.

"We're here to see James Barber," they said.

"Well, you are out of luck," replied his foreman.

"Why is that?"

"He left the job without giving us any notice. I went out on a limb to hire him, and that's how he paid me."

"When did he leave?"

"Last time I saw him was on November 18."

Up to date on the Carmen Colón case, the police knew that this was the same day that Carmen's body was found. When they checked back with Detective Ford, he felt that they were on the right track with this man. Ford checked his records, and, according to the M.E., Carmen was murdered around 5:30 p.m.

So, they now had a viable suspect in James Barber. The foreman was very cooperative, giving them James Barber's timecard for November 16, 1971.

Steadying his hand, the officer took the card. He paused to take a deep breath before looking at it. When he looked down at the card, he let out a gasp.

"Here, let me see it," his partner said.

He handed it to him and looking over his shoulder he viewed it again. What they saw was that Mr. Barber had penciled in his time instead of punching it with the company's automated system.

"Can we get a copy of this?"

"Sure, wait here."

This looked like a solid lead, a very solid one. When they had the copy in hand, they headed back to the cruiser and immediately called in to share what they had found.

Not taking any chances, while the officers had been at Mr. Barber's workplace, another two officers had been sent to his place of residence. When they called in to tell Detective Ford of their findings, they said that he had obviously left in a hurry.

"Why do you say that?"

"Well detective, he hasn't taken anything with him. It looks like he did not bother to take his belongings from the apartment. If I had to guess, he probably took whatever he had on him at work with him."

"Thanks, Guys. Come on in and we will discuss the next step."

Now they had proof that James Barber did not have a feasible alibi and that he was obviously on the run. This gave credence to him being a suspect in the murder of Carmen Colón. As a known rapist, he clearly had the motive to be considered for the crime. A manhunt was soon underway to locate him. They talked to neighbors and co-workers, trying to gather evidence and a lead as to where he could be. They worked hard at trying to locate him, and while that was taking place, they were gathering evidence to connect him to the Carmen Colón case.

To their dismay, after following every lead they had, they did not find him, and eventually the trail ran cold.

Information kept coming in as everyone wanted to help find who killed Carmen Colón. One witness told the police she had called them earlier in the week to report a man she had seen in a car talking to a little girl. They picked her up for an interview, but she admitted she had not seen anything that connected that individual to the murder. They thanked her for her involvement, letting her know that if she thought of anything more, she should contact them.

In the file was a report about checking the Morrell's Cigar Store. They had shown the owner pictures of suspects to see if anyone looked familiar, but he could not recognize any of the people in the photographs. They did the same at Padilla's Market and Cruppe's Dry Cleaners with no luck.

It was obvious that the people in the neighborhood were suspicious of the police and did not want to be questioned. They had their reasons, as some of them were without green cards or visas and did not want to be deported.

Others had personal matters going on that they did not want pried into by the police.

But that did not stop the police. It took a lot of persuasion to get residents to open up and share what they knew. They learned from Ramon Padilla, who resided at Maple Street, that he had six children, and sometime back a guy tried to get one of his daughters into his car. He did not have much more than that to share. He was not specific on the date, nor did he have any description of the man or the car.

It was enough though, to get the police speculating that this could possibly be their guy. Since they had nothing that would point the man out, there was only one way to find him, and that was to keep an eye on the house and hope that he would reappear.

The surveillance went on for the next five days, but to no avail. The suspect did not try it again. A record of the incident and the follow-up was put in the Colón folder.

Then a neighbor from down the street from Carmen's grandparents' house contacted them. He told the officers that he had lived in the neighborhood for over forty years and had seen it deteriorate. Without hesitation, he told the officers he listened to the police scanner at home.

"And why is that?" the officer asked.

"Because Felix and Candida let their grandkids play in the backyard a lot, and I worry about them. Felix and Candida are getting older and cannot keep an eye on them every second. This way I can warn them of any danger."

What could they say but, "Thanks for sharing that and for being a good neighbor"?

The officers were smiling as they left to return to their cruiser. They had dealt with individuals who would not look out their curtains at night even if a bomb went off, and others who would deny any information that they could possibly have on something they had seen. To have someone tell them they looked out for their neighbor was a breath of fresh air.

While suspects were being questioned, there were investigators hunting for Carmen's pants and undergarments. When she had been found, she was not wearing them and, so far, they had not turned up. There would be evidence on the garments that might help further their investigation, so they continued searching.

Once the word got out about the murder of Carmen Colón, reporters stayed on top of the investigation, sensing that, from all the activity surrounding the case, it was destined to become high-profile. The police did not fight it; instead they smartly embraced the attention, knowing that the media would help them reach more people. Maybe by shaking more bushes, more witnesses would appear.

The police were not giving up. They began re-canvassing Carmen's neighborhood in hopes of getting people to talk. When people are crammed into city neighborhoods, there is not much privacy, and neighbors become spectators to one another's personal lives. Living in homes so close to each other the residents know how important it is to create boundaries and respect one another's privacy. But sometimes the outside encroaches, and the neighbors' business becomes theirs, whether they want it to or not.

So, what should they do? They could call the police. But they ran the risk of wasting police time or mortifying their neighbors. Even worse, they figured they could put their neighbors in danger if the police were to accidentally find out they were without green cards or visas. So instead, they simply ignored the issue and hoped someone else would talk.

The police were aware of the setbacks, but they continued to dig for information, giving special attention to the area around the Jax Drugstore, since that was where Carmen was last seen.

"Somebody must've seen something," said Detective Ford, looking around the highly populated area. "Someone knows something or saw something. We need to make them comfortable enough to tell us." He paused, looking at the two officers who accompanied him. They nodded their heads.

As they set out to see what they could learn to help with the case, they quickly realized the neighborhood's attitude had changed. Reading in the newspapers that the little girl Carmen had been abducted and raped right there in their own backyard had opened their eyes, and they told what they knew.

They were really depressed about what was going on, for most either knew the family or had seen them around. They could not help identifying with them now, because if it had happened to the Colóns, it could happen to them. Seeing another family inconsolable fueled the situation and encouraged them to try and help the police.

The investigators were told that officers had never been called out to the Colon home before. "Just an innocent life that was taken, really, for no reason and that's what makes this difficult," said one neighbor.

The question on everyone's mind was why, which, when there was not an answer, caused panic. They knew some killers were motivated by revenge, but that scenario did not fit. Then there were killers who kill just because the opportunity presents itself. If that was the case, they were dealing with the type of murderer who would be the hardest to find.

The news was now out there, and the facts were frightening. Carmen's case riveted the entire nation, so it was inevitable that details would eventually be learned about that day Carmen Colón was running for her life.

Rochester commuters who had witnessed the bizarre and terrifying sight in the breakdown lane of 1-490 West began calling in. They reported seeing a dark-haired little girl, naked from the waist down, racing along the shoulder of the interstate near the Chili-Riga exit. Others remembered seeing the girl waving her arms as if to elicit attention from passing drivers. Still others reported seeing, ahead of her, a car backing up. This was followed by callers saying that when the car was close, a man jumped out, grabbed her, and led the terrified child back to the vehicle. It was noticed that the man was literally dragging her by the arm. And finally, the report was added that they saw the car with the little girl get back onto the highway and drive away.

That is what it took to get the full picture, as there was no way that a person driving on an expressway would have seen the whole incident. Pieces woven together from several witnesses provided the scenario.

In all there were thirty-eight witnesses who saw this drama unfolding on November 16, but not one would report it until November 18, three days later. By then, the lifeless body of Carmen Colón had been found.

The observations of that night would be circumstantial details to add to the file, since there was no actual identifiable proof that it had been Carmen who had been seen running down the shoulder of the Western Expressway. The girl had looked like Carmen. She had been described as naked from the waist down, and the body had been found in that condition. But experience had taught the detectives that, just because it seemed logical, it was not necessarily fact.

Nothing was considered unimportant, as every fragment of information added another layer to the investigation. Justiniano Colón, Carmen's father, stating that Carmen was a very friendly little girl was important. The fact that her grandmother did not understand how anyone could do such a thing to an innocent girl was important. Teachers who saw Carmen as struggling with her English were important. All of this information helped to establish a profile of Carmen.

The investigators started looking into those in authority as possible suspects. They interviewed teachers, counselors, police officers and firefighters who were in the area at the time of the abduction. They looked carefully at church personnel, school staff, social services workers, and other similar individuals, as well as anyone who may have had access to family information.

Nothing panned out.

Then their sights were directed towards someone perhaps posing as one of these authority figures, which led to hundreds more people being questioned, to no avail.

Continuous investigation went on in Carmen Colón's neighborhood. A child raised in this environment would be unusually vulnerable, and the transient nature of residents would make it easy for someone to move about unnoticed. So, they asked questions and followed with interviews of strangers in the area or people acting contrarily. Again, they came up empty.

What did they have, mused Detective Ford as he reviewed the file. The ME report had noted that Carmen had eaten within two hours of her death. This could be how the killer had lured the child into his car. This would explain why her abduction was perceived as a child climbing into a car voluntarily.

Another point of significance was that light-colored cat fur had been found on her clothing. They had checked with the family and learned that neither the grandparents nor her mother had a cat, so this might be trace evidence. A cat might be how the abductor got Carmen into the car. Of course, there was also the possibility she had seen a cat and picked it up at some point.

The incident garnered massive media coverage while the investigators continued canvassing and pursued all leads. Instead of in-house interviews, they began bringing the family and friends into the station, hoping out of earshot of others they could glean more information.

It did not take long before their sights turned toward Miguel Colón, the common-law husband of Guillermina and also Carmen's uncle.

When they called Miguel Colón in for an interview, they were judicious in announcing their intentions. Since the detectives thought of him as a viable suspect, they did not want to scare him off or put him on the defensive. As far as Miguel was concerned, this interview was just another round of fact-finding.

That was true, except they had discovered something that made them suspicious. In previous interviews they had learned that prior to Carmen's abduction, Miguel had purchased a car, so they had asked if they could search the vehicle. Miguel gave them permission.

During that search of the car the investigators detected an unusual smell. Further investigation revealed that the trunk had been recently washed with a cleaning solution. That raised a red flag.

However, before jumping to conclusions, they took the issue a step further. They tracked down the person who had sold Miguel the car and asked him, "Before you sold the car to Miguel Colón, did you clean it?"

"Of course, we cleaned it."

"I mean, did you wash the interior with any detergent?"

"Well, no, we did not go that far. Is that a problem?"

"No. Oh no. Just asking. Thanks. You've been a big help."

The seller was puzzled. Having the police officers ask if he had given the interior of a car a bath was odd and scared him. He calmed down some when they told him he was not in any trouble, but he kept on his guard.

After that interview, the two had been excited, but tried to remain calm as they walked back to the cruiser. Once inside, Detective Ford said, "Okay, so they did not detergent-wash the trunk of the car."

Officer Rodríguez nodded, adding, "and we did find one of Carmen's dolls in Miguel's car."

Feeling confident they now had a good lead, they went back to the station and added this new evidence to the folder.

Continuing to be thorough, Detective Ford made a call to the family to check on the doll they had found in Miguel's car. They were told that Carmen rode in that car frequently after Miguel got it, and she could have left her doll in the car at any time.

At the next briefing, Detective Ford shared what he had learned, and others added more details to the case file. Once everything was in, they began a review of what they knew about the car that had been seen near Carmen, as well as the car seen on the expressway. It was frustrating to realize that there were at least six different descriptions given for the vehicle that passersby had seen on the side of the highway that night, and only one matched Miguel's. As for the car seen in the neighborhood, no one could describe it as it was dark. And now, every piece of possible evidence discovered on Miguel's car was in question, since they could not say for certain this was the car.

The officers had a suspicion that the Colón family was holding back information, but they did not know if what they had not shared was relevant to the case. They continued to contact the family, hoping to glean new leads, and they listened carefully to comments they made. Even though they had no direct tie back to the car, they did not write it off.

The more they prodded, the more obvious it was that the immediate members of the Colón family believed in Miguel's innocence. They told the police repeatedly that Miguel was a truly kind and protective father to Carmen.

So, after a long interview covering timelines and what they had discovered about his car, they released Miguel, thanking him for his help. At that point they felt confident he had nothing to do with the rape or murder of Carmen. Only later did their opinion change.

Countless headlines appeared in newspapers across the country during the last half of November 1971, covering the story of the abduction and murder of 10-year-old Carmen Colón. Two months after Carmen Colón's body was found, billboards with Carmen's school portrait were placed around the area. The leads began pouring in from all over.

By April of 1972, five months after the murder, the number of people questioned in Carmen's case had climbed to thousands.

The leads, added to those collected from family, friends, acquaintances, business owners and employees in the Bull's Head neighborhood, now had branched out beyond the area. Included in that list were known sex offenders living in Rochester, especially in that southwest section of the city.

Keeping in constant contact with the Colón family it became clear to the public that they were not just suffering mentally, but also suffering financially. The police put the word out, and on Friday, November 19, the Gannett newspapers donated $200 to help the family financially.

A hotline set up by the police headquarters kept ringing. Callers were informed they would be assigned an ID number for anonymity. Again, Gannett stepped up, giving $2,500 toward a reward to those providing information leading to an arrest in the Carmon Colón case.

An unsettling tip was received on Saturday, November 20. The police were called to the Sibley, Lindsay and Curr department store at 228 Main Street East, less than two miles from the houses of Carmen's grandparents and mother. The officers quickly rushed to the store and were taken to the sixth floor of the department store. There they were led to the men's room. Their jaws dropped as they stared at the door where in pencil had been written, 'he killed a 10-year-old girl, who will be next?'

"Okay, we are going to need to get fingerprints of everyone who touched this door, so that we can begin to identify and eliminate suspects."

"Okay, but that will be a long list, Sir."

"Doesn't matter." He turned to the investigator who had come with them. "Okay, dust the door and areas around it for fingerprints and photograph everything."

Soon reward money was coming in to support the effort. Citizens for a Decent Community (CDC) donated $1,000, and the Ibero-American Action League, Inc. donated $500. Edward Morrell, the owner of Morrell's Cigar Store, personally donated $100. Other businesses and private reward funds kept being added until the reward had grown to more than $6,000.

It was an all-out effort which thankfully led to many tips.

Chapter 14

Detective Ford's phone rang. He picked it up.

"We found out that Miguel Colón has a criminal record."

They had kept searching for information on Miguel even after they had decided he was not responsible for the murder of Carmen. Upon hearing he had a criminal record, they sent an officer out to bring him back in, but by then he was on the run.

The police received reports of sightings, and each time officers were dispatched to each location. Information coming in took them first to New York City and then to Syracuse, but Miguel managed to evade them.

Detective Ford was studying the case when the phone rang. He picked it up quickly, hoping they had finally tracked down Miguel.

"Hey. Detective Ford, did you hear, Miguel Colón has fled the area?"

Alex sat up straight in his chair, his hands working through the pile of papers to find the interview folder on Miguel.

"No, I had not heard. Do we know where he is now?"

"Yes, the family said he went to Puerto Rico."

Alex was silent, pondering the matter as he searched the paperwork. The police had determined, after numerous interviews, that Miguel Colón had nothing to do with his niece's abduction and murder. There was no value put on the evidence or his demeanor to point a finger at him. It was all explained away. Had he missed something in the interviews?

"So, what do we want to do now?"

The question brought Alex back. "Tell me what you learned."

"Well, after the family said he was on his way to Puerto Rico, I checked with my informant who said he left quickly. It was not planned. When my informant asked him what was up, he told him that he had done something wrong. That was why he was leaving."

"He said he had done something wrong in Rochester?"

"Yes, That is what my informant said."

Trying not to sound too excited, Detective Ford calmly replied. "So, did he tell you where in Puerto Rico he was going?

"Not exactly, but he thought possibly Guayama."

It seemed like good information, since the Colóns still had family in Guayama, Puerto Rico. They had a sister and two nieces on Guillermina's side. Finally, they had a starting point.

"Find him."

The District Attorney, Hamilton Burns, along with two Rochester Sheriff's detectives, a Spanish interpreter and a stenographer from the DA's office boarded a plane at the Rochester Airport headed for Puerto Rico. On the plane they reviewed the case file so that everyone was up to date.

Miguel Colón had a criminal record, and now he had fled Rochester soon after the murder of Carmen Colón. At this point he became suspect number one.

The police had called ahead to make sure the investigation would be conducted with the full cooperation of the San Juan police department, already briefed on the investigation. Meanwhile in San Juan they put out feelers to try and locate his whereabouts.

When they landed and made their way to the San Juan Police Department, the visitors were met with disappointment. The Puerto Rican investigation had hit a brick wall. Miguel was nowhere to be found.

"Now what?"

"I guess we call home and tell them and get instructions on what to do next."

They made the call, expecting they would be told to return home. The area was beautiful and the temperatures warm, but they felt like fish out of water there, so when the word came down that they were not going home, they had mixed emotions.

"We just learned that Miguel is hiding in the jungle." They looked at each other. "Can you hold a minute?"

They turned toward the Puerto Rican police, who were there in the room. "They're saying they have a lead. They were told that Miguel Colón may be hiding out in the jungle."

Through the help of the interpreter they were told, "Guayama is southeastern Puerto Rico. Thorn and scrub vegetation predominates on the drier south side, but there are tropical rainforests covering parts of the north side of the island. Guess they must mean we need to go to the rainforests!"

"Ah, are we going to run into anything, you know, dangerous?"

"No worry. Land animals are mostly confined to nonpoisonous snakes, lizards, mongooses, and the coqui." Seeing their puzzled looks, he added, "a frog that has become a kind of national mascot."

District Attorney Burns smiled and said, "Guess we'll be guests for a little longer."

They were escorted out of the precinct and taken to a resident hotel. The local detective got them a couple of rooms and told them he would be back to pick them up in the morning. "Get some rest. It may be a long day, Officers."

During the interim, the party was brought up to date on what had taken place that had led to Miguel leaving Rochester and going to New York City and then to Syracuse. He had been suspicious after their last interview with him and had fled. Miguel had taken off, leaving his restaurant job, without picking up his pay for the week.

No one knew what this terrible thing he had done in Rochester could be except, perhaps, the murder of Carmen Colón, but that was speculation.

In any case, knowing that the police were getting close, he had no choice but to flee the area and go to Puerto Rico. He felt safe for a while, but then there was a leak to the San Juan Star saying that the police were here from Rochester, New York, looking for Miguel Colón. They made him out to be dangerous, saying he was armed.

Afraid that this would put the family in jeopardy, Miguel went into hiding.

For the police, each lead ended in disappointment and the trail ran cold. With no other leads to follow, the team called home and were told to catch a plane back to

Rochester. Tired, disappointed, and frustrated, they returned home.

Once on the ground, The D.A. was angered, learning that the Democrat and Chronicle in Rochester had contacted the San Juan Star to alert them that a suspect they sought had fled to Puerto Rico. Miguel Colón had gotten wind of the search and fled the area, putting the detectives a step behind Miguel Colón in their efforts to locate him.

After that fiasco, it was time to play hardball. Word went out that the police in Rochester had his mother, Candida Colón, in custody and were going to keep her incarcerated until he turned himself in.

It worked. Miguel Colón was now being sought by the FBI, the police, and the Puerto Rican authorities. He received the news that his mother had been taken into custody in Rochester, and that forced his hand. During the early evening of March 26, Miguel turned himself in to a police drug and narcotics unit in Guaynabo, a town in northeastern Puerto Rico. Guaynabo is part of the metropolitan area of San Juan, lying south-southwest of the city.

The ploy had worked like a charm. The narcotics unit took Miguel to the detective division of the Commonwealth Police Department in San Juan.

Miguel answered their questions and they gathered information about his activity.

When he first got to Puerto Rico, he had lived in the San Juan suburb of Puerta de Tierra, but during the time he

117

was being sought, he moved to at least two other towns, Carolina and Guaynabo.

Once they finished the interrogation and felt sure he had honestly answered their questions, this information was given to the Monroe County Sheriff's office, when they called to inform them, they had Miguel in custody.

From that point things moved quickly. The investigators flew to San Juan and took custody of Miguel. Miguel gave them no trouble as he climbed on the plane and was taken back to Rochester. The group landed in Rochester at nine o'clock the night of March 27, and Miguel was escorted directly to the sheriff's office where the interrogation began.

Questions flew and Miguel had all the answers as he proclaimed his innocence.

"So, why did you run?"

"I did not run!"

"You call taking off with no notice and not even picking up your pay, not running? We know you got word that we were coming after you in Puerto Rico"

Not missing a beat, Miguel said, "I left to visit my aunt. That was it. When I learned that I was being sought, I turned myself in."

"Sure, Miguel, it was urgent you visit your aunt, quickly. We get it." He could hear the disbelief in their voices.

"You don't believe me. Give me a lie detector test so I can prove my innocence."

The officers looked at each other, nodded and said, "Wait right here."

Not wasting any time, they made the arrangements. Miguel took a lie detector test at the state police headquarters in Canandaigua, New York. Everyone waited anxiously for the results, hoping this would give them something to work with, because throughout the six-hour interrogation, Miguel had maintained his innocence.

He passed. The DA, along with the rest of the group involved in the case, had a feeling of being let down. As if grasping for hope, DA Burns argued, "Lie detector tests can lie. They are not admissible in court because of the longstanding debate about their accuracy."

DA Burns knew the questions that had been asked and looked over the results of the tests for himself. He had to agree, from what he could see there was nothing that proved Miguel had murdered his niece, Carmen Colón.

Yet his gut feeling was that Miguel did murder Carmen Colón.

The Rochester Police continued a door-to-door investigation and manned special number tip lines. They constantly rushed off to question a suspect only to find the suspect had an iron-clad alibi for the time of the murder.

Aimlessly they reviewed the files they had accumulated on Carmen Colón's murder. There was information in the file on all the possible suspects, including Miguel Colón, but nowhere in the information collected was enough evidence to secure a conviction on anyone.

In November of 1972, almost a year since Carmen Colón's death, optimism was fading.

The file on Carmen Colón bulged with details that consumed four two-inch-thick volumes containing reports and tips. This was the most difficult type of murder case to solve, because of lack of definitive evidence. There was no definite description of the car, no clues on the body to identify the perpetrator, no physical evidence of any type. There were no descriptions of the murderer to warrant identification, and something of interest, but not definite, was that there may have been a woman with the man.

Proof positive that the incident that had unfolded on the highway involved Carmen Colón came when her crumpled and frozen pants were found in a field in the town of Riga, 200 feet from the Western Expressway, near a barren rest area about a mile east of the Chili exit. Further investigation revealed that this location was a few hundred feet from the spot where motorists had seen Carmen.

The investigation took them to Glens Falls, New York, when they heard that on August 8, 1971, a petite thirteen-year-old named Sandy Ann Wesolowski had vanished on her way to meet friends. She too was still missing. The detectives could not help but wonder if this had been done by the same person, or persons, responsible. Would they find her body, raped, and strangled like Carmen Colón?

The facts were that the Bulls Head area neighborhood was where Carmen was last seen alive, the killer had a car, and Carmen had entered it willingly, which might mean she knew her killer. Only the last was not necessarily fact since Carmen was said to be very friendly.

Other reported details were that Carmen disappeared from New York State Route 33 (Main Street West) and was last seen running just before Exit 3 on I-490 West. It was presumed the killer, after Carmen's escape attempt on the highway, turned off on Exit 3 and headed toward Stearns Road in Riga where he dumped her body, and possibly killed her, less than a mile from New York Route 33A, the Chili-Riga Center Road.

Another logical conclusion was that Carmen had been raped and killed near the expressway, most likely at a rest stop not far from the spot where she had temporarily gotten away. The killer had then taken her body to the dumpsite two miles away on the little-used Stearns Road.

For most of the first month, a dozen detectives and officers were assigned primarily to the Colón case. By late December, however, the decision was made that with all the leads checked out and rechecked they could not justify keeping so many full-time officers on the case. So, December 21, 1971, the size of the force assigned to the case full-time was decreased to three very experienced Monroe County detectives, who were charged with revisiting previous information.

Chapter 15

When ten-year-old Carmen Colón was abducted, murdered, and raped on November 16, 1971, police initially had no reason to believe it was not a horrendous but isolated case. Investigators believed she willingly got into the killer's car, as all evidence suggested she had not been forced.

Taking what evidence and witness reports stated, the proven facts were that the killer had a car and that Carmen Colón entered it willingly. It was possible that the lure dangled before her may have been the offer of a hamburger and a soft drink, since the autopsy showed that she had eaten shortly before her death. Or it may have been a cat that the murderer had in the car with him that made her want to climb in, since cat hair was found on her clothing.

But during the spring of 1973, just as the pencil-wielding Sibley's graffiti-artist had predicted, it happened again.

WANDA WALKOWICZ

Chapter 16

Richard Walkowicz made it into the newspapers several times. The first time was when he was eleven and cut himself on barbed wire while trying to sneak into the Red Wing Stadium on Norton Street for an exhibition game between the Rochester Red Wings and the Baltimore Orioles.

The next time the offense was not so minor. Richard was 21 when, in January 1959, he and his friend, Raymond Pratt, stole radiators from Veterans' Auto Parts lot on Lee Road in Gates. At the time he lived on Weyl Street, in the home of his mother, Mrs. Wanda Walkowicz, for whom his daughter would later be named.

Richard then settled down, and the next time he appeared in the newspapers was on the society page when he became engaged to Miss Joyce Chatterton of Ariel Park, located about 200 yards southwest of Conkey Avenue near Avenue A. That was in May of 1959. The wedding was to take place in August but was later moved up to early March.

It was a happy life in the beginning with the two moonstruck partners pledging eternal love. They were happy, and that was especially true when on Friday, August 4, 1961, a sunny, 82-degree day in Rochester, New York, Wanda Walkowicz was born to Joyce and Richard Walkowicz. The following year her baby sister, Rita, was born. For the next six years they were a strong Catholic family, happy and content with their lives, until tragedy struck.

The tragedy happened when Wanda was just six years old and Rita was five. Richard had not been feeling like himself that evening. He managed to make it to the end of the meal but felt as though he was going to pass out.

Shortly thereafter he had a heart attack. Even though he was rushed to the hospital, doctors were unable to save him, and Richard died. He was only thirty years old, and his death would change the family dramatically.

Joyce was overcome with pain. Her grief overwhelmed her to the point that her capacity to cope was diminished. The loss of her beloved Richard was so disruptive that recovery became complicated. One moment they were saying "I love you" and enjoying each day, the next day Richard was gone. The shock was as palpable as being slammed against a brick wall.

In the first few weeks Joyce awoke each day, remembering that her husband was gone. She spent many mornings crushed by the sadness of coming face to face with his death, almost as if it were the first time.

Yet, as much as she wanted to pull back from life, she could not. Eventually she realized that she was young, pretty, and alone, with two daughters to raise, and that made her anger overpower her loss. His death felt like a punishment.

That proved to be true when the bleakness of her situation revealed her financial difficulty. She had two growing girls to raise and a shortage of cash. That reality slammed her hard in the face. If they were to survive, she would have to do something.

The obvious first step was to find a more affordable place for her and the girls to live. Joyce sat down with the newspaper and made calls on listings of apartments that were available and would fit into her budget. It was a long and depressing project, since her main limitation was price, not location or design. She finally settled on a brown, two story clapboard house located at 132 ½ Avenue D. It was on

Rochester's east side, in the diverse nationality area of the Conkey Avenue neighborhood. There was an upstairs apartment available, and after looking at it, she took it.

The next few weeks were spent packing up their belongings and getting them over to the new apartment. It was time-consuming, hard work, but they managed to do as much as they could on their own and with family assistance. Soon Joyce and her two fair-haired daughters were settled into their new home.

The move did not make a major decrease in their living expenses, as Joyce struggled to survive on the few hundred dollars she received monthly from her husband's social security benefits and a welfare check. With two growing girls it was not easy, but she had no choice. Each day became problematic, as she mourned the loss of her husband while struggling to keep her daughters fed and clothed. It was a lot for a young woman to handle, and eventually she found that having a drink or two made the days bearable. Soon a new pattern developed.

Joyce enjoyed drinking outside her home, and on Thursday, January 27, 1966 she was anxious to be on her way. She peeked out the window and saw it was snowing, but being used to snowy days, thought nothing of it as she rushed her daughters along. She never left them home alone when she went out to the bar.

Rochester gets more snow than any other large city in the United States, with a yearly average of nearly 100 inches because of its location astride common storm tracks, and far enough north so precipitation often falls as snow instead of rain. Add to that the fact that the city is along the shore of one of the world's largest snow-generating machines, Lake Ontario.

It had been a hard week, and as Joyce watched the snow fall, she fought her demons until finally she made up her mind to risk venturing out in the horrible weather.

It was still snowing on Friday, and the reports coming in were calling for a blizzard, so on Saturday, when there was a break in the weather, Joyce bundled up her daughters and ventured out to pick up some necessities.

They did not have far to walk, but the trip was a bit trying with a four and five-year-old shuffling along. Soon she could see the Victorian-style storefront of the Hillside Delicatessen and let out a sigh of relief.

Wanting to stop off at the Shenanigans' Tavern, Joyce changed her mind and took the troop home where they could warm up and have dinner before it was time to get ready for bed.

In the beginning it was just beautiful, big fluffy flakes coming down. As snowy as the days were it was nothing to compare with what they faced on Sunday, January 30th and Monday, January 31st. when Rochester received 27 inches of snow and much of the area got over 30 inches

School closings were announced and lasted for the full week. When Joyce looked out, she could barely see the edge of the front yard. She turned on the radio and listened. They were reporting a total of fifty inches of snow had fallen, and the whole city was on shut down, while plows tried to stay ahead of the storm clean up. Joyce could feel the house shaking as the sixty mph winds churned the falling snow into monstrous drifts, dropping visibility to zero in the process. But that was not the end of it as the storm continued from Sunday until midnight Monday, January 31st. By the time it was at last over, 100 inches of snow had blanketed the area.

Joyce wanted to get out, but it was hopeless. She felt caged in and had finished off what liquor she had had in the house. She was aware that the storm had added to the danger of the area, so as much as she wanted to step out, she dared not leave the girls alone. She never had before. She always took Wanda and Rita with her to the neighborhood bars, so she could keep an eye on them.

Once the storm was over and the area cleaned up, the pattern continued, and Joyce was again seen in the local bar with her daughters in tow. It was inevitable, her being young and pretty, that the male patrons of the bar would notice her.

Though she had not expected to feel this way, she found it was exciting to be noticed, and this offered her a chance to meet someone her own age. It was hard to go unnoticed when you were young and quite pretty, with deep auburn hair. The more her appearance was noticed, the more she found she wanted companionship beyond that of her children. She needed that.

So, a new phase of life began for Joyce. She eventually would have several affairs, including one ending in an abortion. Joyce was now living for herself.

The day came when she met Peyton Raney, known as 'Junior.' She became pregnant and delivered another daughter whom she named Michelle. Peyton moved in with her and the girls and became Joyce's common-law husband, providing a period of stability in the family's lifestyle.

Chapter 17

There are very few good neighborhoods in the city proper, but there are exceptions such as the East End, Park Ave, East Ave, the Neighborhood of the Arts (NOTA), Cornhill and Browncroft Blvd. Living in these areas puts one outside the 'danger zones,' but no city neighborhood is more than a ten minute walk from a blighted area.

Because of the low income of the residents, many slum neighborhoods are on the west side. They include West Main St., Plymouth Ave., Jefferson Ave., Troup St., Thurston Rd., and Genesee St. The north west side area that includes Lyell Ave, is known for drugs and prostitution, while the north east side is worse. The area includes streets such as Joseph Ave., Hudson Ave., North Clinton, Norton St., Clifford Ave., North Goodman, and their connecting side streets.

The residents in the area often speak Russian, Polish, German, Yiddish, and Spanish; almost all of them speak broken English. The shoppers in the stores, the neighbors on the avenue, all the store owners, and everyone who lives in these neighborhoods are at least bilingual.

At one time the neighborhoods were quite respectable, as can be visualized by the size and style of the homes in the area, most of which were, in 1971, already mainly rentals. The reputation of the neighborhood did not bother the Walkowiczes or others living there, because they knew how to be careful, and they taught their children the same. This was the area where Wanda was being raised, and she and her sister were learning what they needed to do to be out of harm's way.

With the help of Junior, the living arrangement on Avenue D became more affordable. Joyce still had a taste for her liquor, and that did not change. She and Junior were drinkers and spent a lot of their money on liquor. So even with Junior's help, the financial situation did not improve much.

Wanda and her sister were getting older, which meant they cared more about how they looked. They also knew there was not any spare money to spend on new clothes, so they figured out a way to help. Wanda and Rita started cleaning houses on their street. Because the children were familiar sights around the neighborhood, it was easy for them to get customers and earn their own money.

The only problem with a job was that going to school became a struggle. Wanda was tired in the morning, and try as she might, Wanda's efforts to be ready succeeded only half the time. It was madness getting up, dressed and out of the house to catch the bus. If she missed it, it was equally hard to force herself to make the two-mile walk that took over thirty minutes. It was not that she was lazy, but there were things at home she had to take care of before leaving for school, and those made her late. Her school record showed her as being truant for almost half the time, but there was not much she could do about it. Wanda enjoyed going to Abraham Lincoln School No. 22, located at 595 Upper Falls Blvd., but it just was not working out.

Wanda's bad attendance led to her falling behind in her class work.

Chapter 18

It was not only Wanda who worried about her poor school performance and absentee record, but the school also had problems with it. That amount of absence put her behind in her class, so they did something about it, transferring her to School No. 8. This school was only .2 miles from her home, and she could walk there in five minutes.

Now Rita and Wanda could walk to school. Together, they could be seen ambling down Avenue D to St. Paul Street, a main street in the area, and from there to School No. 8.

Wanda's attendance improved rapidly. She studied hard, but though she showed improvement in her class studies, she was still far behind her classmates. As a result, she was put into a special, non-graded class. This was not to her liking as it separated her from her peers, but she tried hard and was a good student.

When Wanda was not in school or cleaning homes, She took her sister with her to Maplewood Park. The park, also known as Seneca Park West, was linear, following the Genesee River from Driving Park Blvd. and the Lower Falls to just north of route 104. Its length made it convenient for several neighborhoods, and that made it a safe place to play. It usually took the girls a little over ten minutes to get there, as they walked together heading west on Avenue D toward Harris Street and turning right onto Nox Alley. From there they would continue to Avenue E, turn left and soon could cross the river on Driving Park Avenue, where Maplewood Park was located.

Making these trips helped Wanda to learn safe areas around her neighborhood and short distances beyond. She needed places to go to have fun, and the park was the best place. Sometimes, her friend, Annabel Walker, would join them at the park.

But there was danger. To the east of Avenue D were the railroad tracks. The railroad tracks were a world unto themselves. At first parents warned about the danger of walking down the tracks because the trains traveled in both directions at all times of the day and night. People had died because they were looking for a shortcut or thought it would be fun.

But later, when Wanda was older, she was warned about the concentration of homeless people hanging out near train tracks. When Wanda, who could not envision people living outside with no protection, gazed doubtfully at her mother, Joyce told her that two transients had recently been shot after breaking into a house. They had been living along the railroad tracks. Who knew what these transients would do if they saw a little girl out on her own? That story was enough to keep Wanda away from the tracks.

Wanda learned how to get the things she wanted, and because she was good at it, she asked her mother what she could do for her to earn money. Joyce understandingly offered to pay her for jobs around the house, so several mornings a week Wanda would do little things to earn money. Wanda added on as many chores as she could until, eventually, she was earning around eleven dollars a month.

It was not easy for Wanda to make friends in her new school. Although she was shy by nature, she wanted to have friends. Here was this little red-headed, blue-eyed, freckle-faced girl with a happy disposition smiling at everyone. Her classmates could not help but like her, and soon they became friends.

Her shyness remained intact though, holding her back from volunteering to answer any questions during class, even if she knew the answer. On days when the class had to give an oral report, Wanda was way out of her comfort zone, but if she wanted a passing grade, she had to take part. So, Wanda would ask the teacher in private, "Please, oh please, can you call on me last to give my report?"

Seeing the dread in her eyes, her teacher would agree without asking why, so Wanda was usually called on last.

Her logic was not quite rational, but it made her calm as she stood to speak in front of the class. Wanda thought, being last, she would be giving her report to students who were tired and restless from sitting through several other reports, and therefore they would not be paying attention to anything she said. Most of them did not pay attention anyway

The teachers recognized Wanda was an avid student who did a lot of independent type work, one who put a lot of effort into her assignments, making sure that her work was neat and complete. With her schoolwork improving, and her attendance up, Wanda began earning good grades on her report card. She was a good speller, and that expanded her interest in science, math, and art. The teachers were pleased, and Wanda was happy.

Chapter 19

Wanda looked younger than her age, but she was more grown-up than she looked. She took pains with her hair, making sure it was just so before she ever left the house.

She enjoyed her friends. Feeling as if she belonged was important to her at a young age. Each day Wanda and her friends would hang around together at school and later, when school let out, they would walk home together, making plans for the rest of the day. Though Wanda was smaller and perhaps younger than some of her friends, she was a leader.

By the time she turned eleven, she was mature beyond her years, all sixty-five pounds and four feet, seven inches of her, fussing over her curly, pixie haircut like a teen and playing outside with friends until late on weekends, because she had shown she could be trusted.

Not only was she cute, but Wanda was a tough little redhead, because she had to be to survive. Boys were the main classmates who picked on her because she was small, and at first, they saw her as an easy target. They learned quickly that this was not the case, as she had fought older boys before and beaten the snot out of them. No one who knew her would ever doubt her ability to protect herself and her sister, Rita.

She was bright as well as street smart by the time she turned ten. She had to grow up fast with all the chaos in her life. Having her father, Richard, die when she was only six led to them moving to a less than desirable neighborhood and her mother going on welfare. It was a new life for the family and Wanda, being the oldest, felt it almost as much as her mother did.

Most of the kids were in the same situation as she. They either had only one parent or were becoming aware of the money difficulties at home. But it was this common background that made their friendship comfortable and life enjoyable.

Because she was close in age to her sister, Rita, they did have friends in common, and Wanda liked that. By the time she was eleven, Wanda was familiar with her neighborhood, happy with her friends, and enjoying her life.

She understood that they could not afford much, which was why she liked keeping the place clean even if it looked worn. Not that she had a lot of friends over, but it made her feel better.

Later, when her mother's common-law husband, Junior, moved in with them, Wanda had to adjust once more. She tried to look on the bright side, hoping that this would lessen her mother's drinking, and she would become the mother she used to know.

Joyce did cut down on her drinking when she became pregnant, but after giving birth, she started up again. Wanda had a new baby sister named Michelle.

Again, Wanda hoped this would get the family back to where they had been before her father had died. It did not. Wanda's stepfather and half-sister were not enough to blot out her mother's pain, any more than they erased Wanda's distress. Junior had joined the household, and Michelle had been born. And all semblance of Wanda's sense of self had gone up in a plume of smoke. With her mother not able to manage on her own, Wanda was there, left to pick up the broken pieces. Wanda could not control any of this because her mother had never asked for her opinion.

The one thing that Wanda could control was herself. She could not do anything about her size, but she could build a reputation to protect her. That aim she had accomplished. Some people saw her as a tomboy, full of frenetic energy. But Wanda was more than that. One minute she would be tussling and joking with the boys in the neighborhood, and the next she would be playing with Barbie Dolls.

Wanda knew that every attempt to dull the pain did not work for her mother, not alcohol, not painkillers, not even sleeping pills. None of them. For Wanda, there were even fewer choices, as she wondered why life was so hard. Her mother was constantly in a state of struggle, battling to keep the family's heads above water, but every choice she made seemed to backfire.

Even at her young age, she wondered why it always seemed as if bad things continued to happen repeatedly.

In her neighborhood, having a hard life meant having a life full of difficulties, adversities, and negative experiences. Dealing with hard life situations could be daunting. Emotions like fear, anger, grief, and sadness were part of a hard life. As Wanda found out, coping with such emotions and situations was not easy, especially for someone so young. Whether or not she was aware, however, she had established her own way of coping. She took care of herself, sought friendships, and had her church.

Wanda's mother, Joyce Walkowicz, had been a young widow. Although she had had several boyfriends in the years after her husband died, and had visited neighborhood bars to socialize, her actions did not mean she was a bad mother.

Her mother raised all three of them to be helpful, responsible young ladies who cared about each other and about other people.

Wanda began to appreciate how many obstacles her mother had to scale and, knowing this, she tried her best to be as helpful as she could.

Wanda understood that it was through no fault of her own that her mother had found herself in her current situation. She had hoped living with Junior would rectify the shortcomings in their life, but it had not happened.

So now there were more mouths to feed, less money, and more stress. Sometimes her mother appeared angry and frustrated. When Wanda was younger, she had trouble understanding why her mother yelled about things that would not have bothered her before. Now Wanda understood that her mom worried about paying the bills and keeping food on the table.

Angry outbursts, depression and alcohol abuse had changed her mother, and Wanda wanted to help.

She began her own campaign to help. She took the money she had earned for chores and spent it on practical things besides clothes. She had heard enough conversations between the grownups to know that she should turn out lights, and not keep the water running. Although it had not seemed that important at the time, she tried doing it.

Wanda did whatever needed to be done without expecting to be paid for it. She always tried to be kind and courteous and not argue with her mother. And there were times when she felt that her mother was being too strict, but she did what she was told anyway. That came from the spiritual upbringing that her parents had provided for their children. She knew what was right and what was wrong, and she stayed on the path.

Wanda had learned a lot in her few years. She had garnered skills that would benefit her later in life. Only Wanda did not think that far ahead. She was interested in now, not some time in the future.

Where her mother was concerned, Wanda did not know Joyce's whole story. She had lived with her mother for almost eleven years and been with her through the good and the bad times, but Wanda never thought about before she was her mother. She did not wonder what she was like before she had married and had children.

Because over the years she had never asked, she did not pick up bits and pieces of her mother's life story, though at some point Joyce may have left little breadcrumbs here and there. If Wanda had been asked about her mother, she would say that she cared for her since the day she was born. Would the story have been different if she had known more?

Chapter 20

Wanda's mother, Joyce Walkowicz, was raised in a dysfunctional family, and when her husband died, Joyce's main objective was to keep her family functioning and together. It was hard going, especially since Joyce had no guidelines to go by.

Joyce had survived a miserable childhood. Her mother, Wanda's grandmother, depended heavily on alcohol and men. The situation had become so bad that Joyce and her siblings had been taken from home and put into a series of foster homes. To add to her feelings of inadequacy, when the social worker took Joyce to one family, they had refused to take her in, saying that she was too fat. From that foster home, the social worker took her to the Hillside Children's Center.

Joyce had a hard time coping until she finally decided to run away to New York City. Determinedly, Joyce waited until nighttime before making her move. Quietly she gathered her belongings and cautiously made her way down the hallways to the one exit she knew would not be staffed, the fire escape. Just as she had expected, there was no one there.

Confidently she went over and pulled open the door. The fire alarm was deafening, as she stood there in shock before finally coming to her senses and going outside on the fire escape. She took a deep breath and began carefully climbing down. Her heart was racing so fast she thought it would break free of her chest, but she kept going.

When she was almost to ground level, her escape was halted when the night security guard grabbed her and returned her to her room. From those childhood experiences, Joyce was seen as a wild kid with a reputation as a fun girl, one who did things that made her stand out in an unfavorable way.

Joyce gave up in many ways. She learned early on in her life that she could lessen the pain by drinking, and so she did. Soon she was imitating her mother as she shrouded herself in a life of alcohol and men.

Joyce had enough blows to her ego to leave her with a feeling of being unworthy. When she thought her life was going to continue in that downward direction, she met Richard F. Walkowicz.

When Joyce met Richard, everything changed. She was no longer unwanted and uncared for. She settled down as a married woman, and then later a young mother. At first, she was afraid to relax and enjoy her new life, afraid it would all evaporate. Each morning she woke anxious to begin the next day and then the next, until finally she was able to let the past dissipate. But fate was still not on her side.

When Richard told Joyce he was having pain in his arm, and said he really was not feeling well, Joyce told him he should lie down. A few minutes later she checked on him and he looked awful. Not knowing what else to do, she called the hospital. When the ambulance came to transport Richard, Joyce went to get a few things and then hurried to the hospital, all the time thinking how she would live without him. She was afraid of what her life would look like if he were not right there next to her. She was right to worry. Just as quickly as her life had taken on meaning, while still in her twenties, she became a widow.

Joyce was beside herself, and her previous ways returned. Even though she was now a mother with responsibility for her daughters, she began ushering a parade of men into her home, most of whom she had met in a bar.

For Wanda, the negative side of growing up with a single parent was feeling a sense of neglect at times. The positive side of that same issue, though, is that she learned independence at an incredibly young age. Since her mother was often drinking, Wanda had to grow up a little bit faster.

Wanda learned that doing any major task alone can be stressful and difficult, but with the death of her father at such a young age, it was hard for her mother to adjust.

But Wanda did not complain. She was adjusting just as her mother was. She missed her father and could understand why her mother was sad most of the time and unable to sit them down to a home-cooked meal.

Since meeting her boyfriend, Junior, Joyce spent more time at home and less time at the bar, though she still made the occasional visit. Once Joyce and Junior were a couple, they were not able to afford a babysitter, so Joyce still made Wanda and Rita go with her to the bar. While Joyce drank at the bar, the girls sat across from her, occupying themselves until it was finally time to return home.

That slight change from every day to once in a while was seen by Wanda as an improvement, since she was now at an age when she had learned from her peers and teachers what the average homelife was like, and it did not include taking your children to a bar.

By the time Wanda was eleven years old, she felt the pangs of the pre-teen girl. She felt isolated and distant from her family. No one's teenage years are easy — frankly, they suck. For Wanda, however, her teen angst and turbulent emotions were amplified, because she often felt as if her mom did not care. Joyce had transferred her attention to

Junior and their shared daughter, Michelle. To Joyce, Wanda and Rita were merely part of a separate relationship that no longer involved her.

No family, no matter how many people it is composed of, is ever one hundred percent happy, one hundred percent of the time.

When you are a child, all your attention is focused on yourself and your life. This was true for Wanda, but she did understand her mother's situational change because she had been a part of it.

April 2, 1973, was that fateful day when Joyce sent Wanda to the store, granting her oldest daughter the responsibility of helping her manage the household. What happened next would overshadow all that had happened before.

Chapter 21

April 2, 1973, started out to be a perfect day. The temperature would reach 52 degrees, but by the time school let out, the temperatures were dropping. It had turned into a cold, wet afternoon, but that did not bother Wanda one bit because she had good news.

Wanda hurried home from School 8 with her best report card ever. It was hard even for her to believe since she had missed close to fifty days of school that year. However, she had applied herself and this was the proof.

Her mind flashed back to all the wonderful moments of that day. They made her smile; it made her want to dance as she continued her walk home. She could not wait to tell her mother that her fifth-grade teacher said that she, Wanda Walkowicz, was an average student. Not a below average student, but an average student. But that was not all. Her teacher had said that she was proving to be a little above average in reading.

It was the best day ever. Nothing could darken her spirits today, Wanda thought. Nothing.

When she arrived home, Wanda hurried in the house, and as she closed the front door, she yelled out, "Mom, Mom?"

Joyce, who was in the kitchen, heard her child shrieking and hurried into the front room, thinking something was wrong. "Yes, Wanda, what is it? Are you all right?"

Wanda did not miss a beat as she held out her report card toward her mother. "Look, Mom."

"I thought something was wrong, Wanda. Don't yell like that again." She looked at her daughter's radiant face.

"Okay, what is it?" she said, smiling and matching Wanda's expression.

Joyce walked over to her daughter, and Wanda handed her mother the report card. Joyce took the card from her daughter and smiled. From her daughter's reaction it had to be good news. Wanda stood waiting, trying to be patient. She stood with her weight on one foot, and then the other, anxiously waiting as her mother removed the report card from the envelope, glanced up to smile at her, and then placed the envelope behind the report card before finally opening it up.

Wanda stared into her mother's face, not wanting to miss a minute of her surprise. Finally, her mother looked up, stared off into the distance and then at her impatient daughter. Slowly a smile began to spread over her face until it turned into a big happy grin.

"I knew you could do it."

Wanda was smiling so hard she thought her face would break. When her mother motioned for her to come closer, Wanda stumbled forward and felt the warmth of her mother's hug. At that moment, she was glad she still was a little girl, glad that all it took was a good report card to please her mother. After Wanda pulled back, she was still grinning. "Isn't it wonderful? I am not below average anymore. I am average."

"Yes, and above average in reading. I am so proud of you."

One more hug and her mother walked away with the report card in her hand. She would put it in a safe place and sign it later, so Wanda could take it back to school.

Wanda practically danced to her room where she changed her clothes, and then, since she did not have any homework, and it was cold and drizzly outside, decided to color. She got out her coloring book and crayons and became absorbed in coloring. Ever since she was a little girl, she had enjoyed coloring books. Each page had pictures of animals or people in some setting, and once she filled in the picture, it would come to life. As she filled in the drawings, Wanda would painstakingly work with the crayon, making sure to stay between the lines. She did not like to be messy.

Her concentration when she was coloring was all-consuming. Her mother used to tell her that she was probably going to be an artist when she grew up. Wanda liked to think that was true, as she studiously worked on the picture.

Wanda was concentrating on her picture and did not hear her mother calling her. Joyce called her name three times before she heard Wanda reply.

"Yes, Mom. What is it?"

"Can you come downstairs?"

"I am coming." Wanda quickly picked up her coloring book and crayons and put them on her nightstand before hurrying downstairs.

Her mother waited for her in the front room. As Wanda's foot hit the last step she asked, "What is it? What do you want?"

Her mother had a note tablet in her hand and was writing on it as she talked. "Wanda, I need you to go to the store for me. I need a few things for dinner and some other groceries as well." She paused as she continued writing. "Here, this is what I need you to pick up for me at Hillside Delicatessen. Do you think you can handle it alone?"

Wanda nodded, trying to remain calm. She thought that her mother was so pleased with her report card that she felt her daughter was growing up. Wanda knew her mother considered her responsible, but never had she let her go to the store this late, alone.

Her bubble burst a bit when Joyce added, "It's so cold out, and I am in the middle of making dinner. I really don't want to drag your sisters out either." Joyce paused and looked at Wanda. "Do you mind going for me?"

"No, I don't mind."

Joyce handed her the list. "Will you be able to manage all that?"

Wanda looked down at the list. On it her mother had written down dog food, cat food, tuna fish, two quarts of milk, bread, cupcakes, soup, and Pampers for Wanda's two-year-old half-sister Michelle. Before she could answer the question, her mother asked for the list back. Wanda stood next to her mother and watched as she added a pack of cigarettes to the bottom. Then Joyce asked again, "Can you carry all of that?"

Without really thinking about it, she said, "Yes. I can carry it." She did have her doubts since it was a long list, and some of the items were heavy, but she was eleven, after all, and should be able to handle it.

"Okay, Wanda, thank you, and please hurry. I am out of diapers."

"Okay, Mom, I'll hurry."

Wanda was wearing a blue-and-white dress, white socks, and sneakers. Looking across the room through the window she could see it was still raining outside and thought about changing, then decided against taking the time to change. Instead she put on her red-and-green checked coat and headed out the door.   Besides, it was only three blocks from her home to the Hillside Deli.

It was late afternoon now, close to five-thirty and the temperature outside had dropped to nearly 37 degrees. As Wanda stepped out to make her way to the deli, the change in the temperature made her shiver and she pulled her coat tightly around her. Then she went out into the rainy evening.

She hesitated, thinking she should change into something warmer, but decided to keep going. The rain soaked through her clothing and she could feel the dampness on her skin.

The deli was just past her school three blocks away, so it was a familiar route to her. She had walked it often enough and believed she could walk to Hillside Deli blindfolded. She knew when she was passing the duplexes, apartment buildings, barbershop, stores, and bars that lined Conkey Avenue between her house and the school and the deli. She did not need to see them to know they were there.

It continued to rain, that light misty rain that turns the sky gray. It would be dark soon, but she had no doubt that she would be back home by then.

Wanda tilted her head upward to verify her whereabouts and, as the rain rolled down her face, she saw she had reached her destination. She paused a moment, then turned, and went into the Hillside Delicatessen.

She stood in the doorway for a moment, allowing her body to enjoy the sudden warmth. It felt good. If she could, she would have stayed there until she was dry before venturing out again. But she had promised her mother she would come right home and be as quick as she could. So, with a slight shake, she stepped the rest of the way inside.

It was time to get started. She reached in her pocket and pulled out the list her mother had made for her. She looked it over carefully, and then reached back in her pocket for the short stubby pencil she would use to cross items off as she found them. She did not want to go back without everything her mother had asked her to pick up.

Wanda knew the store like the back of her hand, so, after pausing to get a cart, she began her search down the aisles, stopping in the pet food aisle to put the dog and cat food into her cart. She next came to the coolers and took out two quarts of milk. She turned around and located the next aisle she needed to go down and to purchase the bread and cupcakes. Then it was on to the soup and tuna fish.

Wanda paused a moment to smile at another customer before proceeding to the diaper aisle. She looked over the choices and then back down at her list. It said 'Pampers.' She looked up and as if by fate, the Pampers were right in front of her. She grabbed the size and quantity her mother had asked for. She was done.

She moved swiftly up the aisle and to the checkout.

"Hi Wanda," Douglas Pierson, one of the clerks on duty said.

"Hi, Mr. Pierson. I had to get a few things for my mother, and I am kinda in a hurry."

"No problem," said Paul Wethers, the store owner. "I'll give Doug a hand."

Doug went behind the counter and started ringing up the purchases in Wanda's cart. As he rang each item up, he handed it to Paul who began bagging the purchases, while Wanda looked on.

Wanda looked behind the counter and remembered she was to get a pack of cigarettes. "Oh, Mr. Pierson, I also need a pack of cigarettes."

Both men knew the family well and knew that the cigarettes were for her mom. So, the clerk turned around and took a pack off the shelf and put them on the counter. Paul picked them up and placed the cigarettes in the bag.

Wanda saw they had filled two bags and was not comfortable carrying two bags home, so she asked, "Do you think we could get everything in one bag?"

"Here," Doug said, "I think I can get them all in one back for her."

Wanda watched as Doug took items out and then replaced them until he finally had everything in one bag. He looked at the 65 lb., 4 ft little girl wonderingly. "It's going to be heavy. Are you sure you can carry it?"

"Yes, I'll be fine."

"Okay, that will be $8.52, Wanda."

"Can you put this on my mother's charge account?"

"Sure, no problem. No problem at all."

Wanda stood waiting impatiently while he opened the book where he kept the store customer accounts. He flipped through until he found the page for Joyce Walkowicz and wrote down the date, the time, and each item that Wanda had purchased, along with the cost. He totaled it at the bottom and when he was done said, ""Okay, Wanda, you are all set."

"Thank you, Mr. Pierson. Thank you, Mr. Wethers."

"You are welcome, Wanda."

They watched as Wanda picked up the large bag and worked at settling it on her hip, so that she could get a good grip. They continued to observe as she made her way to the front door and, using her other hip, pushed the door open and left the store.

Outside the chill immediately greeted her, along with the steady drizzle that had not dissipated. Wanda turned left, heading northward toward home. She passed by several people she casually knew and smiled as they watched her struggling with her bag of groceries.

Her grip on the bag loosened and she stopped in front of the barbershop on Conkey, just north of Avenue B. She allowed herself to rest a bit before she was ready to go on her way.

Wanda was street-smart and quite capable. Since the time they were ten and eleven, Wanda and Rita had both become accustomed to interrupting their play to run errands for their mother, walking alone through their lower-middle-class neighborhood. Sometimes they went together or with a friend. But often Wanda went alone if it was her turn to do so, regardless of the weather. The difference now was that she had not been sent out this late in the evening before.

She knew that if her mother asked her, it was because she needed some necessities that evening. That thought pulled her out of her reverie and she was once again on her way.

The rain and cold made the going hard and she was feeling it in her bones when she saw three other friends watching her. She tried not to look as if she were struggling as she smiled, but she could not hold up the front for long. She managed to make it to the front of the school, where she was able to brace the bag against the fence, pushing into it until she could get a better grip.

Wanda continued walking with her head down, almost not hearing her friends as they yelled out and waved at her. She looked up, stopped, and waited as they crossed the street to join her.

"Hey, Peggy," Wanda said, shifting the bag of groceries on her hip.

"Hi, Wanda." Sara and Janey both said together. "Where are you going?" added Peggy.

"Home."

"We'll walk with you."

Together they walked with her to the corner of Conkey and Avenue D, where they parted ways. It was so cold, and her bare legs were freezing as she continued on her way. The paper bag was soaked, and Wanda was careful to make sure she used both of her hands now, moving the bag in front of her and hugging it close, with her hands meeting across the bottom of the bag.

She had to stop again. Wanda looked back behind her, but she could not see her friends anymore. She was alone.

She started out once more, then stopped when she heard someone call out to her. She turned to see a man in what looked to be a brown car which was idling at the sidewalk in front of her.

Chapter 22

What seemed to be an uneventful evening, with few customers coming out in the cold rain, three store employees stood outside watching Wanda as she left the Hillside Deli. They could tell she was struggling with the bag of groceries and chuckled, talking amongst themselves and saying that the bag was as big as she was. When their break was over, they went back inside. Wanda had not seen them.

Just like the three store employees, a woman who also knew Wanda, as the woman had babysat for Wanda's mother on several occasions, sat watching Wanda as she passed by the window of Jimmie's Tavern across the street from the Hillside Deli. She saw Wanda leave the deli with the big bag clutched in her arms. At first, she thought of going outside with her umbrella and walking Wanda home, but did not. It was so cold and drizzly, and she had a few drinks in her. Better to stay where she was. Besides, Wanda had done this alone many times, and she had always managed without a problem.

The three friends of Wanda who had met up with her on the corner of Avenue D, glanced down Conkey when they came out of their store and saw Wanda as she made her way home. They could tell she was having trouble with the bag but were sure she was all right. She was close to home already.

The rain made it hard to see clearly, but when they next looked in Wanda's direction they saw she was leaning against the school fence, and a car that, through the rain, appeared to be a brown shade was almost blocking her from view.

As they looked her way, they wondered if maybe Wanda was tired, and they should give her a hand with the bag. They stood looking at each other, thinking the same thoughts. It was cold, rainy, and growing darker by the minute. They needed to get home.

Janey sighed, looked in Wanda's direction again and turned to her friends. "I don't see her." The other girls looked too. They did not see Wanda or the brown car. All three girls shrugged their shoulders at the same time as they continued on their way.

Joyce was getting impatient. She needed the groceries, especially the diapers. "Where can she be? she wondered. They often went to the Hillside Deli and she knew how long it took for them to make the trip.

Joyce went to look out the window. It was still raining. She went to the door and opened it and could feel the chill of the air rushing in. She closed the door and turned around, calling out. "Rita, can you come here, please?"

A few minutes later she could hear footsteps hurrying in her direction, and soon Rita stood before her. "What is it Mommy?"

"Rita, your sister hasn't returned from the store, and I need those groceries. Do you mind going out to get her?"

"No, Mommy.'

"Dress warmly and take an umbrella. It is quite chilly and rainy out there.

Rita nodded and went to get her coat. She sat down and put on her boots and stood up, as she reached into the pockets of her coat and took out her gloves. While she was putting them on, her mother reached in the closet and brought out the umbrella.

"Now, as soon as you find Wanda, you two hurry home so that I can get your baby sister out of her wet diaper, and we can eat supper."

"Don't worry, I will." With that, Rita was out the door. She barely made it off her doorstep when her friend Annabel Walker spotted her. "Where are you going?" she asked.

"I am going to get Wanda. She went to the deli and hasn't returned yet."

"Want me to come with you?"

"Sure."

Glad for the company, Rita added, "She should have been home long ago, so let's check her friends' homes before we go all the way to the store."

"Sounds like a good idea."

So, along the way, Rita and Annabel knocked at the door of the first home where Wanda might have gone. When the door opened, she asked, "Is Wanda here?"

"No, we haven't seen Wanda. Anything wrong?"

"Oh, no, we just need her to come home."

They left, and making the same inquiry, they got the same answer at the next home they stopped at.

It was indeed cold, but Annabel, being the friend she was, continued with Rita all the way to the Hillside Deli. When they arrived, they hurried inside. It took a moment to stop shaking as they felt the warmth in the store. Rita happened to glance up at the clock and saw that it was now 6:45 P.M.

Trying not to appear worried, Rita walked up to the counter and inquired, "Have you seen Wanda tonight?"

"Yes, she was here."

As an afterthought she added, "Did she buy the groceries for my mom?" Rita thought if she had not, they would get them before they left.

"Yes. Wait a minute."

The store clerk reached under the counter and came up with the record book. He flipped the pages until he came to the record for Wanda's purchases. He pushed the book across so that Rita could look it over. As she did, a puzzled look appeared on her face. If Wanda had that many groceries to carry, no way would she dillydally around before returning home. It was a long list and not just a couple of quick items to pick up.

Trying not to let it worry her and thinking ahead, she asked, "Can I see the list? I am going to purchase them again and take them home with me."

"Sure, no problem. I'll add it to the record and get you a receipt."

"Come on, Annabel. Can you help me?"

Annabel nodded and they went through the store making the same purchases that Wanda had made. They could always use the items, so it was not wasteful. When they were done, the store clerk rang up their order, showed Rita that he had entered it in the record, and put the receipt in one of the bags.

"Since you have help, we evened out the load into two bags for you."

"Thank you. If Wanda should come back to the store, can you tell her Mom is looking for her?"

"Sure, we will."

The two girls headed home, keeping an eye out for Wanda as they went, but they did not see her anywhere. When they arrived at the Walkowiczes', Annabel waited while Rita set her bag down and took the other one from her friend. They said goodbye to each other, and Annabel went home.

Upon hearing the door open, Joyce rushed into the front room. "Wanda, It is about time..."

She paused and looked around, trying to hide her anxiety. "So, Rita, did you find your sister?"

"No, Mom, It is just me. We stopped at a few of her friends' and then went to the store. She had been there and bought the groceries, but since we did not see her, I made the same purchases for you. I do not know where she is.

Chapter 23

Joyce's heart was racing, and it was hard not to show how worried she was as she tried to smile at her daughter. "Thank you, Rita." She started to choke up, so she cleared her throat and added, "Thanks for going to look for your sister for me, and thanks for thinking to buy the groceries."

"You are welcome, Mom. The store clerk said that Wanda had left with the groceries, but because we had looked for her and did not see her, and I knew you needed them, I purchased them again. Ah…"

Rita was about to say that there were two charges on the books for the groceries but decided against it. Instead she said, "I'll go change Michelle for you."

There was no reason to doubt. Her daughters did what they were told, and Rita had said she had checked the homes of some of her friends and had been to the store. Joyce paced, wringing her hands, and looking at the clock. It was almost eight now. Wanda would not be gone this long unless… unless something had happened.

She fought the urge to panic, but it was a losing battle, as she found herself rushing to the phone. She dialed the Rochester Police Department and waited nervously on the line. She understood her neighborhood would not like having the police officers called in, but she had no choice.

""Nine-one-one operator. What is your emergency?"

"Hello, this is Joyce Walkowicz. My daughter, Wanda, is missing."

"Where are you calling from?"

"I live at 132 ½ Avenue D, off Conkey Avenue."

"What happened to your daughter?"

Joyce choked up, then swallowed hard. "I sent her to the Hillside Delicatessen on Conkey Avenue and she never returned."

The operator heard the catch in her voice. "Ma'am, what time did your daughter leave the house?"

"Around 5 o'clock. It takes only a few minutes to get to the Hillside Deli from our house."

"How old is Wanda?" Joyce was growing impatient now but calmed herself to answer.

"She's eleven years old."

"Did she perhaps stop off at a friend's house?"

There was a long pause before Joyce was able to reply. "My daughter would not do that. She knew I needed the groceries, especially the diapers for her baby sister. She would have come straight home."

"Well, It is only been a couple of hours now," the operator said, then paused. "Is there someone who could look around the neighborhood for you?"

"Yes, but they did check all the way to the deli."

"Well, have them check again and call us back."

Trying to keep the scream from coming out, Joyce whispered, "Okay."

Joyce was even more upset now. It was as if it did not matter to the woman on the line that Joyce knew her daughter, knew she would come straight home. You do not wait twenty-four hours to report a child as missing. Did not they know that? You are supposed to call immediately. She had to stop thinking this way. There was nothing she could do but follow their instructions, so she put on her coat, and told Rita she was going to check with the neighbors again.

"I won't be long."

With that she was out the door. She moved quickly in the cold, wet night making her way up the steps of the houses nearby and down further, asking if Wanda was there or if they had seen her. Several mentioned they had seen her, but that was on her way to the deli.

Determined, Joyce headed down to the Hillside Deli, keeping an eye out for her daughter, and stopping at homes of friends to inquire if Wanda was there or if they had seen her. The response was always the same. At the deli she asked the employees about her eldest daughter's visit.

"Yes, Ma'am, she was here, and she left with the groceries. Did something happen to her?"

"I do not know," Joyce tearfully replied. "She did not come home."

"I'll send one of our stock clerks out to look for her. If she comes back to the store, we will call your house. We will also get the word out that you are looking for Wanda."

"Thank you. Thank you very much."

Like Rita, Joyce went to the houses of Wanda's best friends in a futile, frantic effort to find her daughter. But she had no luck.

She hurried back home, not feeling the cold or the wetness seeping into her bones. Once inside, she rushed over to the phone, not taking the time to remove her coat or boots, and dialed nine-one-one again. She then breathlessly gave them the information they needed, adding that she had done as they had requested and gone out and double-checked to see if she could find her daughter, but with no success.

"Can you please help me?"

This time there was no delay, and before she had hung up the phone the police had been dispatched to the area. By then, it was 8:15 p.m.

The word did get around that Wanda Walkowicz was missing, and a massive search and rescue got underway. Police and neighbors were combing backyards, alleys, the railroad tracks, and the entire area between the tracks and Avenue A.

The police questioned the people in the neighborhood thoroughly, hoping for a lead or two. In their questioning they learned that there had been a close encounter for Wanda and one of her nine-year-old friends, just two nights earlier. It seemed that a strange man had come out of nowhere near the railroad tracks, approximately a block away from the store.

It had happened late in the evening. The girls had seen the man, but because they were together, they thought nothing of it until the man had started to run toward them. That scared the bejesus out of them, and they took off running as fast as they could. When they thought it was safe, they slowed and turned to look behind them, and saw the man jump into the bushes.

When they returned home, they each told their parents about the incident.

"What did he look like? Did you see what he was wearing? Was he black or white?"

Neither girl could answer their parents' questions. But they both remembered one feature and that was his shoes.

"What about his shoes?"

"He had buckles on them."

"Oh my god, were you that close to him?"

"No, the light at the railroad crossing reflected off the buckles on his shoes."

Joyce contacted the other mother, and they exchanged information. Both girls had said the same thing about the incident, and the other mother said she had already placed a call to the police.

The mother of Wanda's friend explained that, when she gave them the information, she was told it was too little to go on. It would not be easy to trace the man, but they would give it their best effort by checking to see if anyone else had reported something similar happening in the area. They were told they would get back to them if they came up with any information.

While the search continued in the area where Wanda disappeared, several police officers were dispatched immediately to the areas close to the railroad tracks. They did the search in cruisers and on foot. It was not long before a man was spotted hanging around there, and he had buckles on his shoes.

They called the news in over the radio. "We have the guy that chased the girls. We're going to keep checking the area for the little girl, while the other officers take him in for questioning."

Making their way back to the Walkowiczes, they knocked at her door, and Joyce opened the door immediately.

"Can we come in?"

"Yes. Have you found her?"

The officers stepped inside. "No, not yet. We wanted to ask you a question."

"Yes..."

"Are you aware that Wanda and a friend had been followed by a stranger on the previous Saturday night?" He paused and looked down at his notebook. "Around 10:00 p.m., on March 31st. "

"Yes, my daughter told me about it, and her friend's mother called it in. Do you think…?"

The words flew incoherently from Joyce's lips. "That doesn't make any sense. Why would she walk in the rain from the deli, past our house, and go a block farther away to the other side of the railroad tracks? She was carrying a heavy bag of groceries, for goodness sake. She knew I needed them right away." Tears now flowed freely from her eyes as she paced about the room.

"We do not know anything yet, so let's not jump to conclusions."

The officer looked down at his notes. "We also spoke to a Clarence Byrnes, who is a director at the local recreation center on the other side of the railroad tracks. He said that Wanda and her friends frequented that area a lot on warm, summer days."

Joyce interrupted. "I told Wanda it was not safe and to stay away from the tracks, but…"

"That is not important now. I mention that because Mr. Byrnes does know who Wanda is, and he said he thought he had seen Wanda on that side of the tracks at around 7 o'clock."

"Well, he's wrong, she would not have gone that far."

"We do not know, Ma'am, but we have to check out every lead."

Joyce was becoming distraught, and fear welled up in her as she sobbed out, "She's gone for good, isn't she?"

162

As they watched the woman in front of them crumble, they became worried. They forced her to sit down in a chair and called for an ambulance. They stayed with her until the ambulance arrived, and the EMTs said the woman appeared to be in shock, and they would take her to Rochester General Hospital.

The officers then talked with Rita, and on their way out, made arrangements with a neighbor to check in on the family. That done, they went to the patrol car.

And check every lead they would, knowing that eyewitnesses are a powerful form of evidence for convicting the accused. But every witness is subject to unconscious memory distortions and even prejudices, no matter how confident he seems to be. So, though they would follow every lead, they kept in mind that some of what they heard would not be useful.

Chapter 24

"Do I know you?"

"Yes, I live a few blocks from you. Looks like that bag is heavy, and wet. I can give you a ride home if you like."

Wanda hesitated. She tried to get a better look at the man in the car, but she could not see much through the rain and darkness of the evening. She moved closer, watching as the man leaned across the seat to open the car door.

The bag was heavy. The paper was wet and might rip. If it did, she did not know what she would do. She could not carry all those groceries home in her arms. Wanda looked around her but saw no one.

Wanda leaned in closer, resting the bag on the seat of the car, so she could get a better view. Suddenly his hand reached out and grabbed hold of her coat. His movement was so fast she was unable to move back quickly enough. She felt his other hand reach over and pull her inside the car with such force that the minute her body was beyond the car door, it slammed shut behind her.

She was in trouble. She knew it. She fought, punching him in the chest as hard as she could, but he did not let go. Instead, he untangled his hands from the grip he had on her coat, and, before she could attempt to back out, his hands wrapped tightly around her neck.

Wanda could feel the pressure on her throat as she fought, grabbing his hands, and trying to pull them away from her neck. But he was too strong. The pressure on her neck was enough to stop her breathing, as she desperately fought against him.

She struggled vigorously to get a breath of air, but her efforts only made him squeeze harder. Her throat was on fire, and it felt as if there were pins and needles of ice sticking into her fingers, her toes, her arms. The hands continued to squeeze her neck until she felt pressure behind her eyes just before everything went black.

Wanda was not aware of the car starting up, or aware of it driving away from her neighborhood. They traveled north on Conkey Ave toward Ave D, where the driver made a right-hand turn. He continued to Lux Street, steering cautiously along the vacant roads in the wet darkness of the evening. Soon he was turning left onto Portland Ave, then making a quick right and another left before turning right again toward Ridge Rd. Every now and then he looked over to check on his passenger, making sure she was still unconscious. He was almost there now as he turned right on Bay Shore Blvd and then left toward Irondequoit Bay. He had made the little over five-mile distance without being noticed, and without his passenger causing him any trouble. He pulled the car into the rest stop.

He was anxious now but being careful was more important than his desires. He looked around him, thinking that he needed to move the car further back. Where he sat now the car could be seen, and someone might stop, thinking he was having car trouble. Slowly he drove deeper into the rest stop, checked again, and was satisfied. Now if anyone saw the car, they would assume he had pulled off to get some rest. That made him chuckle.

Finally, he was able to turn his attention to his captive, who was beginning to stir.

Wanda moaned softly as she tried to remember what had happened. She tried to turn on her side, but her body would not move. She lay there waiting, until finally she felt the feeling returning to her body and she remembered.

Her eyes flew open and she stared up into the cold piercing eyes of her assailant.

"Make a move and I'll kill you," he rasped, baring his teeth. Knowing what he could do, she obeyed. She forced herself to lie still as he stuffed a cloth from his pocket into her mouth, tied another around her head as a gag, and reclined the driver's seat of the car in order to force her body into the back seat. Terror paralyzed her and she was like putty in his hands, as he held her tightly and thrashed about, trying to get his body over the edge of the front seat and into the back. With success he landed on top of Wanda.

If it had not been for the weight of his body on her chest, and the gag in her mouth, she would have screamed.

He pinned her arms down and stared directly into her eyes as he growled, "Do not even try to fight me, little girl. If you annoy me, I'll push this knife all the way into you." As he made this terrifying speech, she saw the flash of a blade dangling in front of her face.

Over the next two hours the man repeatedly raped her. At one point he put his penis between her hands and commanded her to stroke it. Then he raped her again.

"Isn't this good?" he whispered into her ear.

Wanda had never had sex before and now her body ached from his manipulations. She hurt so badly she just wanted to die. It was then that she saw her attacker held something else in his hand. She looked to see what it was. Up until that moment she had kept her eyes closed, trying to take herself away from what was happening to her.

As she stared up, she saw the man had a wire with handles attached at the ends. She could not figure out what it was, until he took the instrument and placed it around her neck.

Her body numb with pain, she was helpless as the wire dug deep into her neck, cutting off her air. Instead of struggling she prayed silently. "Everlasting Son of God, for the sake of Thy love towards St. Joseph, who didst protect Thee so faithfully on earth, have mercy on us all and on those who are dying. Our Father, Hail Mary, Glory be to the Father…"

Thankfully, it was over.

Chapter 25

No one wanted to stop the search, as the police, friends and neighbors walked along streets, side paths and knocked on doors.

The investigators talked to everyone in the proximity of where Wanda had last been seen. They asked what, if anything, anyone had witnessed. Then they questioned what time it had been when people saw her, and, if they had noticed something happening, how long did they think it had gone on.

He could see the witnesses' expressions change with each question, so they hurried through their inquiries before they totally shut down.

What did you see? Where did it happen? Can you identify the person or persons involved? Did you hear what was being said, or see anyone else in the area at the time who might have seen what you did?

Doggedly, the investigators continued their queries until they met with success. Some people reported seeing what they thought was the abduction of the little girl. Knowing their last question would be the most difficult to answer, the investigators went on: "What did you do after witnessing the incident or behavior?"

As the evening drew on the men were exhausted, and the investigation ended.

"I think we need to call off the search for now. It is getting late and everyone is cold, wet and worn out."

The lead detective agreed and sent out a radio call to the police. He told them to get the word out to everyone that it was no use continuing into the night, but they would resume the search in the morning.

Slowly the streets emptied as friends and neighbors returned home to get some rest. As much as they wanted to find Wanda, at this point they had to admit it was best to start fresh in the morning.

The police cars pulled away and silence descended on the neighborhood.

It was raining again on Tuesday morning, April 3. This was to have been a day of celebration in the Walkowicz household. It was Rita's tenth birthday. Rita woke that morning all happy and excited at first, until she remembered Wanda was missing. She had stayed up late to care for her baby sister while her mother had joined the search for Wanda. Now as she sat up in bed, she could see that Wanda was not in her bed, but perhaps that did not mean she was not home.

Quickly she put on her slippers and robe and dashed downstairs to see if Wanda was there. All thoughts of it being her birthday vanished as worry built up inside her.

Her mother was already in the kitchen feeding Michelle. Joyce, hearing Rita come into the kitchen, turned around. "Dear, get something to eat."

"Wanda?"

Joyce stared off into the distance. "Nothing yet. Nothing."

Joyce left the kitchen before Rita had a chance to see how worried she was. She went into the front room where they had a radio scanner.

It was common in this area to have a radio scanner as it could be tuned in to hear news of any police activity. Since this was not a safe neighborhood, it paid to keep abreast of what was happening, whether it be a fire or streets being blocked off for some other type of emergency.

In all the time she had listened in, Joyce never thought she would hear about something happening to her own family. Joyce now searched the scanner, stopping when it detected a signal on any of the frequencies. Hopefully, she listened in until she was sure it was nothing concerning Wanda. She then continued searching the police radio frequencies. Joyce knew that when a patrol car called in to report a problem, the scanner would stop on that frequency so one could hear the conversation.

She was still listening when there was a knock on the door. She quickly went over to open it and found her neighbor standing there. She invited her in, and before she could close the door, other friends and family began showing up on her doorstep.

It was evident that nobody had slept a wink the night before. Some tried to cover their yawns, but their eyes gave them away. Hearing the voices in the front room, Rita went to see what was going on. There was already quite a gathering of people surrounding her mother, and instinctively Rita knew they were not there to celebrate her birthday.

They were there to offer support to Joyce and the girls in their time of need and were huddled around a scanner tuned to the local police frequency. Rita soon found herself fetching coffee and keeping an eye on her baby sister. Everyone was anxiously waiting for news about Wanda. When the police had called off the search the evening before, they had asked everyone to wait in the morning, so that they could organize the search and not have everyone stepping on top of each other.

At the police station, they were gearing up to continue the search for Wanda, knowing that the longer she went missing, the less chance they had of finding her alive.

"What's the plan?"

"Well, let's get our photographer up in the helicopter to take pictures of the area."

"Have you looked outside? I cannot imagine they will be able to see anything out there. It is still raining."

"We at least have to try."

There was a slight pause before the officer added, "Are you thinking about the Colón girl?"

Detective Ford, paused, looking at the officer who made the inquiry. "Ah, Officer... is it Clancy Thomas?"

"Yes, it is."

"Well, in answer to your question, I am thinking about the Colón girl, but until there is reason to believe these abductions are connected, we need to keep our minds on Wanda Walkowicz for now.

"I understand. I'll send up the helicopter."

Soon the search was again under way. The police photographer flew around taking aerial photos of the areas between the Conkey Avenue Neighborhood where Wanda lived, and all the way to the Emerson Street Landfill located in the western portion of the City of Rochester, bounded by Lexington Avenue to the north, Lee Road to the west, Ferrano Street to the south, and Colfax Street to the east. As he flew, he took pictures to record the most probable paths one could take to get from one location to another.

The photo mapping would be a great time-saver. It was quicker taking photos of the area than having to drive around and write it all down. It was important to have good shots to make a model of overlapping aerial shots that would be transferred to the map compilation sheet. The photographer was careful to make sure the photos were taken with a section of one photo visible in the previous photo. This overlapping would make it easier to orientate when looking back over them. There were additional shots to identify where a rape or murder could have taken place without being discovered.

Back on the ground he returned to the station to look over the photos, hopeful they would help to compile medium scale maps. He was to be disappointed. Because of the weather the pictures did not come out well, and plans were made to make another attempt later.

But they were all ready to go on to plan B. As frustrating as the news of the photographs was, they had to move on. Soon the patrol was busy looking at other maps of the area.

While they worked on the mapping, they received a call reporting that the man who had been hanging around the tracks had been found, and he had been identified.

"Finally, some good news," Detective Ford replied. "That is great. What do you know about him?"

"His name is Randall White, and he's a known sex offender so he just might be our man."

"Did he say anything about the Walkowicz girl?"

"We showed him her picture, but he says he never saw her and did not take her."

The detective paused. "Well, take his picture, and send it out to the police who are canvassing the area. Tell them to show the picture and see if we can get anyone who can put him in the area at the time of the girl's disappearance."

"Wait a second," Detective Ford said. "Does he have a car?"

"What do you think?"

Of course, he did not. If he did, he would not be living around the tracks. "Oh, well, let's follow the lead anyway."

Randall White was not being cooperative when the men tried to take his picture. He kept fidgeting and lowering his head until they had to force him into position. At one point they started to pull out his old photo, but he looked quite different now.

Copies were made and distributed to each detective canvassing the neighborhood. The man was distinctive in that he had big ears and a big nose, so if someone had seen him, they would probably remember.

Hours passed and the outcome was anything but satisfactory. No one had seen him around.

While the search continued, there were other officers working on possible alternatives. Police wondered, if Wanda did get into a car with a stranger, what might cause her to do that?

"Well, it was raining. It had rained all that evening, and she was returning home from the deli with her big bag of groceries."

Catching on, another officer piped up. "Maybe she was worried that the bag would get soaked, and the grocery bag would rip, so she ran into one of the houses she passed on her way home."

Several officers nodded. "But what about the car? I mean, if we think back to Carmen Colón, there was also a car…"

"Okay, Men, Detective Ford, said that we need to set the Colón case aside for now. So, what else do we know about Wanda?"

There were investigators who did not believe Wanda got into a car. They did say, however, that the car disappeared and when it moved, there was no Wanda on the sidewalk.

"This is a smart little girl. She would have struggled and drawn attention to herself if her abductor were a stranger, and as far as we can tell no one saw anything that registered an alarm."

Thinking aloud, an investigator added, "We are quite certain that Wanda was not carrying any money on her. None changed hands in the deli, so she was an unlikely victim for a robbery."

Another officer piped up. "She also was not considered a good candidate for running away, either."

Theory after theory was formulated to help in the search. It was important if they were to think like Wanda and get into the head of the person who had abducted her.

The search for Wanda Walkowicz was in full swing long before that dreadful day, April 3, 1973.

Chapter 26

Members of the Rochester and Monroe County police began the official investigation of a missing 11-year-old girl when the missing person report was filed for Wanda Walkowicz. The response was immediate: local police, firefighters, rescue squads, and volunteers began an intensive search for her. The search covered her neighborhood and nearby areas where Wanda was known to frequent. The search continued into that cold night of April 2, 1973 until a call was received on April 3 from State Trooper Cameron that he had spotted something "Ten miles east of Conkey Avenue, near the Irondequoit Bay Bridge, on a hillside next to a Route 104 access road." Cameron had exited the expressway to get a better look before calling in again to say he had found a body. He believed it to be that of Wanda Walkowicz.

The Irondequoit Bay Bridge is a continuous truss bridge that spans the Irondequoit Bay in eastern Monroe County, New York. The bridge has six-lanes carrying the Route 104 traffic from the town of Irondequoit on the west side of the bay to the town of Webster on the east side. Although it is a major thoroughfare, visibility is limited in the areas below and surrounding the Bay. The stretch where the body was discovered is thick with brush that supports wildlife inhabitants.

So, it was indeed lucky that State Trooper Cameron happened to be looking in the right direction and spotted something white on the hillside near the rest area, something that made him go to investigate. It was early that day, around 10:15 am when he called it in on the police radio.

Cameron would tell Detective Ford that he had exited the expressway and driven down to the area, careful to park on the shoulder a slight distance away. As he made his way up the incline to have a closer look, his heart started pounding faster. The closer he got, the surer he was. Then, careful not to contaminate the area, he moved nearer to the small body lying face down. The body was fully clothed, and there was a coat with a patterned design lying nearby. The body had on a blue and white checkered dress and green shorts. In his opinion, the clothing on her was disheveled in a way that made him think she might have been re-dressed after her clothes were removed.

As quickly as he dared, he went back down the incline to his patrol car. He climbed in and immediately he made the call.

Detective Ford could hear that Cameron was clearly shaken and having a hard time talking about it, but he did manage to report that he had gotten up close enough to see the red hair, and that was what had verified that this was indeed Wanda Walkowicz.

When the responder said, "Stay put. Officers on the way." State Trooper Cameron said he was finally able to breathe.

While State Trooper Cameron waited, he wondered how the body had arrived at this position. He looked above him at the bridge and thought it was possible that the body had been thrown over a railing and had rolled down the embankment. From where he stood, he figured that the body was seventy-five yards from Route 104 and about twenty-five feet from the rest area.

It was only seventeen hours since Wanda had disappeared and finding her so soon meant the press had not yet had time to report her missing. This was a good thing.

Soon the locale was swarming with Crime Scene Investigators. The area around the body was taped off to avoid any contamination. Because there is rarely more than one opportunity to obtain evidence, the investigation by the CSIs was methodical and complete. They collected any evidence from the crime scene that may have been touched or microscopically "contaminated" by the suspect or suspects. They also took samples of fibers, dirt, and dust, including tire prints along the perimeter. They eliminated those made by State Trooper Cameron, as well as his footprints.

After a preliminary search, the crime scene was photographed before being measured. Artists and other officers made detailed notes and drew sketches, all of which would help later in cataloguing the evidence.

Once the area around the victim had been thoroughly processed, the coroner was able to approach the body and begin his investigation. The body was checked for latent fingerprints, stains, hairs, fibers, and other trace evidence. It was moved carefully in order to take photographs of the front, sides and back of the body. Meanwhile the CSI's completed their reports with descriptions of the body's position, clothing, and any other details they felt necessary.

At the signal from the coroner, the body was finally removed and brought down to the roadside. Detective Ford asked them to stop, and, turning to the Coroner who stood next to him, he asked, "What do you think?"

"It is definitely the Walkowicz girl."

"So how was she murdered?"

"I would say she was strangled both manually and with an object."

"What kind of object?"

The Coroner moved closer to the body and said, "See this red line?"

Detective Ford nodded.

"Well, that would be the marking left by a garroting instrument. My guess is it was that or something similar."

The detective replied, "I see. Thank you."

He watched as the coroner turned and left the area. Behind him came CSI Jamison.

"So, what? What's your call on this?"

"Well, as far as I can tell at this point, I think that she was raped and strangled elsewhere. I do not think someone would be so brazen as to commit such an act in or near this rest area." He looked up. "They would be seen by passing traffic."

Detective Ford followed Jamison's eyes and observed above him. It was a good theory, but as he considered the area around them, he thought it was well off the highway, and it was nearly dark at the time of Wanda's abduction. If the urge to rape a child struck, perhaps the killer was willing to take his chances. He wrote on his pad Jamison's take on the scene.

As Detective Ford made his way back to the cruiser, he could not help thinking of Carmen Colón. He tried not to put the two cases together, telling himself at this point nothing about the two matched. Most noticeable, unlike Carmen's, Wanda's body was found fully clothed.

It was at 10:15 that morning that Joyce heard the news. She had not been far away from the scanner since turning it on, listening to reports coming into the police station. She had been steps away, folding laundry, when something coming over the radio caught her attention. Stolidly she moved closer, hesitated, and then came to an abrupt stop. She glanced at the clock and moved closer to the scanner, visibly shaking as she put her ear to the box.

"This is officer Cameron. I have a Code 8."

"What's your 10-20?"

"Ten miles east of Conkey Avenue just east of the Irondequoit Bay Bridge on a hillside next to a Route 104 access road."

"What's your 10-13?"

"I think I found her."

"Stay put. Officers on the way."

Joyce grabbed the edge of the table, frozen in time. The shock took over her body immediately. She spoke aloud, "No, it cannot be. God have mercy, it just cannot be." She was alone, her children were at school, and there was no one with her when she collapsed in a heap on the floor, literally losing her ability to stand or get up again."

Once Chief of Detectives Ford was sure that the body was Wanda, he immediately dispatched officers to the house. Officer Ferrell pressed the doorbell and stepped back, as they waited for the door to open. After several minutes, Officer Ferrell moved toward the door and lightly knocked. There was still no response. He waited a few minutes and then pounded heavily, calling out, "Ms. Walkowicz, Ms. Walkowicz, It is the sheriff's department. Please, open the door."

He put his ear near the door and finally heard movement within, just before the door opened.

Inside, Joyce had regained consciousness and managed to get to her feet. She stood, trying to remember how to breathe and unable to speak as the sound of thunder bounced around inside her head. She tried to calm herself down, but she could not. When the knock came at the door, she barely managed to open it to allow the officers in. One look at her and they realized she already knew why they were there.

Barely reaching out in time, Officer Ferrell caught Joyce Walkowicz as she collapsed in front of him. Carefully, he worked his way inside and moved slowly across the floor until he could lower her into the nearest chair. Then he reached for his radio.

Not waiting, he said into his radio, "Send an ambulance to 132 ½ Avenue D. It is off Conkey."

"What's happening?"

"I am at the home of Joyce Walkowicz, and she just fainted."

"The ambulance is on its way."

Then Officer Pitt went into the kitchen and returned with a glass of water. Joyce had recovered and was moaning when he returned.

"Please, Ms. Walkowicz, drink this."

Joyce took the glass and, with the officer's help, managed to bring it to her lips and take a drink.

"Ms. Walkowicz, where is your coat?"

She pointed to the hall closet and Officer Pitt went to fetch it. Luckily, there was only one coat that was not a child's, so he knew which one to pick. He carried it over to Joyce and between them they managed to get it on her.

Shortly thereafter there was the sound of the ambulance siren outside. Officer Ferrell went over to open the door, and in a low voice apprised the attendants of what was happening. Then the police officers both stood back and allowed the EMT's to do their job. Soon Joyce was on the stretcher.

"Stop, please, my girls," she said.

"Do not worry, Ms. Walkowicz, we will make sure someone takes care of the girls for you."

Joyce then allowed them to take her outside and wheel her into the ambulance. Soon they were on the way to Rochester General Hospital.

Joyce was awake as the attendants took her vital signs in the back of the ambulance. While one attendant performed the examination, the other was writing down information: patient had fainted; pale clammy skin accompanied by a rapid. thready pulse and rapid shallow breathing; patient exhibits dizziness, seems confused. The final notation noted that Joyce Walkowicz was suffering from shock.

While the activity was going on around her, Joyce's mind was churning, trying to find answers. It had been fourteen hours earlier that she had first called in the missing person's report, and she had felt hopeful that her daughter would be found unharmed. But as dusk had turned to dawn, she knew. Even before the devastating news had broken over the scanner, before her family had even identified Wanda's lifeless little body, Joyce had realized her first child would not be coming home again.

Chapter 27

With the discovery of Wanda Walkowicz's body on April 3, 1973 near the Irondequoit Bay Bridge in Webster, what had been the search for a missing child now became an investigation of a murder.

In November 1971, when Detective Ford was alerted that a child was missing it turned out to be Carmen Colón.

Now another girl, Wanda Walkowicz, had been reported missing, also in the city of Rochester. Detective Ford led the search party for Wanda. He forced himself to concentrate on the evidence and not try to match the two cases. If he did that, he might miss something that could identify the person who had murdered Wanda, who might or might not be the same person responsible for the death of Carmen.

What was known was that Wanda had been strangled both manually and with a weapon, possibly a garroting instrument.

Wanda's body was found at the rest area near the bridge over Irondequoit Bay in Webster, but based on observations at the body recovery site, police had reason to believe she had been raped and strangled elsewhere.

Detective Ford was not totally in agreement with this theory. From walking the area, he felt the rest area was well off the highway, plus it was nearly dark out at the time of Wanda's abduction.

With more information in his possession, Detective Ford now considered the possibility that the murderer was the same one who had abducted and raped Carmen Colón. He pondered this theory, reviewing the details. The only item that stood out was that Carmen had been found undressed, while Wanda had been found fully clothed.

Flipping through papers on his desk, he reviewed the interviews with people who might have seen Wanda. There were her friends who had seen her pausing in front of the school fence, as if trying to get a better grip on the groceries she carried. They had also reported seeing a brown car near Wanda, but when they had turned and looked back the car had been gone and so had Wanda. They had not seen her get in.

The detective was glad that in this case the body was discovered before the press had an opportunity to report she was missing. He hoped this could lean in their favor.

Detective Ford tilted his head to the side as a thought hit him. He jotted down the fact that in both cases the girls had been sent on an errand by their parents, in the late afternoon. That might mean something. For now, it meant that the killer might not necessarily have known the girls, since they were not abducted at their homes.

Detective Ford got up, stretched, and walked around the room to get his circulation going before sitting down again. This time he turned to the evidence bag.

He paused when he came to an evidence bag that was noted as containing cat fur found on the clothing of Wanda. It was listed as white cat fur.

Detective Ford leaned down and opened his desk file where he searched around until he found what he was looking for. He laid the folder on the top of his desk and began going carefully through its contents.

"Yes... ah..."

He turned to the report on the location of the body. The exact location was noted as on a hill seventy-five yards from Route 104 and about twenty-five feet from the rest area. He picked up the sheet of paper and read aloud. "The body had been dumped about seven and a half miles from where she was abducted, and she was thrown over the railing and her body had rolled down the embankment."

That meant there were no tire tracks near the body, or footprints of the killer. That was not good.

He made some notes on his pad and then, picking up the autopsy findings, continued to read. "Wanda Walkowicz was four feet tall, weighed 65 pounds. She had been raped and strangled, possibly with a belt."

He leaned back in his chair. Just then the phone rang.

"Detective Ford."

"Yes, Detective, this is Jamison…I was the crime scene investigator."

"Yes, I remember you."

"Well, in our report we mentioned that we found feces near Wanda's body."

Detective Ford rested the receiver between his shoulder and his ear as he leafed through the contents of the folder, looking for something pertaining to feces.

"Yes, go ahead."

"Well, we heard back from the crime lab, and it was verified as human and found to contain Seconal." Not waiting to see if the detective was aware of what this was, he continued, "It is a barbiturate that is a popular recreational drug and is known as 'reds.'"

Detective Ford sat up straight in his chair. This was new and something to keep to themselves. "Listen, let's keep this under wraps and not let this get out to the papers or the public."

"You got it."

Everything was moving quickly, and possibly this time they would catch the murderer. And maybe it would be the same person who had murdered Carmen Colón. He turned back to the medical examiner's report.

ME Jonathan Walker, who performed the autopsy, verified that the girl had been raped and strangled, possibly with a belt.

Dr. Walker found custard in Wanda's stomach. It had not been custard, but other food had been found in Carmen's stomach as well. The stomach stops working after death, creating a gastronomic time capsule of the victim's last moments. Though digestion varies from person to person, a meal is typically fully digested and the stomach empty six hours after eating.

The detective stared at the notation, as he mentally analyzed the finding. Where could she have gotten custard? He looked through the file until he found a copy of the groceries she had purchased. "No custard," he said. "She could have bought a custard herself... no, she had no money, none at all. She charged the items she bought for her mother."

The coroner's report said that Wanda had eaten custard shortly before she was murdered, so she did not eat it at home before she left.

"Okay, so what is left?" He had to assume she was taken somewhere for a treat by her abductor. That rang a lot of bells. Would Wanda have eaten the custard if she were afraid of the person? Maybe, but it made more sense if she was with someone she knew or trusted.

It was late, but he had to make a call. Home at last, Joyce was seated in the front room, with the lights off. When the phone rang, at first, she was not going to answer it, but decided to go over and pick up the receiver.

"Yes."

"Is this Ms. Walkowicz?"

"Yes. Who is this?"

"It is Detective Ford. I am heading the investigation on your daughter's case. I need to ask you something."

"Anything. Go ahead."

"They found custard in Wanda's stomach. Do you know where she might have gotten it?"

There was silence for a brief minute. "No, I do not. Wanda had an incredibly nervous stomach and could not possibly have eaten something in her...in this situation. If she did, she would vomit it up."

The detective looked over the notes. No mention of Wanda vomiting appeared.

"Thank you, Ms. Walkowicz."

"You are welcome."

After hanging up the phone, the detective pushed his chair back and, picking up the folder, put his feet to rest on the desk in front of him. On the pad in his lap he noted what he had learned. He surmised that maybe an individual, a stranger, or an acquaintance, who lived or worked in the area had seen Wanda struggling under the weight of her load and had approached her. He may have done it in a way that made her think he was coming to her rescue, offering to carry it back into his house... or place of business, so he could give her a new bag.

He paused, working the idea in his head. He began writing again. As soon Wanda had stepped over the threshold of the killer's home or store, he had raped and strangled her there.

He looked over what he had written, then thought it made sense. It had been late so it was probably dark out, so the rapist could be quite sure he would not be seen as he took her limp body out to the car. He had then driven until coming to the area where he had thrown her body over the bridge.

That part agreed with the scenario that Wanda had been raped and killed somewhere else and not at the site where she had been found. He remembered seeing something else in the file and searched until he found it.

"Yes," he said aloud. "The coroner said that the killer had put her clothes back on after he raped her."

It was getting late but having asked everyone to work the case as quickly as possible, he also had to do the same. He picked up the folder and read on. Wanda had been strangled from behind. He carefully laid the folder down and picked up the one containing information on the Carmen Colón case.

He found what he was looking for. Carmen had been strangled from the front, face to face. This was a significant difference. Either there were two killers or one. Now there were two differences to contend with: Fully clothed versus naked and strangled from different positions.

He read, "There were marks on the neck and elsewhere on the body indicating there had been a struggle." He leaned back. Carmen was such a tiny little thing. He did not think she had been capable of putting up much of a struggle, but that was important. If she had struggled, it might be because she did not know the person who took her. It could as easily mean she had known him, but when he had started taking off her clothes, she was shocked.

Now he tried to put his thoughts together. The last time the kids who had been walking a block or two ahead of Wanda had seen her, she had been leaning against the fence, struggling to manage the grocery bag. That had been on Conkey Avenue. They said that a car had been approaching, going in the same direction Wanda had been walking. Then the girls had turned away and later, when they had looked back in that direction, both Wanda and the car had been gone. There had not been time enough for a stranger to have pulled up, rolled down his window, and persuaded Wanda to get into his vehicle by showing her a cat. Everyone said that she had been a smart little girl who knew how to be safe on the street.

But, he conjectured, if a gun had been pointed in her face, or if she knew the driver well, she might have climbed in without hesitation.

That rang true, but still, there was no evidence to indicate whether she was abducted by a vehicle driver or by someone on foot.

It was time. He had the preliminary survey, the narrative description, the administrative notes, photography, sketching/diagramming, and the evidence recovery log. Before he knew it, the office was filling up, and he had been there, working on the details, all night. He grabbed a cup of coffee and the files and took them to the War Room. He started with the interviewed witnesses, then he took out the scene diagrams and photographs. He next pulled out the details of the crime scene, making note of any trace evidence, body fluids, hair and fibers, and fingerprints that had been collected. This was a major investigation, and it might be connected to the Carmen Colón case, so he began creating a link chart on the wall, showing people, locations, cars, etc., some connected by lengths of string. When he was done, he turned and, for the first time, realized that other officers had joined him. He watched as they moved forward and studied the board, nodding. Every now and then someone would add something to one of the areas. Detective Ford moved to the side and waited.

When the last officer took his seat, Detective Ford led the discussion on what they needed to do that day. In a matter of minutes, they were out of the office to begin the work of tracing down the murderer of Wanda Walkowicz.

By Thursday night April 5, they all met again at the precinct.

"So, what do we have?"

"Well, I do not think that the Carmen Colón murder is connected to this one."

"Why is that?" asked Detective Ford

"I believe that Miguel killed Carmen. I know we do not have evidence of that, but I still think so. Plus think about it: Carmen was found naked and Wanda had all her clothes on."

"Plus, Miguel Colón fled to Puerto Rico. Why would he if he was innocent?"

There were nods of heads around the room. Detective Ford referenced this fact on the board, bulleting the differences.

"Okay," Detective Ford interjected, "Let us not try to link the two just yet. Let us go with what we have on suspects in Wanda's case."

"What about James Barber? He's a known sex offender."

Detective Ford flipped through the file in front of him, but before he could find what he was looking for, another officer chimed in.

"Yeah, I thought that was a good lead too, but in follow up, I learned that James Barber had left Rochester before Wanda Walkowicz was murdered."

"I am checking on Joseph Naso but haven't anything substantial to report."

The investigation continued with the police given plenty of leads to pursue. The phone rang with anonymous callers reporting they saw a young girl they believed to be Wanda being bundled into a Dodge Dart. Then there were two young girls who told the police that on the Saturday before Wanda's murder a man had attempted to lure them into his vehicle. Hoping for a connection, they asked if the girls could describe the car. They reported the vehicle was a Ford LTD, not a Dodge Dart.

One of the more hopeful leads was from a caller who said he had seen the body being dumped. The officer took down the information and shared it with the group. The final report received was from a caller who said he had seen Wanda crying in a green Pinto driven by a tattooed man.

What was real and what was not were questions not even considered during the initial investigation. Instead, each lead was acted upon as if it were pertinent to the case.

Each officer reported what they had so far, and Detective Ford wrote the information on the board. It turned out there were a few promising leads, but still no suspect.

"The fact that we did not find any groceries that had spilled out of the bag on the ground near the abduction site bothers me."

"Any theories?"

"If we are leaning toward the theory that Wanda knew her killer, because the consensus is that she was too smart to get into a car with a stranger, then it does make sense. But if the man grabbed the bag of groceries away from Wanda, then they could be expected to spill since the bag was said to be very full."

Another officer added, "He could have convinced her not to scream, but she would have been unable to get the groceries back.

"Yeah, if he grabbed them and her and she could not get away, there would be evidence of the struggle."

"He could have put the groceries in the trunk and then forced her into the car."

Detective Ford added, "If she was being forced into a car with a bag of groceries in her hand, I cannot see how some of the groceries did not fall on the street in the struggle and no one saw anything. A sex pervert does not plan that much ahead."

Several officers nodded, and one added, "I would think he was on the prowl, and therefore he would have an immediate need that must be satisfied."

"Yes, and the fact that the girl had to walk by her school is important because schools tend to attract these kinds of people."

"Good. Any more ideas?"

"The brand of cigarettes is Pall Mall," said New York State Police Investigator, Winston James. "What if the killer got rid of the other grocery items and kept the cigarettes?"

Detective Ford looked at him. "What are you saying?"

"Just that we should see if anyone saw a man smoking that brand of cigarettes in that area. I know It is not much, but…"

"Okay, add that to the list of investigative questions to ask."

By the morning of Thursday, April 5, city, county, and state police were working around the clock trying to find a link between the victim and the killer.

Chapter 28

On Friday, April 6, the obituary for Wanda Lee Walkowicz appeared in the paper. The sad part was that this little girl, eleven years old, was survived by her paternal grandmother, Mrs. Carl (Wanda) Kabelac for whom she was named; her maternal grandmother, Mrs. Lee Chatterton, and her mother, Mrs. Joyce Walkowicz. In the party of mourners would be her sisters, Marie, and Michelle, along with aunts, uncles and cousins.

It was raining that day, a soaking rain that did not let up for a minute. It was a sorrowful gathering that prayed at the wake held at 8:30 that morning at the Richard L. Felerski Funeral Home located at 1005 Hudson Avenue, Rochester, New York. Wanda's casket was heartbreakingly small, white, and gold with etched flowers. The family and many friends had come to say goodbye to a little red-headed, freckle-faced child who was taken before she had a chance to live.

The Mass was scheduled to start at 9:00 that morning at the lofty Gothic church of St. Michael's, at 869 Clinton Avenue North. The family rode in the black limo at the head of the procession as they made their way to the church. The cars headed south on Hudson Ave toward Weyl Street and turned right onto Ave D. The procession drove slowly down the street and then turned left onto N Clinton Avenue, covering the little over a mile distance.

Car doors opened and closed with their occupants making their way into the church, filing in silently and taking their seats. As soon as the attendees were seated the procession of the priest, sprinkling holy water, the coffin, and the chief mourners moved up the aisle toward the front of the church. In attendance at the mass, sitting in the front pew, were twenty-five of Wanda's classmates from School #8. Hanging from the pulpit was a hand-made paper and burlap Lenten sign that read, 'Penance is Love.'

The priest delivered an introductory rite, commemorating Wanda Walkowicz's short time on Earth.

First there were prayers and the opening song with the St. Bernard's Seminary Choir singing, 'Around and Around,' followed by Gelineau Psalms, 'I am the Bread of Life' and concluding with 'Amazing Grace'.

Readings from the Bible were from Lamentations, which consists of four elegies and a prayer. At the end of the readings the Father spoke, "But we know our little friend is with God. She has returned to her Heavenly Father, and she has left her mother to go to her Father."

Joyce broke down. and her sobs could be heard throughout the church. The priest continued: "She was the Temple of the Holy Spirit and that temple was violated. We pray that the yoke of fear be lifted from the neighborhood. We pray that the courts deal out justice swiftly and effectively, and that the criminal and pervert turn from his ways and be cured."

The group rose to take Holy Communion, which was followed by more prayers, before the coffin holding Wanda was taken back down the aisle and out of the church.

Those who planned to go to the gravesite climbed into their cars, and the procession headed north on North Clinton Avenue toward Clifford Avenue, taking the ramp on the left and following the signs for Rt 104 West. From there they turned right onto Lake Avenue and arrived at their destination, Holy Sepulchre Cemetery, located at 2461 Lake Avenue. The procession of approximately twenty-five cars carried about a hundred mourners.

Chapter 29

By now the full squad on the case included upward of fifty detectives. From the initial briefing, they had identified similarities between the families of the Colóns and Walkowiczes. They were both Catholics, both the girls academically challenged, both with low incomes and living in challenging neighborhoods. On these points everyone agreed.

Now it was important that they set up a line of command that would include Wayne County, along with Rochester and New York State law enforcers. This would allow the information to be dispersed quickly to each area with few hiccups. In order to keep the investigation going forward, it would be important to use the Records Management System (RMS) faithfully at all levels and in all areas, so that any matching data would be easily recognized and retrievable, especially since they were looking back at the Colón case as a reference point. That system and getting used to using the computers would in the end save them a lot of time in spotting details they had already covered.

Detective Ford always wanted everyone kept up to date . There were police officers, deputy sheriffs, and state troopers who were all working together on the case, and the overlapping of assignments required open communication channels as well as checking for up-to-date information in the RMS system.

Detective Ford studied the list of uniformed officers, detectives, state police and highway patrol officers, sheriffs and special jurisdiction police already involved in the case. Each one was needed if they were to get anywhere in solving the murder. He paused, leaning his head on his hands, but he quickly identified the investigators whom he would set up as the contacts. The phone rang and Detective Ford picked it up. "Yes."

"Hello, Detective, this is the D&C and we are wondering if you could give us a statement on the Wanda Walkowicz case?"

This was the part of the job that he hated most. It was bad enough having to deal with the people who just wanted to be part of the investigation, taking up police time because they knew the police had to listen to them. But the press....

He took a deep breath. "Who is this?"

"Oh, sorry, this is Thomas Clark with the Democrat & Chronicle. I would just like a statement to keep the public informed on the case."

"I bet you would..." Detective Ford whispered.

"What was that?"

"Oh, nothing. There is not much to tell except that we are focusing our full attention on the case. We will be giving our investigators a composite drawing of a suspect today."

He could hear he had piqued the attention of the reporter. "Who is the drawing of?"

"We do not know yet."

"Where did you get the information for the sketch?"

"All I can tell you is we have promising leads to follow, but no suspect identified as yet."

"Is that all?"

"Yes."

"Well, thanks, Detective Ford. I'll let you get to your work then."

Without a reply, the detective hung up the phone. It was time to meet with the team.

After discussing the officers who would be the leads in the various areas, they went on to bring everyone up to date and hand out assignments.

"We have sketches on the table back there," he said, holding his hand up and pointing toward the back of the room. "Make sure you take them with you. One sketch is from a witness who says she saw the suspect. We had her come down to the station and work with a sketch artist on it."

He paused, staring down at his file. "Oh, yes, we also have sketches made from the Carmen Colón case..." Seeing the reaction of some of the officers, he added. "I am not saying there is a connection, but we need to assume there may be, or we might miss something important. We have been working this case as an individual crime, so now considering the two as possibly accountable to a single suspect will not interfere with the investigation into the Wanda Walkowicz case."

"Does the press have these?" someone asked.

"Not now. Neither the new ones, nor the ones from the Colón case, have been released. We do not want people going around accusing each other."

"There's a rumor out there that you and Detective Barnes have a witness being questioned by authorities who claims to have seen Wanda's body being dumped in Webster."

"Yes, we heard that rumor too. It is not true. That is why I have assigned individuals who will be the liaisons between us and the press, as well as the lead contacts for each group of investigators. They will be given the phone numbers of the reporters covering the story. In this way, we can be sure to limit contradictions and misinformation."

"If there's nothing else, everyone out on the streets."

On Saturday, April 7, there was a feeling of optimism. A suspect was in custody and in the interrogation room.

The interrogator asked, "Are you warm enough?"

"Yes, I am fine."

"Would you like a cigarette?"

"Ah, no. I just want to get this over with."

"Okay. You were reported as being near the rest stop in Webster where the body of Wanda Walkowicz was found. Can you tell me what you were doing there?"

The suspect went into a narrative explaining the reason he was in that area while the detective listened and watched him closely.

Being careful not to put him on the defensive, the detective asked non-specific questions that did not point a finger.

"So, did you see the body of the little girl?"

The suspect straightened in his chair as he practically yelled out, "No."

"Okay, I just had to ask."

The detective slid a photo in front of the suspect. "Can you point out where you were standing from this photo."

"God…"

The detective thought the man was going to vomit and stepped back, grabbing the photo as he did. "Sorry. Are you okay?"

At this point he knew that this suspect did not commit the crime but thought he might have some information that could help with the case. "Is there anything else that you can tell me about this?"

The suspect gulped and rubbed the front of his head, as if trying to get the image out of there. "No, I am sorry, but I did not see anything or hear anything. I cannot help you."

The detective walked out and joined Detective Ford, who had been watching through the one-way glass.

"What do you think?" Detective Ford asked, knowing the answer.

"This isn't our guy."

Detective Ford nodded.

On Sunday, April 8, almost a week after Wanda's murder, all optimism had evaporated, and the following day when the officers regrouped, they were told that a suspect had been interrogated for ten hours.

"So, what…"

Detective Ford swallowed. "We thought we had our man, but he had a solid alibi and passed a lie-detector test."

He saw the disappointment on the faces in front of him and added, "He was, however, charged with endangering the welfare of a child."

The heads rose with questioning looks.

"It was a 1972 incident involving a child, but unrelated to Wanda's murder."

The officers looked at each other, feeling discouraged. "Listen, when It is not the guy, It is not the guy, so now, we need to go on."

"So, what next?"

"More of the same. That was our only real lead in the case. So, we keep on doing what we were doing, as if we were back to square one. We regroup and start in again. We will continue to get together early Monday and rehash things."

There was an audible groan.

"Sometimes the second time around you pick up something you missed before."

Detective Ford paused. "Any questions?"

He waited and when nothing was said, he added, "Okay, everyone out on the streets."

As he made his way back to his desk, the phone rang.

Chapter 30

The day Wanda's body was discovered the D&C opened a special Secret Witness anonymity line. The line was not connected to the newspaper's switchboard. Each call would get a number and the callers did not have to identify themselves unless they wanted to.

For those who were still apprehensive about making a call, the D&C set up an address where tips could be mailed in. Similarly, a number would be required for the letter, so that the individual could be notified if the tip led to an arrest, making them eligible for the $2,500 reward established by Gannett Newspapers.

Since there were dozens of companies and individuals wanting to support the effort, another address was set up for sending donations to the fund. For the papers, this was not a money-making effort, but more a way to reach out. They could supply information and share it with the public. The reporters took it one step further by doing some investigating on their own

The paper questioned neighbors, hoping to get a lead they could turn over to the police. Not all information turned into a lead, but the paper allowed everyone to say what they wanted to say. One gentleman who worked at the Avenue D Playground-Recreation Center, located just on the other side of the railroad tracks, reported that he saw Wanda almost every day and that she was a leader, not a follower. He said he frequented Shenanigan's Tavern and was an old drinking buddy of her parents. This information was shared with the police.

One reporter spoke to Wanda's father's sister. She told the reporter she was afraid something like this would happen. When asked why, she shared her fears, which started a conversation between them.

"As you can see, this is not the best neighborhood, and often Wanda was unsupervised."

"I see…"

"Did you know that Wanda had been stalked 48 hours before she disappeared?" She paused. "Knowing that, why did they allow her to walk around by herself?"

"So, what did you say, if anything?"

"I told the girls not to go out at night, and especially to stay away from the railroad tracks."

"That is good advice."

Wanda's aunt nodded. Again, this piece of information was shared with the police as soon as it was received.

It was important that they try and work side by side and not on top of each other. In that way they could gather more information and keep leads fresh.

Thomas Clark had been busy gathering information wherever he could, and on this day possessed one piece of data he knew was important evidence, so he made a call to Detective Ford.

"Detective Ford?"

"Yes, this is Detective Ford. Who's calling?"

"This is Thomas Clark from the D&C," he said, then added, "I spoke to you earlier."

"Yes, I remember you. What do you want?"

"Well, I heard there was a report of a light-colored Dodge Dart and an armed man who was seen struggling with a girl with red hair who looked like Wanda Walkowicz."

"Yes, we heard about it and checked it out. We found the report to be without basis, and repeated attempts to get the tipster to call back with further details were in vain."

"So, you think it was not a light-colored Dodge Dart?"

"No, I am saying that the bad weather might have made it hard for identification, and the person who reported it obviously is not sure just what he saw. But we are not writing it off just yet."

"So, what now?"

"We continue to follow up on leads and work toward solving this murder."

Thomas hung up the phone feeling frustrated. He understood what Detective Ford was saying, but he had been so sure there was something to this. He wanted to call the detective back and give him the name of the person who had divulged this lead, but the informant had said that he did not want any hassle, and would only tell him what he saw if he promised not to give out his name.

Chapter 31

One of the first suspects questioned was an old man brought to their attention by Peyton Raney, Wanda's stepfather.

"Do you know his name?"

Peyton, known as Junior by the family, took a moment, his suspicions showing on his face. "Now, why would you think I knew the man's name, huh? I do not know his name."

"Well, can you describe him."

Peyton looked down at his hands that were constantly rubbing against each other. Finally, he looked up. "Do not think it will help, but Wanda told her mother he was dirty, wore a red plaid shirt that was way too big for him, and his hair was longish and dark." He stopped for a minute before adding, "That is all I remember. You should ask her friends. They were there."

Officer Pete Taylor took out his pad. "Good. What are their names."

"They're Peggy, Sara and Janey."

He wrote the names down, then raised his head. "Do you know their last names?"

Junior thought for a moment, "Ah, yes, Peggy Logan, Sara James, Janey Foster."

When Taylor finished writing down their last names he tried for another piece of information. "Do you happen to know where they live?"

"Oh, no, just in the neighborhood, but you could ask at the school. They go to School 8, where Rita and Wanda go…" He paused, a sad expression transforming his features. "Ah, I mean, went."

"You've been a big help. Thanks. "

Officer Taylor was excited. This was a good lead, and he did not want to waste a minute. He drove back to the precinct, afraid to call it in over the radio. He had barely stepped through the doors when he called out to Detective Ford.

"Detective, can I have a word with you?"

Detective Ford nodded, finished what he was doing and then walked the officer back to his office. "What's up?"

Taylor pulled out his notes and filled in Alex on all the details that he had gotten from Junior. Then he asked, "Can you send another officer to the school with me to talk to the girls?"

Alex knew Taylor and could tell by his manner that he was more than confident in what his witness had told him. They had been involved in cases where a relative had attempted to flip the attention away from themselves and onto someone else, but because Junior gave names of other witnesses to attest to what he said, it was obviously not the case here.

"Come with me," Alex said. He took Taylor back into the front room and looked around to see who was available. His eyes landed on Officer Clancy Thomas. "Clancy," Clancy looked up, "Can you accompany Officer Taylor to check out a lead on the Wanda Walkowicz case?"

He had hardly gotten the words out of his mouth before Clancy popped out of his chair. "Sure, Boss, sure."

Pete walked over to Clancy, and a few minutes later they were out the door. Pete filled him in on the way to the school, and when they arrived, he knew as much as Pete did.

The two officers entered School No. 8 and headed straight to the main office. They showed their badges, stating their reason for being there.

"We are working on the Wanda Walkowicz case and have been informed that three of the girls who attend school here may be able to help us with some information we received."

They were asked to take a seat. They watched as the woman from the front desk went over and knocked on the door of the principal. They continued to stare in that direction as she disappeared. They were happy with the speedy reaction as the door almost instantly reopened and the principal appeared. "Hello Officers. Martha is calling the classroom now. We are having the girls brought here. You can use my office to speak with them."

While this was happening at the school, Detective Ford sent two other officers out to the railroad tracks to see if they could come up with something, anything that might lead to the person who had been hanging around.

The officers spoke to several people in the area, but with only a vague, verbal description to inquire about, they did not come up with anything worth reporting.

But that was not the case with Officers Taylor and Thomas. When they arrived at the principal's office, the girls had a lot to tell them. Officer Taylor made a call to the station to speak with Detective Ford. Detective Ford responded. "Consider it done."

Then Taylor went back into the principal's office. "Say, Girls, would you like to take a ride in a patrol car?"

He knew the answer before he asked it. While the girls went back to get their coats and school bags, Officer Taylor told the principal they were taking them to the station to talk with a sketch artist. When they were done, they would bring them back to the school.

Peggy Logan, Sara James, and Janey Foster were having the best day of their lives. They described the man they had seen, giving as much detail as they could. When the artist had finished his drawing, he turned it around so that they could see it, and they all nodded and said, "Yes, That is him."

They had learned from the girls that this had happened a while back, but they had since seen him hanging around the tracks another time and had stayed clear of him. In case the girls saw him again, the officers had taken down their home addresses and given them a card. They were told to call if they saw the man again.

This time the officers were sent out to the tracks with the description and the drawing prepared by the sketch artist. Detective Ford scheduled a twenty-four-hour surveillance of the area near the tracks that continued for several days before a man finally showed up. Within minutes he was in custody.

"Sir, can you tell us your name?"

He did not answer, just looked extremely uncomfortable as he asked, "Why am I here? What did I do?"

"Sir, your name."

He looked around the room again. He felt caged in as he replied, "It is Anthony Cymery."

The officers looked at each other, wondering if this was his real name. It did not seem to fit a homeless person, but then, it was not a name someone would make up.

"So, Mr. Cymery, we hear that you were telling little girls that you would give them each a dime if they would kiss you. Is that true?"

Anthony had been leaning back in his chair, but now sat up straight. "Now, wait a minute, there. I did not mean any harm."

There was a knock on the door and one of the officers went to answer it. They had done a background check on Anthony Cymery, and he did not have a record. The only notation about him was that he was a vagrant and sometimes slept at a local shelter.

Officer Taylor, hearing that they had brought in a man, anxiously went to the viewing window to look at him. The man did not resemble the drawing at all. The old man had a fringe of grey-white hair around his balding scalp. He had a shriveled face and a slight hunch in his back. Each time Anthony Cymery moved, his bones creaked painfully, and his attitude was not of one who would harm a child. Even if he did try, he was obviously too weak to succeed.

Now, after checking his background and finding nothing suspicious, they released him with a warning not to talk to or touch any little girls or he would be right back in the station house.

Detectives Sanders and Ford could see Officer Taylor's annoyance, and went over to explain to him that while the man had not matched the description, he had been hanging around the tracks, and they thought it wise to question him. They would continue surveillance at the tracks for the man the girls described and hope he would show.

So, the investigation continued, going back over areas and interviews covered previously. Detectives Sanders and Ford heading the Rochester investigation team, and Captain Barnes heading the investigation for the state police, kept the channels open.

They set up roadblocks at five o'clock in the evening on Conkey Avenue and asked the motorists if they had seen anything suspicious on Monday night, April 2.

Officers in unmarked cars took down license plates of individuals who seemed to be attempting to avoid the roadblocks. These car owners were later questioned to find out if they were hiding anything.

Even with this intense search going on, by day four they still had not uncovered anything more, but they did not give up. Any lead was taken seriously. Therefore, when a rec center worker said that, although he could not swear to it, he thought he had seen a little girl who looked a lot like Wanda near the rec center at around seven o'clock that Monday evening, he was brought in for further questioning. It was later determined that from the time she had left the store to where her friends had last seen her, she could not have walked all the way to the rec center that evening. They thanked the man and told him if they needed anything further, they would be in touch.

The consensus of friends, family and acquaintances of Wanda's were all confirming she was fairly intelligent and definitely not the type of girl to get into a car with a stranger.

The hunt for the murderer was frustrating. It seemed that no one could say they saw Wanda get into a car, and no one remembered seeing her between her disappearance and when her body was dumped in Webster.

In the beginning, the investigation had focused on Wanda's neighbors and pulling in known sex offenders. All were asked to provide an alibi and once verified, the alibis checked out.

As for the information coming in from the city newspaper's secret-witness phone line, during the first twenty-four hours seventy-two calls were received. Those calls mainly described automobiles spotted in the vicinity of the Hillside Deli where Wanda had last been seen, and others covered incidents involving other neighborhood children.

As could be expected, people were scared and nervous, and speculations were epidemic. The public understood whoever murdered Wanda did not look like a monster nor would he be easily distinguishable, and this put them on edge.

Detective Ford, Captain Barnes and Detective Lt. Sanders had felt sure that the neighborhood was too populated for someone not to have seen something. But they soon learned that, while this may have been true on a nice, sunny day when everyone was outside, the day Wanda disappeared was cold, wet, and miserable, not a day for people to be mobile.

Detective Lieutenant Terrance Lopez and Detective Les Velazquez from the Monroe County Sheriff's Office had been part of the investigation team on the Carmen Colón murder. They were a welcome addition to the Wanda Walkowicz case, since now the detectives were working the cases together because the similarities might point to a single murderer.

The similarities were amazing. Both girls were nearly the same age; both came from poor family backgrounds; both had been abducted while running late-afternoon errands for their mothers; and both were found by the side of a road, raped and strangled to death. The investigators would be lax if they did not consider this possibility.

Repeatedly, the Webster and Irondequoit investigators scoured the Irondequoit Bay Bridge area where Wanda's body had been found, looking for clues, and hoping that the murderer might come back. City and state investigators concentrated their efforts on the northeast side of the city, revisiting, and interviewing people in the neighborhood on the chance someone would remember something they had forgotten to mention.

Along with their hopes of a fresh lead, they looked for evidence of any connection between the two girls that might lead to the murderer.

It was a revolving door of suspects that the authorities brought in for questioning. There were known sex offenders who lived in the area, the same men who had been questioned in the Carmen Colón murders. Their hopes were high when they learned that an ex-con who had attacked a young girl in the late 1960s was now living in the area where the two girls had disappeared. He was brought in and questioned, but when they had verified his alibi, they had to let him go.

It was frustrating as they repeated their steps talking with family members, teachers, and friends, only to hear the same information. Just the same, the team met and reviewed their findings.

The team questioned each other to gain new perspectives.

"Do you think Wanda would accept a ride from a stranger?" But as before the answer was always, "No."

"So, what would make her accept a ride from a stranger?"

After giving it some thought, several replied, "Well, perhaps if he was dressed like a police officer, postman, clergyman, or fireman, she would."

Several present nodded in agreement.

"Maybe if he was dressed like a woman," someone added from the back of the room.

The officers looked at each other, and then forced themselves not to let out the laughter that bubbled up in them.

"Okay now, Men, we need to be serious."

Another officer piped up, "Talking with one little girl, she said that Wanda would have put up a fight if someone had tried to force her into a vehicle."

"Okay, so what can we draw from that?"

"Maybe that it is a strong possibility that Wanda knew her killer and went willingly with him."

"Anything to support that?"

The room grew loud as the officers addressed the issue considering what they had learned about Wanda. The consensus was that even if she were carrying a bag bursting at the seams in the rain, she still would not have accepted a ride from a complete stranger.

"Okay, is there anything that would support her getting into a car with a stranger?"

"Yes, Wanda was only two-tenths of a mile from her house when she was last seen. Maybe she thought, going that short distance, what's the harm?"

That conclusion met with disagreement.

People in the neighborhood were anxious and they had reason to be. Even though the police were everywhere, residents still felt uncomfortable. Cautiously, they changed their routines, causing traffic jams at the local elementary schools at both the beginning and end of the school day. The concerned parents of walkers decided to drive their children to and from school, watching them go safely inside and seeing them safely all the way back home.

In the area of Conkey Avenue, where the children were usually seen out playing, they were now kept indoors. Occasionally, you would see boys on the streets; but young girls either walked in groups or with their parents.

The outpouring of support continued. The secret witness program received nearly four hundred phone tips and letters that were turned over to the police. From the Citizens for a Decent Community (CDC) who initially offered a reward of $1,000, the amount was increased to $6,000, while the Rochester Auto Dealers Association contributed $5,000 to the fund.

Old leads took on new life. One tip from an anonymous caller came in on the secret witness line on Thursday, April 5. The caller claimed to have seen a man forcing a red-haired girl into a car at the corner of Conkey Avenue and Wanda's street between 5:30 and 6 p.m. three nights earlier. The car he reported as a light-colored Dodge Dart. A different individual called in to say he had seen a similar car at the rest area where Wanda's body was found. Still another person reported seeing Wanda dumped from a similar car at that spot.

Each call was followed up, with bulletins going out to be on the lookout for a light-colored, Dodge Dart-type vehicle. Unfortunately, when police appealed to the first anonymous tipster who allegedly had seen Wanda enter the car on the street corner, he never called back, and the two related tips from other sources did not pan out either, leaving investigators wondering why the first witness did not call back, and if what he saw was related to the case or not.

On Friday, April 6, police questioned an Avenue D man for twelve hours. The suspect had been charged five months earlier with endangering the welfare of a child, and city detectives were hopeful that this would be their big break. In fact, Alexander Ford was sure this was the culprit and they would be arresting him over the weekend. But the man passed a polygraph test and provided a solid alibi, so he was cleared, much to the chagrin of the authorities.

It is normal to become desperate in a situation like the one the police now found themselves in and to start grabbing at straws. At about the same time the previous year, when the man from Avenue D had been charged with child endangment, another murder had occurred across the road from School 8 on Conkey Avenue, less than fifty feet from where Wanda had last been seen alive. In that incident, Jose Bas, the owner of a store at 262 Conkey, had been shot in the face and killed during an alleged attempted holdup. The killer had never been found, and with no witnesses police could only speculate that burglary was the motive. But what if the reason Bas had been silenced had something to do with his having witnessed another crime? What if he had been killed because he was aware of another neighborhood child being molested, for example?

Everyone felt the tension, and by Wednesday, April 11, a week after Wanda's murder, it was evident in the community when the rewards leading to the killer's identity climbed to $9,951.

Just as they had done for Carmen Colón, the CDC sponsored five billboards offering a $10,000 reward for information leading to the killer. It was sensible to assume that anyone in that lower-middle-class neighborhood would come forward anonymously, if not for ethical reasons, then certainly for the financial incentive.

The leads did keep coming in. There were several potential suspects identified in the homes along Conkey Avenue that Wanda passed on her way to and from the deli, and each one was methodically checked out.

Then came a lead that looked promising. A couple of ten-year-old girls said they had been approached the Saturday before Wanda disappeared by a man about thirty years old, with a black beard and a mole on his forehead, wearing a long, black coat. He had tried to get them into a 1971 Ford LTD that was black on the top and white on the bottom. This incident had happened across the river, west of where Wanda had disappeared. Police were sent along the Genesee River, searching both sides, but they came up with nothing.

Two weeks after Wanda's murder, a gas station attendant told police he had seen a green Ford Pinto pull into the parking lot with a young girl inside. She was crying and looked as though she was trying to get out. The driver was white and about forty years old. He had a tattoo on his right forearm. Other people called in regarding the same scene, so the police appealed publicly to the driver to come forward for questioning, but he never did. The identity of the girl in that car has never been determined. But police continue to wonder why, if the driver of that vehicle had nothing to do with the crime, had he not come forward to clear his name?

Chapter 32

Seventeen months had passed since the death of Carmen Colón, and still the police had not found the killer, who now they thought was the same person who had killed Wanda Walkowicz. After a month of constant area surveillance, interviews and news coverage, Wanda's killer still eluded law enforcement officials. Now they had two unsolved murders of preteen girls, both under remarkably similar circumstances. Now two families had been shattered, and two neighborhoods had been turned topsy-turvy.

The most promising break in the Walkowicz case came when a neighborhood man with a previous arrest for child endangerment was brought in and questioned for twelve hours. Everything pointed to him being the murderer; however, after passing a polygraph, the suspect was released, and the murder investigation of Wanda Walkowicz went cold.

Wanda Walkowicz had vanished from the neighborhood near her Avenue D home. She was found slain the next day in an isolated area at a rest stop in Webster

The police knew that there are times when, no matter how long the investigation lasts or how hard the investigators work, the suspect is never found. There are also cases where there is a lack of evidence for the police to either find a suspect or make an arrest. But knowing this did not make it easier.

At the next briefing, the officers entered with long faces. There were Chief of Detectives, Alexander Ford, New York State Trooper, Thomas Cameron, CSI, Dominick Harris, Detective, Peter Barnes, Wayne County Sheriff's Detective Sgt., Howard Clark, RPD Lieutenant, William

Sanders, New York State Police Investigator, Winston James, Monroe County Medical Examiner, Jonathan Walker, Monroe County Director of Mental Health, Michael Barnes, State Police Captain, Anthony Maloney, Wayne County Sheriff's Investigator, Louis Richards, Monroe County Sheriff's Detective, Jamie Foster, State Police Investigator, Harold Hill, D&C Investigative Reporter, Thomas Clark, RPD Sergeant, Robert Newport, Detective Lieutenant, Patrick Ward and Detective, Walter Simmons.

The room was bathed in silence until Chief of Detectives, Alexander Ford, stood to address the group.

"Gentlemen, we need to recapitulate and go over what we know at this point. Nothing is off limits. By that I mean if you have a theory, please share it."

"I'll start," said Detective Peter Barnes.

"Both victims were girls aged ten and eleven. Each victim had been sexually assaulted and murdered by either manual or ligature strangulation before her body was discarded."

RPD Sergeant, Robert Newport, spoke next. "Whereas Carmen Colón was found naked, Wanda Walkowicz was fully clothed."

RPD Lieutenant, William Sanders, added, "Yes, there are differences. An autopsy revealed that, in addition to having been raped, Carmen had suffered a fracture to her skull and one of her vertebrae before she had been manually strangled to death. Furthermore, fingernails had extensively scratched her body."

State Police Investigator, Harold Hill, added, "Yes, It is true there are differences between the cases, but there are more similarities. Both girls had several strands of white cat fur on her clothing, although one of the families did not own any pets. And both girls were on errands for their mothers, which means that the killer could not predict the time or place. To me that speaks to it being someone in the neighborhood."

"Can you add anything to this, Doctor Walker?"

"Yes, both girls had food in their stomachs, but only Wanda had fingernail scratches."

"Are you sure they were from human fingernails?"

"Yes, without a doubt."

New York State Police Investigator, Winston James, spoke up, "Each girl attended a Catholic school. I cannot say that adds much, but we are saying that we suspect both Carmen Colón and Wanda Walkowicz willingly got into a car with their abductor. This leads us to a suspicion that the killer was probably someone who appeared to be in a position of authority — such as a police officer or firefighter — or perhaps was someone posing in those roles."

There were nods all around before D&C Investigative Reporter, Thomas Clark, spoke. "I hope you meant we could present anything."

Detective Ford spoke up. "Yes, we meant anything. What are you thinking?"

"Okay, here it goes. Under similarities there is something else to consider. Both girls' first and last names are the same initial: Carmen Colón; Wanda Walkowicz." Seeing the reactions, he hurried ahead. "And, they were found in areas that matched their initials. Carmen Colón was found in Chili…"

"It was not exactly in Chili; it was on the border in Riga."

"Yes, I know, but bear with me. Wanda Walkowicz was found in Webster. I am just saying that if we haven't already done so, we need to check out places where someone could research this information, like social workers or welfare workers for instance."

"Thanks, Tom. It is something to think about."

RPD Lieutenant, William Sanders, said, "I think that we need to consider that the killer had a car and that the girls entered it willingly. It may be that he offered them food of some sort, and that was how the killer got them into his car." He paused, then, thinking aloud, "How could the killer have anticipated the movements of the Colón girl and the Walkowicz girl? They were on their way to the store on errands, late in the afternoon. Was the killer ready to sit there all-night waiting for them?"

It all was valid information that would get them thinking again. As for the girls having the same initials, well, they had been picked up on the street, away from their homes, so a stranger would not have known their initials. It was not as if they had worn their initials on their clothing.

No one could say there was a lack of coordination between investigation agencies in these two cases. Unfortunately, the information sharing in the cases still resulted in two unsolved homicides, for which no suspect was apparent within a reasonable period.

MICHELLE MAENZA

Chapter 33

At 25 Webster Crescent in Rochester, NY, sits a 1,018 square foot house built in 1900 on a 2,250 square foot lot. The house has two upstairs windows that are spaced like eyes, looking out on the neighborhood, and below them is a modest front porch surrounded by skirted panel sides giving privacy to the family. Oil fuels the hot air heating system, and the house is kept warm and cozy. This house is no different from the ones around it, except this was the home of Christopher and Caroline Maenza.

Inside this imposing structure are three bedrooms and one bathroom, and it was where Christopher and Caroline Maenza would bring their baby girl, Michelle Maenza.

After celebrating Thanksgiving on November 23, 1961, there would be one more celebration close on its heels. Michelle was born on Tuesday, November 28, in Rochester, New York, and would be their first daughter after having two sons, Stephen and Angelo. Three years later, Caroline would give birth first to Marie and then to a final baby daughter whom they named Christine, making Michelle the middle child of the family.

Life went on happily for a while, but each day the realization that they could not continue this way became apparent. It was hard to accept, but the family was facing a real dilemma. Caroline could sense things were off balance, but she tried to ignore it since there was nothing she could do to change their situation.

Christopher was asking himself, "I feel as if I need to leave and end this, but I cannot be sure it is the right thing." It was not as if it was a decision just between himself and Carolyn. No, it was a decision between them and the five children they had created. Christopher knew he could not provide for the family. If he left, they might be better off. Some days he felt confident this was the solution to their problems. He knew that a lot of people would be affected by what he decided, so he wanted to figure out the best way to handle it.

The night he told Caroline what he planned to do, he knew by her reaction that she felt the same. It was easy for them to work out the arrangements that would be best for everyone. Christopher would take the two older boys to live with him, while Caroline would stay in the house with their three daughters. She had her welfare check and received food stamps, so they would manage quite well on their own.

The change did not have an adverse effect on Michelle. True, she lived in a broken home, but not a broken family. Her mother, Caroline, had custody of her and her two sisters, eight-year-old Marie, and baby Christine. Her brothers, Angel, 14, and Stephen, 13, were in her father, Christopher's custody, but they were not far away.

The most noticeable change was how empty and quiet the house felt, but she would adjust just like the rest of the family. What was unchanged was that she felt safe in the cul-de-sac house on Webster Crescent.

It happened slowly, but in time, Christopher moved out, taking his sons, Stephen and Angelo, with him. They moved to 21 Hall Street in the city, leaving the rest of his family in the home they had shared together.

It was not far to her father's place as it was just over a mile away. They would head east on Webster Crescent to Webster Ave and then turn right onto Webster Ave. From there it was a quick left onto Parsells Ave and then a right onto Baldwin Street. Going down Baldwin across Hayward Ave and taking a left they arrived at East Main St. There they continued down Main Street to Hall Street and turned left. If they walked, it took around twenty-five minutes.

They say life was simpler in the '60s, and for the most part it was, especially if one was a child. The neighborhood was not the best, but it was all she knew and accepted it as such. Her mother, Caroline, was a protective mother. She always had her three daughters with her wherever she went, whether she was going to the laundry, a store, or a friend's house, until Michelle became part of the headlines in 1971.

Chapter 34

The Beechwood community on the east side is in the southeast quadrant of the City of Rochester. The area is bordered by Bay Street to the north, Atlantic Avenue to the south, Culver Road (CSX Railroad tracks/Atlantic Avenue) to the east, and North Goodman Street to the west.

A visit to the area and you will see the neighborhood homes, an interesting mix of old and new. Many houses were built in the early 1900s and still retain classic architectural elements like American gumwood trim and stained-glass windows within. The owners have modernized other houses to attract more tenants. The area was named for a local post office and the famous Beech-Nut baby food and chewing gum company that had been located on East Main Street.

This is a "rainbow community" filled with young families as well as older, long-time residents. There are many established businesses in the area, including the German Swan Market on Parsells Avenue that opened in the early 1900s.

Rochester has always been a magnet for immigrants, especially during its boomtown era as a manufacturer of flour, clothing, and cameras. Its mix of immigrant residents includes Africans, Asians, and Latin Americans. It generally has a bad reputation, due to the high levels of poverty.

The houses sit close together, and there were many children living near the Maenza family, but for Michelle it was lonely beyond her home. She began gaining weight which made her a focus of ridicule. To compensate for not being accepted by her peers, Michelle began to hang around with younger children who looked up to her and accepted her just as she was.

Such poverty and family issues may have made these children vulnerable. In addition, the transient, chaotic character of the neighborhoods in which they lived may have made it easier for someone to move about unnoticed.

That being the case, Mrs. Maenza usually walked Michelle home from school. Sometimes Mrs. Maenza would drive in the afternoons to School 33 where she would pick up Michelle and her sister.

She would often be seen taking all three daughters with her to the grocery store, or the laundromat, or just to visit neighbors.

Though it was not the best part of town, their actual neighborhood was quite safe, especially where their house was located on the 'little bent street' as it was often called. It was an innocuous area for kids, since there was no through traffic, allowing the children to play safely in the street.

It was made even safer because the neighbors sometimes sat on their porches with their feet propped up on the railings, just enjoying the best part of the day and watching in amusement as all the kids ran around playing. It was the best way to spend the day and most took advantage of it.

Chapter 35

Michelle would start out her school days at Corpus Christi School on Main Street East, a Catholic School that was located some distance from her home. Here she worked hard at her studies and was comfortable. She felt confident that it would be the same when she transferred to School 33.

John James Audubon School No. 33, located at 500 Webster Ave, is a kindergarten through sixth grade school operated by the Rochester City School District, making the student body quite different from what she had experienced at the Catholic school.

School 33 was only a half mile from their home, as it was located at 25 Webster Crescent. With her girls in tow, Caroline would walk east on Webster Crescent toward Webster Ave and turn left onto Webster Ave. On a good day, the full trip would take them three minutes.

At school, Michelle was an average student who paid attention in class and followed the rules. She was friendly to her peers though they tended to pick on her.

Because she was overweight for her age, Michelle was constantly being teased. Then, to add to her torment, they picked on her for having to walk to school with her mother and her baby sisters. That had them taunting her, laughing, "Here comes the baby."

Children can be so cruel, and Michelle was an easy target. She was chubby and slow and that made her an object for spiteful jokes. She weighed in at around ninety pounds and stood four foot seven inches. If it were not for her family, she would have suffered even more, but her mother would comfort her, saying that she would grow out of it. When Michelle asked, "But when?" her mother always replied, "In time, Michelle. We love you just as you are, and that is all that matters."

However, the intensity and the drama of a pre-teen—especially for girls—can be frustrating. From the complex social dynamics at school to the physical changes that can confuse and embarrass a 'tween, age eleven often means big physical changes. For Michelle, puberty started early.

Already suffering from her increase in weight, reaching puberty added more body fat. No matter how she tried, she could not get the pounds off, and often she would be crying in the bathroom. The fact that other girls were experiencing puberty did not help. For them it seemed exciting to be developing larger breasts and wider hips. To add to her problems, Michelle possessed active sweat glands.

But Michelle was used to being picked on by her peers, so the friends she made were younger. These children enjoyed her attention, which allowed Michelle to become a quiet but happy-go-lucky, and friendly little girl. The unfortunate outcome was that she became emotionally immature compared to other girls her age, since girls her age would not hang out with her.

Transferring from one school to another did not make it easy for a girl like Michelle, who had problems making friends. This time of life is hard enough for a girl who is comfortable with her weight, but for one who is suffering from the stigma of being overweight and shy, it becomes an even more precarious time.

To make matters worse, Michelle, and soon her younger sister, Marie, were tormented by their classmates because they obviously were not required to bathe regularly. The children at school began calling them both 'Stinky'.

The school guidance counselor tried to help.

"Michelle, you need to take a bath. Washing and bathing are important."

Michelle nodded.

Not sure the child was getting the message, the guidance counselor continued, "Maintaining cleanliness is also important for your self-confidence, and for physical and emotional well-being."

Michelle whispered something.

"What was that, Michelle?"

"I thought it was to remove dirt."

"Yes, that too." The counselor paused. "Is there a reason you aren't bathing?"

Michelle nodded again.

"Can you tell me?"

In response she said, "Not enough time."

The counselor started to say more but thought better of it as she looked at Michelle. Her clothes were ragged and dirty. Even if she did decide to bathe, her clothes would still make her stink.

"Okay, Michelle. That is all for now."

She watched sadly as Michelle got up and left the room.

Some mornings when she was getting ready for school, Michelle would stand in front of the mirror and gaze at herself. She saw her hazel eyes and long brown hair that she usually wore in two side ponytails, with thick bangs covering her forehead. She would smile, but that would force her eyes down to take in her large nose, chubby cheeks and, worst of all, the beginnings of a double chin. That made her sad.

Michelle was no different from other girls her age when it came to wanting more independence and less coddling by her mother. Sure, she hung around with younger girls so that she could feel accepted, but that did not mean she was not age appropriate in her thoughts.

Luckily for Michelle, at home Caroline was taking care of not only her, but also her sisters. With Michelle and Marie being close in age, only three years separating them, Caroline had her hands full. Having baby Christine to contend with also made it harder for her to keep up with each of her daughters as she used to.

Having been put into special ed classes, Michelle withstood being called stupid by her peers. Later, when she advanced to regular classes, she thought the torment would stop but it did not. Academically, Michelle worked hard, and that relentless work paid off. She was not the smartest child in her class, but she was an average student falling into the normal range and making satisfactory progress.

Michelle had not learned how to accept advice or ask for help. Life would have been better for her if she had heard what her counselor had said about her personal hygiene and taken it to heart. That was something she could have changed for the better. The counselor could have suggested a plan for her to learn how to take care of her body and would have told her personally and privately.

Dressing herself was a bit of a problem because she did not have the money to buy new things, but as she got older this became one of the most important choices that might have changed her life. Her mother did her best, but when one is eleven, the wrong clothes become a point of ridicule with one's peers. But if Michelle had tried a little harder, maybe she could have learned how to wash and take care of her clothes.

Then there was her weight problem. Michelle needed to have better eating habits. She could not control what her mother fed her, but she could learn to eat less.

There were so many ways that her friends, family and school could have helped Michelle to have a better life if she had only listened.

Luckily, Michelle was not one to let life issues get her down for long, so she continued to do her best and ignore the taunts of her fellow classmates. Of course, there were a few children her age who accepted her, and Michelle played with them on occasion. But, at their pre-teen age, when the other children picked on her, they tended to shy away into the background, not wanting to have those children also turn on them. At times, Michelle understood, but other times it hurt too much to endure. So, Michelle learned how to fend for herself.

One thing she could not change and that was her mother, Caroline, walking up Webster Avenue to School No. 33 each afternoon, with Christine in a stroller, to accompany Michelle and Marie and another neighborhood girl home from school. Even though her mother knew that Michelle's fifth-grade peers teased her about walking home with her mother and called her a baby, the girls' safety meant more to Caroline than teasing by the other children.

Michelle's mother was supportive of her attempts at independence. She had tried to prepare her for the time when she must leave home and lead her own life. Caroline thought that giving in to Michelle's request for independence, her efforts to teach her how to solve problems and not take being harassed to heart, would benefit her daughter, not harm her.

Repetition and practice make doing things and going places independently possible, and Caroline knew she could not always be at Michelle's side. It was just plain impossible to let Michelle go around on her own without practice, and practice meant she would have to give her that freedom. Since Michelle was good at memorizing what streets to take to get to her school, the tracks and her father's house, her mother did not worry she would get lost. However, she only dealt out little bits of freedom from time to time.

It was true, Michelle had a good memory, but her mind, like everyone else's, wandered occasionally. On her final day at school before her world fell apart, Michelle had been teased relentlessly during recess. When she could not take it any longer, she left her classroom and spent most of the afternoon crying in the nurse's office.

Chapter 36

Monday, November 26, 1973, presented Rochester with a misty rain and 36 degrees. During the month, over five inches of snow had fallen, but most of that was gone. What remained now was the snow plowed back off the road and sidewalks, all dirty and unappealing.

Coming off the four-day weekend of Thanksgiving, Michelle was moving slowly as she prepared for school. She seriously had not heard her mother call out, "Get up, Michelle," or later the pounding on the door. It was her mother's final announcement that Marie was on her way to the one bathroom in the house, that made Michelle jump up and hurry down the hall. She reached it just ahead of her sister.

She closed the door and went to the sink to brush her teeth with the baking soda kept in the cabinet. When she was done, she reached for her washcloth and held it under the water while she stared into the mirror.

When she heard Marie knock on the door, she came out of her stupor and quickly wiped her face, grabbed her hairbrush, and ran it quickly through each ponytail. After a quick brush of her bangs, she opened the door, and Marie squeezed in after her.

Finally, Michelle was on the fast track, grabbing her clothes that had been strewn around the room and putting them on as quickly as possible, so she could eat before they had to leave.

After hurrying downstairs, Michelle made a beeline for the kitchen. There was oatmeal in a pot on the stove, and she stuck the spoon into the pot, blew on it and stood there eating until her mother's final plea, "Come on Michelle, hurry up. We've got to get a move on."

"I am coming."

In the front room there was a hassle as she tried to get into the closet, jousting with Marie to claim her outerwear. With a little pushing and shoving, Michelle finally found her long purple coat with the silver trim. She swung it over her arm as she scrounged around on the closet floor and came out with her knee-high black boots. As if it had been planned, she was wearing her favorite purple slacks with a zigzag pattern that went great with her coat.

Caroline stood watching the struggle, with baby Christine already bundled up and in her stroller. She reached over to help Marie with her scarf, then, before she could yell once more for them to hurry, the girls were ready.

They shuffled through the doorway and then helped Caroline get the stroller down the steps to the sidewalk. Finally, they were on their way.

It was nice walking together, especially because, when they passed by other students, no one picked on her. It was not until her mother had left with baby Christine that the harassment began.

Michelle went to her locker and took off her coat.

"Hey Fatty, how did you get your butt into those pants?"

Those who heard the remark started giggling. Michelle could feel her face getting red, so she kept her head turned toward the lockers. She leaned over to take off her boots and listened as the giggles turned into loud laughter. She knew her shirt had pulled up and she wanted to reach back and pull it down, but she knew that would only make them laugh more. So, she continued to place her boots in the locker, along with her scarf and hat. She fiddled with getting her books out until she heard the bell. Then she slammed the locker closed, replaced the lock, and headed toward the class, her tormentor close on her heels.

Her classmate did not stop but continued to sling insult after insult. When she called her 'stinky', that was the last straw and Michelle pushed her, pushed her hard. The girl started to push her back, but that was when the teacher caught them.

"Girls, stop it! Stop it right now."

Surprised, they looked up to see the teacher. "You are eleven, not five. I expect you to act your age."

"Yes, Mr. Hampton, but she started it," Michelle protested, pointing at her tormentor.

"I do not care who started it. Matter of fact, I do not have time to deal with this now. You are late for class. You are both going to detention after school. Am I clear?"

"Yes, Mr. Hampton."

With that, they entered the classroom and took their seats.

Mr. Hampton was not ignorant of what had happened that morning. He knew who the troublemaker was, and who was the brunt of the jokes, but he had no choice but to punish them both.

As the day wore on, Michelle worried about having to stay after school. She wondered what they would tell her mother when she came to get her. However, she did not wonder for long as she got caught up in the class, trying not to miss anything.

She suffered through more ridicule at lunch, keeping her head down and keeping to herself, wishing the day were over. Then she remembered that it would not be over for her, not until after detention.

At the end of the day, she watched the students filing out to go to their lockers and get out their coats and boots, while she and her tormentor, Adrienne, remained in their seats.

Mr. Hampton stood up behind his desk. "Okay, Girls, I do not want to hear any excuses for what happened, and I do not want either of you to talk. Open your books and start working on your homework. You will be here for an hour, so I hope in that time you learn how to be nice to each other."

Adriene turned and gave Michelle a look that said, "Just you wait."

Mr. Hampton saw that look and said, "You are both to blame, and if one of you would like to be more to blame, keep acting up."

With that, both heads went down. In the silence that followed the only sound was the scratching of a pencil on paper and the rustling of turning pages.

Mr. Hampton read. Every now and then he would get up and move about the classroom before taking his seat again. He would peek over at the two students, watching them work. He knew that Adriene had been written up on more than one occasion for picking on students. She had developed a reputation as a troublemaker at the tender age of eleven.

On several occasions her parents had been made aware of the issue, but whether they had tried to correct this behavior was unknown, because Adriene persisted and she had acquired the label of troublemaker.

When Caroline arrived to pick up her daughters, only Marie was waiting for her. "Where is your sister?" she asked, but Marie did not know. Caroline pushed the stroller up to the school front door and waited while Marie opened it. They went directly to the front desk.

"I am looking for my daughter, Michelle Maenza,"

"Wait here, and I'll find out where she is," the receptionist replied.

Caroline watched as the receptionist disappeared. When she returned, she had the principal with her.

"Ms. Maenza, I am sorry. Someone should have told you that Michelle was being kept after school."

Puzzled, she asked why.

"Well, she was fighting with another girl in the hall."

"That cannot be. Michelle does not fight. There's been a mistake."

"No, the teacher caught her and another girl fighting in the hall, and they were given detention. She will be free to come home in an hour if you wish to wait."

Caroline was a little upset, knowing that Michelle was not a problem child and that someone else must have picked on her. But she knew that the school was already aware of this, so instead she said, "Please send Michelle home as soon as she gets out. I'll meet her at home."

The principal said they would deliver the message, and, with that, Caroline turned the stroller around and waited while Marie held the door for her to go through. Soon they were on their way back home.

Caroline preferred to walk the girls home, but she knew that Michelle would be fine walking the short half mile home. It would still be light out when Michelle could leave, later that afternoon.

Philip Maenza, Michelle's uncle, did not ask for much in life, but when he had the opportunity to buy a gas station, his attitude changed. It changed again once reality set in. He did not earn anything from the gas part of the business, so he had to have an alternate plan to earn enough just to keep the station going. With that in mind, he set up a mini mart where he sold beer, cigarettes, snacks, drinks, and other items that would help him make a living.

The gas station was at the intersection of Webster Avenue and Melville Street, a few hundred feet from Caroline's home, so he took to keeping an eye on her and her daughters. It was not the best neighborhood for children, or for a gas station, and for that reason there were few customers. As his business did not warrant help and he could not afford their salaries, he had no employees working for him. Most mornings and afternoons he would take a cigarette break, and he would see his sister-in-law and nieces walking by on their way to and from the school. If they saw him, they would wave at each other.

So, on the morning of Monday, November 26, 1973, Philip had waved to Caroline and the girls as they headed to the school. That afternoon he waved at them again when they passed by on their way home, and he noticed that Michelle was not with them this time.

Just then a car pulled up at the pumps. Philip did not have time to wonder where Michelle was as he dropped his cigarette on the pavement, stepped on it, and went over to take care of the customer.

In the classroom, Michelle worked diligently on her homework until Mr. Hampton announced they were free to go. Michelle had no doubt that Adrienne would make her pay for having to stay after school, so she quickly stood up and, in one swift motion, gathered her books and papers.

Michelle knew Adrienne was faster than she, so there was not a minute to spare as she rushed out of the classroom repeating to herself her locker combination. She ran down the hallway, coming to a quick stop at her locker and taking a deep breath before fumbling with the combination.

It opened on the first try. "Thank you, God," she said as she practically jumped into her coat and boots. She stuffed her book and papers into her backpack and slung it over her arm as she looked at the hallway clock. It was 3:20 p.m. That meant there would still be people in the office. She did not want to get another detention for running in the hallway, so she slowed down her pace as she headed toward the door.

Michelle had been so anxious, rushing out of the classroom, that she had not heard Mr. Hampton say, "Adrienne, please wait. I'd like a word with you."

Michelle's heart did not stop pumping until she had pushed the front doors open and stood outside, feeling the cold air on her face. Not hearing the doors open again, she knew she had made it, and allowed herself to relax as she started walking toward home. Adrienne knew that her Uncle Philip would be watching and would not dare start something.

Michelle did not mind walking home alone, in fact she liked it. It made her feel like a grown up. As she ambled, her mind drifted. She thought about just the day before when her mother had taken them shopping at the Super Saver store in Goodman Plaza. Michelle smiled; it had been a fun day. She walked a few more steps, before remembering that when they returned home her mother had realized she had lost her purse.

This made her frown as she recalled how her mother had hurried them up. "Come on girls, I need you to help me find my purse." They had retraced their steps through the plaza, keeping their eyes shifting from side to side as they made their way back to each store they had visited. While they continued looking around the store, Caroline went up to each store manager to ask if anyone had turned in a purse.

Caroline knew the answer before she heard it. This was just not a neighborhood where someone would turn in a purse if they found it. But she had to ask.

"No, ma'am."

"Thanks."

Michelle thought how miserable her mother had appeared when she finally took them home. Michelle could not get that image out of her head now as she headed toward home. When she came to the intersection of Webster Avenue and Ackerman Street she paused. It was only a five-minute walk to Goodman Plaza.

Michelle's eyes sparkled as she shivered inside her coat. It was getting even colder now, but she had an idea. What if she could find her mother's purse? What if she went to the plaza before going home and found the lost purse?

So, at the corner of Ackerman Street and Webster Avenue, Michelle turned left. She kept her head down, looking along the way, hoping to see her mother's lost purse as she continued to Heidelberg Street. There she paused to adjust her book bag before turning left onto North Goodman Street.

"Hi, Michelle."

Hearing her name startled her at first, but she recovered when she looked up to see two of her neighborhood friends, Nina Jones, and Leslie Warwick.

"Hi, Nina. Hi, Leslie."

"Want to walk with us?"

"No, I am looking for my mother's purse. She lost it somewhere near here."

"Oh, Okay. We are going to buy some candy. We will see you later."

"Okay. See you later."

Michelle smiled, feeling good. It always made her feel better when she realized she did have friends. Sure, there were kids that picked on her, but she did have friends who liked her. She was still smiling as she headed toward the short entrance road leading to the plaza, cutting through the barren corner lot adjacent to the parking lot.

Unbeknownst to her, Philip had seen his niece as she turned the corner at Ackerman Street and Webster Avenue, not heading in the direction of home. Wondering where she was going, he followed her and caught up with her at the plaza.

In the parking lot of the Goodman Street Plaza, Michelle heard a car horn blowing. She ignored it, but it was persistent, so she turned to look. At first, she did not recognize the car, but peering inside she saw it was her uncle.

"Hey, Michelle, what are you doing?"

"Looking for mom's purse. She lost it here."

"Okay, why do not I wait and give you a ride?"

"No, Uncle Philip. I am here now, and I want to check around and look again on my way back home."

Hesitantly, he said, "Okay, Michelle, but hurry home."

"I will, Uncle Philip."

Michelle watched as her uncle drove away before continuing to check along the parking lot and the sidewalks. She stopped in several stores, hoping that maybe later someone had turned it in, but each time the answer was the same. No one had turned in her mother's purse.

She refused to give up as she went into the Super Saver where her mother had done the shopping. She walked through the store, stopping to look under shelves, hoping that, after her mother paid the bill, the purse had slipped out of her pocket when she had left the store. Someone walking along might have kicked it under a counter. Not finding it, she went to the front and asked the cashier if anyone had turned in a purse. She got the same answer again.

Michelle, trying to be optimistic as she left the store, began checking the route they had taken the previous day on their way home, even though it was the same as the route they had taken back to the plaza.

Her head was down, swiveling left and right as she moved slowly along the way, crossing the barren corner lot adjacent to the parking lot of the plaza, just as they had that day. She was startled when she heard someone call out to her.

The voice came from a vehicle that she again did not recognize, but she did not recognize most cars. She stared at the car trying to see who was inside, but she could not, so she decided to just keep going and ignore them.

The voice came again. "Michelle, can I give you a ride?"

Michelle stopped. They knew who she was. They called her by name. It would be rude to ignore them now. Michelle walked over to the car to get a better look.

Her hands pressed against the side of the door as she peeked inside.

"Hi, Michelle."

"Hi." She had seen him before, she thought, probably in the neighborhood, but she could not remember his name.

"Would you like a ride?"

"Well, I am looking for something…." She paused. If she had not found it on her way here, why would she find it on her way back? Besides, she was cold, and it was getting dark, "Sure. Thank you."

Michelle walked over to the passenger side and opened the door.

Inside, the car was warm, and Michelle leaned back against the seat, enjoying the comfort, until she raised her head and looked out the car window.

"Ah, Mister, this isn't the way to my house."

"Oh, do not worry, Michelle. I know where you live, but I need to make a stop first."

"But…" She stopped mid-sentence. The car was turning onto the expressway. The first bit of fear settled in her stomach.

"Sir…"

"Listen, I need to pick up some food and then we can go back." He paused, then added, "I'll get you a hamburger. Would you like that?"

She had not eaten since lunch and she was hungry. She had been so absorbed in finding her mother's purse that she had not thought of eating. Now, at the mention of food, her stomach growled.

Michelle nodded her head. She continued to stare out the window, not knowing where she was or where she was going. She read the signs as they passed them. For a long time, it seemed they were on the expressway until finally taking exit 23. When they turned onto the road ahead, she saw a sign that said NY-441, a road she had not heard of before.

She could make out houses that were shaped much like the ones in her neighborhood, but further apart and sitting back off the street behind front lawns that seemed to go on forever. The man continued driving. She watched as he turned on his blinker and then turned into a plaza.

In the plaza he drove around until he found a parking spot near a fast food place. He shut off the engine and turned toward her. "Wait here. I'll go in and get the food, and then we will head back."

She watched the man walk into the fast food restaurant, wondering what she should do. She did not know where she was, and they had been driving for some time. She did not even know which way home was. Not knowing what else to do, she sat and waited.

Soon she saw the man coming toward the car with a white bag. He opened the door and handed the bag to her before climbing back in behind the driver's seat.

"Open it up. There's a hamburger for you inside."

Michelle smiled. The fragrance coming from the bag made her stomach churn. This was a treat, a real treat for her. Not even taking the time to thank him, she opened the bag and pulled out the hamburger.

She put the bag down on the console while she sat, carefully opening the wrappings, not wanting to spill anything inside his car. Finally, she grabbed the sandwich with both her hands. She took a big bite.

"Good, aren't they?"

Michelle nodded, her mouth full. She chewed, and when her mouth was empty, she thanked him for the hamburger. Then she quickly returned to the sandwich, not wanting it to get cold.

The man started up the car and they were back on the road. When Michelle finished her hamburger, she carefully folded up the wrappings, wishing she could have another, but thought that would be rude to ask. So, she stared out the window. It was dark out now, and she could barely see outside. She leaned closer to the pane and noticed they were on a road where she could not see any houses.

"Where are we?"

No response.

"Sir, where are we?"

Still he said nothing. That funny feeling returned to the pit of her stomach again. Michelle slid over as close as she could to the passenger door, her forehead leaning against the glass. She saw a sign that said, 'Eddy Road.'

"Where is Eddy Road?" she asked, panic evident in her voice. "I do not know where we are. Can you please take me home? My mother is going to be worried."

Still nothing. She felt the car slowing down and that scared her more. She had never been in a situation like this before, and she did not know what to do.

The man eased the car over to the side of the road. There was nothing there, not even a house. Michelle turned her head from side to side, looking around. When she turned back toward the man, she watched frozen in place as his hands came up. He put them around her neck and started choking her.

Finally, able to react, she swung her arms and legs at him, fighting as hard as she could to make him stop, but he was so much stronger than she. When she felt his hands release her throat, she was weak, and before she could act, he swung something over her head and began choking her with it.

She wanted to scream, but when she tried nothing came out. She continued to fight as he pinned her down and began taking off her clothes and tossing them aside.

He pushed her down onto the seat, and as she stared with terrified eyes up into his eyes, he penetrated her. This time Michelle did scream.

She squeezed her eyes shut and prayed for it to be over. It seemed like hours that she lay there, helpless and in pain, before he finally came out of her for the last time. She could not move, nor did she care anymore. She just let him toss her back and forth as he put her clothes back on. Her only thought was, 'It is over. I am going home'.

That was her last thought before he strangled the life out of her already limp body.

Once he was sure she was dead, the man dragged her body from the car and tossed her over the edge of the road, watching as her body rolled down into the ditch. Then he hurried back to the car and climbed in. He took a deep breath and started driving up the road, looking through the rear-view mirror to see if anyone had seen him.

No one was around, but as he started to turn to face front, he saw the child's coat. Without hesitation, he slowed the car down as he reached into the back seat and grabbed the coat. He carefully pulled the car over to the side of the road and stopped. He waited, looking around the area and, seeing no one, not even a car's headlights, he rolled down the window and threw the coat out.

Nervously he looked around him again as he rolled up his window, started the car and pulled out on the road, carefully increasing his speed as he made his way to safety.

Chapter 37

When Michelle had not returned home by five that afternoon, Caroline began to worry. It was not like her daughter to stay out late. Where could she be?

Caroline called friends, relatives, anyone she could think of. "Is Michelle there?" she asked. "Have you seen Michelle?" Call after call provided no concrete help in locating Michelle.

Caroline was at her wIt is end. Her mind ran through all the hopeful possibilities for her delay before she dared to think of the worst that could happen. Had Michelle been abducted? Did she run away? She refused — then and later — to think that her daughter might have died.

She called her husband, Christopher. "Is Michelle with you?"

"No. Was she supposed to come here today?"

"No, I cannot find her. She did not come home from school. I do not know what to think."

"Stay by the phone. The boys and I will go out looking for her. We will call you the minute we find her."

Christopher paused. "Did you check with Philip?"

Trying to stay calm, Caroline replied. "Yes, I called Philip. He said he saw her earlier and offered her a ride home, but Michelle refused."

"Okay, we will find her. She could not have gone far."

Caroline hung up the phone. Her back was to the entranceway of the kitchen when she heard Marie call out. "Mom? Did they find Michelle?"

Caroline cleared her throat. "No, not yet. But they will."

She knew only a few neighbors, and those she had called to see if they had seen Michelle. They had not. It was during one of the calls she made that the neighbor said, "It is like that other little girl, Wanda something... I mean..."

Caroline sucked in air and put a hand against the wall to keep herself upright. She squeezed her eyes tight, pushing all the tears out before she hung up the phone and faced Marie, who was standing right behind her. She could not let her daughter see her cry. She had to be strong. When she turned to face Marie, she was back in control. "Nothing yet."

Caroline tried to think of something more she could do, but she could not. The boys were out looking for her daughter now, and she was confident they would find her. She needed to be near the phone in case someone called with news, or if Michelle called home.

Caroline looked at the clock. She had been waiting and hoping so long that it hurt. She kept telling herself that Michelle would walk through the door unhurt and hungry. After all, she had missed dinner.

The phone rang, and Caroline rushed across the room to pick it up. "It is about time," she said over her shoulder.

"Caroline."

"Yes, Christopher", the words rushed out of her mouth. "Did you find her?"

"No, not yet." Her heart sank.

"So why aren't you looking?"

"I have been and will, but I wanted to tell you to go ahead and call the police. We haven't been able to learn much of anything, and I do not want to wait any longer."

Caroline felt as if her heart had stopped beating. She was so distressed she was hardly able to speak. She could not control the sobs that built up in her throat as she responded, "Okay. I will."

Meanwhile, Christopher and the boys walked all around the neighborhoods asking if anyone had seen Michelle. No one had as far as they knew. The cold that had seemed mild at first now numbed his face and extremities. What heat his body had retained was gone, and his thick winter jacket and boots were not up to the task of preserving his body heat. Christopher and the boys had split up to cover more territory, and now they convened in a huddle after an hour of fruitless searching. He did not want to wait any longer before getting the police involved because every minute counted. He was aware of what could happen if they did not find his daughter soon.

Caroline had trouble thinking, as she stood there trying to make the call. Instead of dialing the phone, she pictured Michelle out there in the cold, freezing and unable to find her way home. That had to be it. She was just lost.

Her birthday would be in two days, and her Michelle would be twelve years old. Michelle would not miss that day, oh, no; she lived for her birthdays, thought about them days and days in advance.

Caroline smiled. She said aloud, "She will be back. Yes, she will be back for her birthday."

She picked up the receiver and started dialing.

Chapter 38

On Monday evening, November 26, Caroline Maenza called the Monroe County 911 emergency line to report her 11-year-old daughter, Michelle Maenza, was missing. The time was 5:40 p.m. when she was connected to the Rochester Police Department.

"911, what is your emergency?"

"My daughter is missing."

"What is your child's name?"

"Michelle, Michelle Maenza."

"How old is she?"

"She's 11 but will be turning 12 in two days." Caroline paused to get control of herself. "Can you send someone to help us?"

"Yes, Mrs. Maenza. What is your address?"

"It is 25 Webster Crescent."

"That is in the city?"

"Yes."

"How long has she been missing?"

"I am not exactly sure. She had to stay after school today."

"What school does she attend?"

"John James Audubon School No. 33 on Webster Ave."

"Good, Mrs. Maenza." The speaker paused as he made notes.

"Okay, Mrs. Maenza. Can you tell me Michelle's height and weight?"

Caroline considered for a moment, then said, "She's a little overweight. I would say she is around 90 lbs. and about 4' 7"."

"And what does she look like?"

"Michelle has hazel eyes and long brown hair that she was wearing in two side ponytails. Ah," she added. "She has thick bangs covering her forehead, and her face is chubby like, but sweet. You know…"

"Yes, Does she have braces or wear glasses?"

"No"

"Any medical problems? Does she take any medications?"

"No."

"Does Michelle walk a certain way that would make her stand out?"

"Not sure what you mean, but there's nothing different about the way she walks."

"Okay, does she have a mole or birthmark?

Caroline paused, thinking. "No, she does not."

"Great. Now, Mrs. Maenza. What was she wearing when she went missing?"

"Ah, her long purple coat. It has silver trim. Um, her black boots. They go up to her knees. And her favorite…" She choked up, swallowed hard and gained control. "Her favorite purple slacks that have a zigzag pattern."

"That is all we need for now. The officers should be there any minute."

"Thank you."

As soon as she hung up, she went upstairs to get the photo album. They had her 6th grade school picture, and she got out the manila envelope and took out one to give to the police. She stared down at her first-born little girl, and a tear fell onto the photo.

She heard the door open and Marie's voice. "Hi, Daddy. Hi, Stephen. Hi, Angelo. Mom will be down in a minute."

Caroline allowed herself a minute to release the tears, as she wondered how something like this could happen to her daughter. She had tried her best to keep her kids safe and, until now, she thought she had succeeded. She heard a knock at the door. Quickly, she wiped her arm across her eyes to erase her tears and took a deep breath. She rushed down the stairs and, in the bathroom, grabbed a square of toilet paper to blow her nose. Then she joined the family in the front room. She was hugging her sons when there was another knock on the door. Christopher went over and opened it

Although she had been expecting the police, when she saw them, her legs went numb and her body swayed. One of the officers reached over to steady her and guide her to a chair.

She sat, dumbfounded, while one of the officers went into the kitchen and asked Marie to get her mother a glass of water.

The small living room was full: Stephen and Angelo, her two older boys, her ex-husband, Christopher, and the police officers. In seconds, Marie joined them with a glass of water that she handed to her mother.

The officers introduced themselves. "Hello, Mrs. Maenza, I am Lieutenant Sanders from the Rochester Police

Department, and this is Detective Lieutenant Gunnar from Monroe County. I know this is hard, but we need to get as much information as we can."

Caroline nodded, keeping her head down as she tried to compose herself. She lifted the glass of water and gulped, sending her into a fit of coughing. Stephen went over to his mother and pounded on her back until Caroline raised her hand to let him know she was okay.

"Are you sure you are okay?"

"Yes," Caroline said, her voice gruff from the water going down the wrong pipe.

"I would like to go over what you told the operator, if that is okay with you. We want to make sure everything is correct."

Caroline nodded.

"Yes, stop me if something is not right."

Caroline nodded again.

"Your daughter's name is Michelle Maenza and she is eleven. She weighs about 90 pounds and is four foot, seven inches tall."

Lieutenant Sanders paused to turn over the sheet of paper he had in his hands.

"She has hazel eyes and long brown hair that she was wearing in two side ponytails, and thick bangs covering her forehead."

"She wears it that way to make her face look smaller," Caroline interrupted, a sob escaping as she did. "She has a sweet, chubby face."

"Is that a picture of her you are holding?"

Caroline had forgotten she had the picture. Now she looked down at it and smiled.

"Yes, this is Michelle," she said as she extended her arm out so that the officer could take the black and white picture.

"What a cute little girl," Officer Sanders said.

Then he continued reading. "Michelle does not wear glasses or have braces, and she does not take any medication for a medical disorder. And finally, she does not have any birthmarks."

He paused and looked at the family. "Is there anything else to add to this description or anything that needs to be changed?"

"No, That is all correct."

Detective Lieutenant Gunnar stepped forward. "Mrs. Maenza, I see that she was wearing a long purple coat with silver trim, high black boots and purple slacks that have a zigzag pattern."

Again, she nodded.

"I know this is not easy for you, but I must ask if Michelle might have run away."

"No. Absolutely not."

"Was it possible that she was dealing with something that happened in school, or maybe at home, that bothered her?"

This time Christopher replied. "She deals with the kids picking on her every day, and it has been happening for a long time, so she is used to it."

That satisfied the officers and next they turned to Christopher. "Sir, you and the boys have been out canvassing the neighborhood. Our men are out there now, but can you tell us what you found out?"

"Nothing much. Michelle was at the Bullshead Plaza this afternoon, is all we know."

Caroline stood, whirled around looking at her family. "What? What was she doing there?" asked Caroline.

Christopher turned toward her. "Philip saw her there and offered to give her a ride home, but she said she was looking for your purse and wanted to walk, so she could see if she could find it."

"Pardon me, Mr. Maenza. Who is Philip?"

"Oh, Philip is Michelle's uncle and owns the gas station at the intersection of Webster Avenue and Melville Street, just down the street from here."

"So, he did not give her a ride?"

"No and he was upset when I told him she was missing. He felt it was his fault. That if he had given her a ride, Michelle would be here now."

"Anything else?"

"No, most people we spoke to said they had not seen anything."

The officers both stood, shook hands with Christopher, and assured Caroline that they would find her daughter. Christopher saw them to the door.

The details the officers had gathered from Caroline were dispersed to the investigation team out canvassing the area. Everyone was informed that this was a little girl who was missing. For now, they should assume foul play and check everywhere. He handed out the description he had verified with the mother. They were looking for Michelle

Maenza, who had hazel eyes and shoulder-length, dark brown hair with bangs. She had last been seen in the vicinity of Webster Avenue and Goodman Plaza wearing a long purple coat with silver trim, black boots that went to her knees, and purple slacks with a zigzag pattern.

Lieutenant Sanders went back to the station and delivered the information they had collected from the mother, along with the photograph. Soon a flyer was produced and copied. Lieutenant Sanders took a handful and returned to the Webster Crescent area to distribute them.

Homes in the neighborhood were visited, and back yards checked. When that search yielded no results, volunteers and investigators spread out, canvassing parking lots, parks, and deserted areas. Hours passed as they continued relentlessly, and when there was no success in the areas adjacent to Webster Crescent, a massive countywide search was launched that night.

Investigators checked out reports that a girl who looked like Michelle had been spotted near the plaza entrance, running along Parsells Avenue and Stout Street toward Webster Avenue. They thought it had been around 4:30 in the evening. Another person reported that they saw her playing near Burrows Street at 5:30 that evening.

Each lead was taken seriously, and officers dispersed to check the areas mentioned, but they came up with nothing.

Unfortunately, the authorities had no clue that the perpetrator had hopped across the county border with his young victim, so the concentrated search efforts east of downtown that night were all for naught.

Chapter 39

Solving murder cases is extremely important for many reasons, not least of which is that making an arrest can prevent a killer from committing additional homicides. The police agencies invested time and officers and used their experience to help set up a crime analysis of the abduction. Time was significant not only in preventing future abductions and protecting the safety of the community, but also in finding Michelle Maenza alive and well.

Each lead was taken seriously until it had been proven unworkable. That meant a lot of calls, legwork, and discussions among all the investigators.

The search area enlarged when a report came in that a girl who looked like Michelle had been spotted in a car around 4:30 p.m., at Carrol's Restaurant, a burger joint in Panorama Plaza in Penfield. A woman had seen a man walking toward a car with a bag of food.

"Can you describe the man?"

The woman said she could, and gave them a description. She said the suspect was a white male maybe twenty-five or possibly thirty-five years old, but no older. She thought he was on the tall side and figured him to be around six feet tall. When asked about his weight, she added, "I would say around 165 pounds. He was skinny."

"Anything else?"

"He was wearing a blue or dark colored ski-type vest and jeans, and his jeans were tucked into a pair of brown cowboy boots with belt buckles on the side."

"Thank you. Ah, what's your name?"

"It is Terry. I mean Theresa Lockport. My friends call me Terry."

"Well, thank you, Terry. We usually do not get this much information. You have been extremely helpful." He paused, cautiously asking his next question. "Tell me, what made this man catch your attention?"

"Oh, he just did not fit in. People do not dress like that around here. Plus, I listen to the news and was aware you guys were looking for that little girl. Seeing one in his car, well, I just paid attention."

"We are glad you did."

"One more thing. I want to make sure I tell you everything."

The investigator's ears perked up. "What is it?"

"The man had dirty hands."

The investigator hid his smile by lowering his head. Then he asked, "Terry, if you have the time, can I take you back to the precinct and sit you down with a sketch artist?"

Terry looked at her watch before answering. "Sure. Anything to save that little girl."

The officer was aware of this sighting being similar to the one earlier, but in a different part of the city. He could not help wondering which one was accurate. It really did not matter at this point since both would be investigated, but at least there were some details to work with from this one.

Amanda Walker could tell that Terry was tense, so began by saying, "Terry, my name is Amanda, and I am a composite sketch artist. We do sketches when we do not know who the person is, and we do not have a picture to distribute. Do you understand?"

Terry nodded.

"Before we get started, I want you to know that the point of the sketch is not to make a portrait or an identical match. The point is to get to a resemblance, so that people can look at the drawing and be reminded of someone that they have seen recently or in the past."

Terry listened, relaxing some. She sure did not think she remembered that much about his face to help the artist draw the man.

Amanda started by asking Terry to recall everything that she did that day, leading up to the moment she had seen the man with the fast food take-out bag. To her surprise, she was able to remember pretty much everything, including what she ate that day. Then Amanda questioned her about the plaza and whether there were a lot of people around, before finally inquiring about the man.

At first, Terry had not remembered much about him except for what she had already shared with the officer, so she repeated that to Amanda.

"Okay, Terry, Let us get started on the sketch. Tell me, what was the one thing about the man that stood out?"

Terry thought a minute. "That he had dirty hands... oh, yes, and his eyes."

"Good. Now tell me about his eyes."

"Well, they were slits, under thick eyebrows."

Amanda kept asking questions and managed to pull out more details about the man's eyes. Soon she held up the sketch so that Terry could see it.

The drawing was dead on. Terry nodded in disbelief at how accurate the sketch looked like the man's eyes.

Amanda moved on to other prominent features like face shape, nose, mouth, cheekbones, jawline, eyebrows, wrinkles, smile, and teeth. Literally every single feature on a person's face was addressed, including the symmetry of it.

There were times that Terry could not really describe the feature, but Amanda would then point to the feature on her own face and then have Terry look in a mirror and try to put words to what she saw. This method worked, and Terry was proud of how she could describe the same features on the man when she thought she could not have done such a thing in a million years.

It took some time, but the finalized sketch was so accurate it was scary.

Terry was proud of herself, especially since she had not been able to tell the officer anything about the car when they asked. She did not know the model or even the color. She admitted she had been too busy looking at the girl.

The investigators were appreciative and gave Terry a ride home. At the precinct, copies of the sketch were being made and soon were distributed to all law enforcement. Even if this turned out not to be the man they were looking for, they at least had something to go on.

Information continued to pour in. The next good lead came from a witness who said she had seen Michelle. Janice Walker reported seeing Michelle sitting in a car at the corner of Webster Avenue and Ackerman Street. Janice said Michelle was sitting in the passenger seat of a beige or tan vehicle that was speeding up Ackerman. It slowed down to make a turn onto Webster Avenue, and she got a good look at the passenger. It was Michelle, and she was weeping. When asked about the time, she reported it to be around 3:30 p.m.

There would be two more sightings of Michelle that day, and every single one of them was followed up.

Then there was Alfred, who reported that he had seen a man in a car parked on the shoulder of Route 350 near Walworth. It was the evening of Michelle's abduction. Wanting to help, Alfred said that he had stopped, thinking the man may have had a flat tire. So, he had gotten out of his car and gone over to offer assistance. That is when he had seen a girl who resembled Michelle sitting in the car. He did not know at the time about the missing girl, but he remembered seeing this girl's chubby face. Later, he had put two and two together.

"So, what happened?" The officer asked

"Well, it went like this. I asked, 'Sir, do you have a flat?'"

He replied, 'Hell, no. I do not need your help.'"

"What did you do then?" asked the officer.

"Well, I told him I was just trying to be a good neighbor is all, and then got back in my car and drove away."

"Did you get a good look at him? I mean, do you think you could describe him?"

"You bet I can. Someone acting so ignorant, I would not forget what they looked like, for sure."

"Wait here a minute."

Officer Thomas walked back to his car and got out the folder. He searched through the papers, found what he was looking for, and carried it back over to where Alfred stood.

"Does this look like the guy?" he asked, holding out the picture that Amanda had drawn.

Alfred looked at it and then looked up. "Yes. That is him. That is the man I saw. Who is he?"

"We do not know yet."

"Well, I hope you find him."

"We will. It is just a matter of time."

Detective Sanders sat at his desk going through the file they had accumulated on Michelle Maenza. He picked up another file on his desk and opened it, reviewing the contents. It was the folder on Wanda Walkowicz. Her abduction had happened just six months prior. Now someone had grabbed 11-year-old Michelle Maenza off the streets near her Rochester home on Webster Crescent. If they did not want the same outcome, they had to find Michelle soon.

The State and Rochester police force worked assiduously. No one liked that another young girl was missing, and they did not have a suspect. Everyone studiously investigated and analyzed any data and information gathered. Over and over they evaluated the allegations, examined the complaints, reviewed the facts of the case, and conducted interviews.

Her description was broadcast hourly over police radios in patrol cars throughout that first night. The northeast part of the city was immediately and thoroughly searched. Special attention was given to Michelle's neighborhood, where several door-to-door searches continued.

The report of a sighting of Michelle at the plaza entrance felt hopeful but led nowhere. The Burrows Street report of her playing around there was improbable. For one thing, it was all the way across Rochester on the other side of the Genesee River, and Michelle would not have been playing along railroad tracks when she knew she had been expected home two hours earlier. She was a very eager-to-please child and would never have purposely given her mother cause for concern like that. Nevertheless, they checked out this area, over two miles away from her home.

They also checked out along Child Street and Lyell Avenue and then Ames Street, covering West Avenue and Glide Street, but they found nothing.

Another report came in from an individual who told police she had seen a frightened girl who looked like Michelle in the passenger seat of a dark green pickup traveling down Browncroft Boulevard, five minutes east of Webster Avenue. When asked when, she stated it was around 5:40 P.M. This too was investigated, and the information posted and shared over the police radios.

Other reports came in about seeing girls crying in cars on the day Michelle vanished, which was just as there had been in the Wanda Walkowicz case. And, as before, none panned out.

From the start of the report of her being missing, the investigators worked the case nonstop, never giving up hope that they would find her. But as the clock ticked, the family and authorities became less optimistic that Michelle would be found alive.

It was too much for Caroline Maenza. Like Joyce Walkowicz and Guillermina Colón before her, she collapsed and was rushed to the hospital where she was placed under sedation. She would rest, while the police continued their meticulous manhunt.

Chapter 40

Christopher Hendricks, Fire Chief of the Walworth Volunteer Fire Department, was starting out early on his way to pick up Richard Stalker. The plan was to go look at a new fire truck, and Christopher was eagerly looking forward to seeing it. When he set out on Wednesday morning, November 28, 1973, he had no doubt this would be a great day.

Already it was in the mid 40s and it was predicted to be going to 65 degrees, almost ten degrees above average. Sure, they predicted it was going to be a windy day. As he climbed into his vehicle, he guessed the wind was already close to thirty miles per hour, but wind, a little fog and a little rain could not dampen his spirits.

Christopher took the scrap of paper out of his pocket to double-check; Richard lived at 476 Eddy Road. He climbed into his vehicle and started the engine. He tried to remain calm as he drove, but inside he was excited. He turned onto Route 350 and then made the turn onto Eddy Road, without seeing a single car or truck as he went.

That suited him fine; he enjoyed the feel of open roads and no traffic. This expanse was a lonely stretch, mainly fields with no houses blocking his view. He liked that feeling of being totally alone, as if he were the only person in the world, out for a drive and taking in the scenery.

Christopher allowed himself to relax and enjoy the view. He gazed out the window, and suddenly his eyes squinted. He saw something in the grass on the north side of the road that did not blend in with the scenery.

"Wonder what that could be?" he said, as he steered the truck over to the side of the road.

The drive had been so peaceful and inviting, Christopher was no longer in a rush to get where he was going. He climbed out of the truck and went to get a closer look. He walked closer to the edge of the road, pausing to stretch his body and take in a deep breath. As he lowered his eyes, the breath stuck in his throat. Transfixed, he stood staring down at what he had glimpsed from his vehicle. He now could identify it. He was looking at a motionless body…a dead body. "Oh my God!"

Aware of police protocol, his first thought at seeing the body was not to go near it. He did not want to taint the area or ruin any evidence. He had worked with law enforcement in emergency situations and knew crime scene procedure.

Christopher hurried back to his truck and leaned in to pick up his two-way portable radio.

He waited patiently, and when he had contacted the sheriff's department, he said, "This is Christopher Hendricks, Fire Chief of the Walworth Volunteer Fire Department. I need a deputy at the north side of Eddy Road, about seventy yards from the intersection with Mill Road in the town of Macedon. Send someone to this location, stat."

That was all the information he gave, knowing that many civilians listened in on the police band lengths, and he did not want to say any more than that.

The men at the precinct knew Christopher, so when the dispatcher gave them his name and the location, they did not hesitate. It was 9:15 in the morning on Wednesday, November 28, two days after Michelle Maenza had last been seen alive

The crime scene investigators arrived and canvassed the area, looking for any evidence that would help determine what had taken place. The crew investigating the area around the body pulled out the picture that had been circulated. There was no doubt; this was Michelle Maenza. Her badly bruised, fully clothed body was lying in a ditch in a rural area of Wayne County about seventeen miles east of where she had last been seen.

One of the investigators carefully made his way up the hill to where Detective Sanders stood. "It is Michelle Maenza."

"What can you tell me?"

"It looks like her body was dumped here. She is lying on her side, as if tossed out of a vehicle, and she rolled down the side of the road into the ditch."

"Why do you think that?"

"The bruises on her body for one thing. But this is a preliminary assumption. Also, her clothes are askew. They do not look like they should, somehow."

Detective Sanders listened. "You mean as if she was re-dressed by someone?"

"Yes, that would explain it. Several of the snap fasteners on her shirt are torn, but that could happen during the assault."

While the local CSI's scoured the area around the body, others were working from the Carrols' restaurant where Michelle had been reported being seen by several people, and along the likely path from the restaurant to Eddy Road where she was found.

It was a slow, tedious business, but they took their time, not ignoring anything that might be a clue. When they had finished, the possible evidence they had collected filled the beds of several pickup trucks.

The side of the road was now a parade of vehicles when another CSI pulled his car over and walked up to Detective Sanders. In his hand he was carrying something in a large bag.

"We found this in the ditch about a half mile up the road."

He held the bag out to Detective Sanders. Sanders took it, looked at the investigator, and then lowered his eyes as he opened the top of the bag. He raised his eyes and said, "No doubt about it, That is the coat they said she was wearing." He handed it back.

CSI Dominick Harris had worked on several cases where the victim had been murdered, and he knew what to look for. He went up to Detective Sanders, verifying what Sanders had thought all along.

"She was re-dressed like Wanda Walkowicz. This probably means the killer either left the coat at the scene of the crime before dumping the body elsewhere, or he noticed it still in his vehicle after disposing of the body, and tossed it out the window as he drove away, the same way it appeared Carmen's had been discarded."

In that one sentence he had connected all three cases: Carmen Colón, Wanda Walkowicz and now Michelle Maenza. Dominick did not have to tell the detective that he had worked on the other two cases, Sanders knew that, and That is why he trusted his opinion on the similarities.

With the CSI working diligently around the area, Detective Sanders put his time to good use. He went to his car and headed up the road. He could see a house there, and if he could see it, maybe the resident could have seen something that would help the investigation.

He climbed out of his car and went up to the front door. He shook his shoulders, relieving the tension that had built up, and then reached out and rang the bell. He was careful to step back from the door. Almost instantly a woman opened the door, a good sign, Sanders thought.

"What's going on?" she asked.

Though she had not asked, Detective Sanders took out his badge and displayed it before speaking.

"Ma'am, we wonder if you saw or heard anything unusual last night?"

The woman hesitated a minute, as if trying to decide what to say before she spoke. "Well," she said, "My dogs woke me up around one o'clock in the morning. That was Monday morning, I think." She paused. "Yes, last night was Monday. Anyway, they were barking, and they usually are quiet, but something upset them. So, I came in here to see what had riled them up. I could not see much as it was dark, but I heard what sounded like a vehicle door slamming."

"You did not see anything?"

"No, sorry, just the sound of the door slamming."

Detective Sanders was a little disappointed but tried not to let it show as he thanked her for her help.

The houses were spaced some distance apart, so he climbed back into his car. He continued checking in at houses, asking if they had seen or heard anything that night. Another local resident had seen a slow-moving vehicle going down the road around 10:30 the evening of the 26th. The location was so remote, with few buildings, that canvassing the neighborhood was finished in a snap.

Three neighbors had potentially useful information. One reported seeing a light-colored 1966 Chevy parked on the Eddy Road shoulder facing the wrong way at 5:30 p.m.

on Monday, November 26. In that rural stretch of Eddy Road there was rarely traffic, so people were alert to anything unusual.

Then, at 5:30 p.m. there was another sighting. This time on Route 350 in Walworth. The witness said he saw a man on the side of the road, standing next to a large beige or tan vehicle. The trunk was open, and the man was holding a girl who looked like Michelle by the wrist.

He rolled down his window to see if the guy needed any help, and basically was glared at by the individual. The suspect and vehicle description matched those reported earlier.

While Detective Sanders canvassed the area, the body of Michelle Maenza was carefully lifted onto a gurney and put into the ambulance. The EMT's informed the investigators on-site that they would be taking her body to the Newark-Wayne Community Hospital in Newark, NY.

On Wednesday, November 28, at 2:55 p.m. Michelle's dad, Christopher, accompanied by her Uncle Philip, began the drive to Newark-Wayne Community Hospital where the body of Michelle had been taken. They had agreed to view the body for identification. As they started out, they headed for the expressway. They had been given written directions to the facility, and every now and then Christopher looked down to make sure he was on the right road. They drove in silence, taking the thruway to State Route 21 north in Manchester where they exited onto NY-31 east and Stebbins Rd. They knew they were close. Christopher peered over at Philip to see how he was doing, but he could not see anything beyond the side of his face as Philip stared out through the windshield. A half hour later they were pulling into the parking lot of the hospital.

The Newark-Wayne Community Hospital was a twenty-four hour. inpatient treatment program, jointly licensed by the New York State Office of Mental Health and the New York State Department of Health. It was the closest location to where the body had been found.

Once at the location, both men were hesitant, having never done this before, but if they did not do it, Caroline would have to, and she was in no shape to handle the task.

An investigator on the case met them at the front of the hospital, and along with a member of the staff, they were taken to the morgue. The actual identification of the body took less than a minute; it was Michelle Maenza. After the verification they found their way back to the car and headed toward home.

The neighborhood that had previously been cautious of the dangers around them, was now even more vigilant. Where it had seemed safe to send a child in daylight down the street to the neighborhood store to pick up a few things, this was no longer the case. More children than before were now being walked to school by their parents or were taking the bus. At home, the children were warned to play only in their own yards.

As for the police, it was not easy to keep their minds from drifting back to previous events. In their open cases there were the November 16, 1971 murder of Carmen Colón, the April 2, 1973 murder of Wanda Walkowicz and now the November 26, 1973 murder of Michelle Maenza. The thought of there being a serial child killer chilled their bones, but until they could prove it, each case had to be viewed as separate from each other. There was a lot of evidence to go through, but with no positive suspects connected to that evidence, they were still miles away from the serial killer angle.

Serial murders are a relatively rare event, estimated to comprise less than one percent of all murders committed in any given year. A serial killer is typically a person who murders three or more people, with the murders taking place over a significant period of time. While most authorities set a threshold of three murders, others see it as up to four or as few as two murders.

Although psychological gratification is the usual motive for serial killing, and most serial killings involve sexual contact with the victim, there are other motives to consider, such as attention-seeking, anger, thrill-seeking, or financial gain.

Points to consider in determining if one is dealing with a serial killer are the murders being done in similar fashion, or the victims having something in common such as their appearance, gender, or race.

Yes, there was much to consider before jumping the gun and viewing these murders as the work of a serial killer. If they were too hasty, they might overlook evidence that would point the finger at the killer in at least one, or even all the murders.

Because the murders had now crossed the county border, the Wayne County Sheriff's Office came on board as the lead agency in Michelle's murder investigation. Their officers would be working alongside the Rochester Police Department, the NYS Police Department, and Monroe and Wayne County Sheriff's offices.

Chapter 41

On Friday, November 30, Michelle Maenza was laid to rest. The days leading up to the funeral were heart-wrenching for her family as they prepared the service to say goodbye to Michelle. Caroline and Christopher picked out a little brown casket for their daughter's final resting place, the last purchase they had ever thought they would be making for their eleven-year-old daughter, Michelle. They then met with Msgr. John E. Maney of the Corpus Christi Church to make the arrangements.

On the morning of November 30, Caroline dressed for her attendance at the Profetta-Nanna Funeral Home on North Goodman Street.

There was not much traffic that morning as the limo pulled out from in front of the Maenza residence on Webster Crescent and headed east toward Webster Avenue where it turned left. As she passed the John James Audubon School #33, Caroline lowered her eyes, trying not to cry. She kept her head down, raising it only to see the beautiful marsh area of Lucien Park. She watched as long as she could the two swans swimming lazily, before the limo turned onto Empire Blvd.

The four-mile trip took ten minutes, but to Caroline it was much too short a time to prepare for what lay ahead.

At the funeral home, Caroline would remain a permanent fixture as four hundred mourners paid their respects for ten hours each day and two hours during the evening. When the clock ticked the final minute, Caroline was gratefully exhausted and ready to go home for a good night's sleep before the mass to be held the next day.

Being from a family of good Catholics, Caroline had attended many events at Corpus Christi Church and knew it would be another long day. Yet, though she tried, she could not get to sleep. On Saturday morning, December 1st, Caroline prepared herself for the 9:00 morning mass, which would be her final goodbye to her daughter.

The limo driver waited patiently for his passengers to embark and then headed east on Webster Crescent toward Webster Avenue. They were soon on their way to Corpus Christi Church at 34 Teresa Street, a short one mile from Michelle's home.

It was too short a time for Caroline to prepare herself. By the time they pulled into the church parking lot she was already feeling overwhelmed. It was all too much to handle. Recognizing she was struggling and feeling very tense when they arrived at Corpus Christi Church, Caroline was given a moment, and then was supported as she climbed out of the limo. She was overtaken with wrenching sobs, forcing her knees to buckle, as two men assisted her to the pew at the front of the church.

Caroline was in a daze as the Introductory Rite began, followed by the procession of the priest, sprinkling holy water, the coffin and close to sixty mourners.

Caroline and Christopher had met with Msgr. Maney to select the songs and Bible readings, but now she could not recall what they were.

Caroline mechanically stood with those around her for the songs and prayers. She sat during the readings from the Bible. When it was time for Holy Communion, she let herself be guided to the front, her eyes fixated on the small coffin the whole time, until she was guided back to her seat for more prayers. She did not even try to control her tears as she watched the coffin being taken back down the aisle and out of the church.

She could see her sweet daughter in the black dress and white top she had chosen for her. Every feature of Michelle ran through her mind as if she were trying to preserve her image.

So often she had consoled a friend as they had attended the funeral of a loved one. Now she was the one being consoled, as she sat grieving at the end of the mass. No one rushed her. They waited patiently until she was ready, and then they assisted her as she walked down the aisle and out of the church.

Michelle's father, Christopher, was last to leave the church. He sat, staring off into space, until he was touched on the shoulder.

"Come on, Man, It is time to go to the cemetery."

Christopher looked up, his voice choked as he said, "She was a sweet little girl."

On the drive from Corpus Christi Church to Holy Sepulchre Cemetery at 2461 Lake Ave, Rochester, Caroline, and Christopher could not hold themselves together. The five-mile drive to the final resting place of their daughter was pure agony. The limo left Teresa Street and turned left onto Coleman to begin the thirteen-minute trip to the entrance of the cemetery.

Slowly they proceeded to the gravesite, where the other mourners were patiently waiting. It was thirty-three degrees outside with a slight wind, but no snow or rain. Caroline shivered, pulling her coat closer around her body as she sat down.

Christopher did his best to remain strong and help Caroline through the Rite of Committal, prayers said at the graveside marking the end of life on earth for their daughter, Michelle.

Not one, but many of the mourners had noticed a strange man in a car parked in front of the church. He seemed to be observing the mourners as they entered and later exited the church.

"So, what do you think?" Jack asked.

"I do not know. It looks suspicious. Listen, I am going to give the cops a call as soon as I get home."

"Me too."

As soon as the call came, an officer was sent to Corpus Christi Church, but the man had left before they arrived.

Later, back at the station, Officer Clancy Thomas of the Rochester Police Department reported his findings after checking up on the reported 'stranger.' "I think it was the police officer assigned to attend the funeral that they saw. He was out of uniform, so he could observe anyone watching or appearing odd or out of place at the funeral. I am sure he was trying his best to observe without being conspicuous about it."

And so, Michelle Maenza was laid to rest in Section So 27, Lot 14, Grave 23.; Carmen Colón was laid to rest in Section So 27, Lot 9, Grave 58.; and Wanda Walkowicz was laid to rest in So 21, Lot 29, Grave 42. Three little girls who never had a chance to grow up and experience life, now rested in Holy Sepulchre Cemetery.

There is no sense to be made of the tragedy. All our usual "sense-making" beliefs and notions fail. All we know is that our assumptions are shattered, especially the ones that affirm children should outlive their parents.

While for most, this was the end, for the police, it was just the beginning.

Chapter 42

Every action was taken to solve the murders. Because Monroe County Medical Examiner, Jonathan Walker, had conducted the post-mortem procedures on Carmen Colón and Wanda Walkowicz, he had been asked to attend the autopsy of Michelle Maenza. The purpose was to have him look for possible similarities between the cases that his familiarity with all of them could earmark. Crime Scene Photographer, Theo Jones, took photographs to document the autopsy.

While the autopsy was being performed, Detective Sanders sat at his desk looking over the information in each of the three files.

Carmen Colón lived at 746 Brown Street with her grandparents. She had gone to JAX Drugstore at 898 West Main Street to pick up a prescription for her baby sister at around 4:20 pm on November 16th, 1971. She was ten years old. She had been seen running east of the rest stop on 490W, east of the Chili exit (about a mile east of Riga) around 5:30 pm the same day. Her partially clothed body was found around 4:30 pm on November 18th, 1971, in a ditch on Stearns Road in Riga near Chili. She had been wearing a red coat which was found on November 18th, 1971, around 11:40 pm slightly north and west from where her body had been found. Her pants and underwear were found days later just north of 490 at the Chili exit. Carmen Colón had been sexually assaulted and manually strangled from the front.

The detective paused a moment before turning to the next folder. Wanda Walkowicz lived at 132 1/2 Avenue D and was last seen alive at the Hillside Delicatessen at 213 Conkey Avenue at 5:30 pm April 2nd, 1973, where she bought groceries for her mother. The groceries were never found. Her body was found at the Bay Bridge Rest Area off Route 104 in Webster at 10:15 am on April 3rd, 1973. Wanda Walkowicz had been raped and strangled. She was eleven years old when she disappeared just blocks from her home. Her body was fully clothed and lying face down in the grass. She was wearing a multi-colored coat with a pattern on it, a blue and white checkered dress, and green shorts. Among the evidence collected they had a semen sample and a pubic hair.

He leaned back in his chair to stretch before opening the final folder. Michelle Maenza lived at 25 Webster Crescent and was last seen in a car on Webster Avenue & Ackerman Street, at 3:30 pm on November 26th, 1973. She was 11 years old. She was seen at Carrol's Restaurant in Panorama Plaza in Penfield at 4:30 pm on November 26th, 1973. She was also seen on Route 350 in Walworth less than a mile north of where her body was found on Eddy Road in Macedon, 70 yards east of Mill Road at 10:30 am on November 28th, 1973. Her coat was found on Eddy Road in Macedon – about a half mile West of where her body was found on Eddy Road at 1 pm on November 28th, 1973 Detectives also recovered key evidence of semen from Michelle's body and her underwear.

Now looking over what he had noted, he added that it was seventeen months after the abduction of Carmen Colón in April 1973, that Wanda Walkowicz had been taken, and six months after that when someone had grabbed Michelle Maenza.

He picked up his coffee and the folders, along with his notes and headed for the task force meeting. He, like others on the inside, felt sure that the same person had committed each murder, but there was still a lot to go over before reaching that determination.

In the meeting, Rochester Police Detective, William Sanders, shared his notes and then added, "I see Michelle Maenza's case is almost a duplicate of Wanda Walkowicz's; taken late afternoon on a school day. That raises the question of whether it was just a chance selection, since it was not part of a routine for either girl."

Several officers nodded as Detective Sanders made note of this on the whiteboard.

Another officer piped in. "And we have them being picked up in an urban area and dumped in a rural area."

Still another added, "Both were raped and strangled." He flipped over a piece of paper he had in front of him. "Michelle had marks on her face, neck, and one arm. She would been beaten. It appears she had been strangled by both a belt and hands, and it was done from behind. That is just like Wanda."

"Everything is the same between these two. Both re-dressed after being raped."

"We need fingerprints. I read recently that the FBI has been doing research on methods to develop identifiable latent prints on human skin. They've been at it for some time now."

"How?"

"Well, from what I read, these researchers applied a coating of baby oil and petroleum jelly to their hands and then touched areas of skin on cadavers. They set a timer and begin at different intervals to attempt to develop these latent prints, using primarily the iodine/silver transfer method."

"What does that involve?"

"Well, it has five steps. Let me read what it says," he added, flipping through a pile of papers in front of him. "The steps are to heat iodine in an iodine fuming gun, directing the fumes onto the skin. Then you lay a thin sheet of silver on the skin.   You remove the silver plate and, finally, expose the plate to a strong light, which causes the prints to become visible."

"So, can we do it?"

"We did. We gave it a try."

"And…"

"I tried it," ME Jonathan Walker said, "and I found something on Michelle's neck. I found an impression and it was promptly photographed with a New York State Police fingerprint camera."

"So, what now?"

"We have to figure out what the print is of. My best guess was that a wrist and a small portion of palm had made the print. Although the print had some crucial detail, it was still impossible to determine if it was a right or left wrist."

He added, "Partial prints were also found on Michelle's boots and coat, but these turned out to be useless."

Now the talk went back to the autopsy finds. "Do we have anything else to add to our list?"

"Yes," replied Jonathan Walker. "We found the remains of a cheeseburger in Michelle's stomach. The food was largely undigested, which means she would eaten the burger approximately an hour and a half before she died. It was definitely not lunch."

"One more thing," the ME added, "Semen was recovered during the Michelle Maenza autopsy. So, we now have three semen samples since we found semen on each victim."

Jonathan could see the interest peak in the room. "And, all the samples had something in common, not a blood type, but a blood group, which means he is either A, B, AB or O.

"Great. So that means that Michelle had to have eaten the burger between the time she left school and when she was abducted. So, she must have been with her killer when she ate her final meal."

"So, this also ties the Maenza and Walkowicz cases together. Wanda was found to have eaten custard shortly before her death, a meal fed to her by her killer."

The room agreed. "What about Carmen Colón?"

The ME flipped through some pages. "The contents of Carmen Colón's stomach indicated that her final meal had been consumed at home."

This was noted, giving room for doubt that Carmen's killer was the same as the one who had killed Michelle and Wanda.

"Now wait. Think about the evidence. What we do know is that the killer probably either left the coat at the scene of the crime before dumping the body elsewhere, or he noticed it still in his vehicle after disposing of Michelle's body. In either case, we can assume he tossed it out the window as he drove away, the same way it appeared Carmen's coat had been discarded."

That made the connection of Carmen to these two murders seem more possible.

With that done, they begin looking over the evidence called in or collected. First, they went over the eyewitnesses that were at the top of the list.

Office Patterson started. "I think the three neighbors had potentially useful information." He flipped through his notes, then continued. "Ah, there's Mr. Alfred Porter who reported seeing a light-colored 1966 Chevy parked facing the wrong way on the Eddy Road shoulder at 5:30 p.m." He paused again, found what he was looking for.

"Another, Mrs. Eleanor Langston, said that after her dogs' barking woke her up around one o'clock on Wednesday morning, November 28, she thought she heard a 'bang,' like a vehicle's door slamming."

A few seconds passed and he continued. "The third, Ms. Hope Lang, reported she saw a car driving by slowly. She said it was around 10:30, Tuesday night, November 27, the day after Michelle's abduction.

"Then there was the local man, Peter Foster. He said he saw a slow-moving vehicle going down the road around ten-thirty that evening. which could mean the killer slowed down to throw the body out of the car, or if he did not do that, dragged it a short distance off the road."

The list of witnesses grew, and each member of the task force listened, writing vigorously in their notebooks. Then it was time for the Medical Examiner's Report.

ME Jonathan Walker added that the autopsy showed that Michelle was murdered on November 26 and her body was found on November 28, exactly 36 hours later, in Macedon.

"After hearing the results of the autopsy report, I think we can say it was in fact Michelle who was spotted at the Carrol's Restaurant in Penfield," said Wayne County Sheriff's Detective, Sgt. Howard.

There was a lull in the conversation, broken by CSI Jamison who said he would like to offer his profile of the murderer.

"The killer probably leads a normal life but is sexually immature and terrified of women. He is a psychopath who fears rejection by women, and he acts on an irresistible impulse that comes over him."

ME Walker then took the floor again.

"We have three semen samples, one from each victim, and they all have something in common, but not the blood type. What they do have in common is a blood group. I would conjecture that the killer is either a secretor or a non-secretor." Seeing some puzzled expressions, he added, "A secretor is a person who secretes their blood type antigens into their body fluids, such as saliva or semen. While a non-secretor does not."

ME Walker paused, took a drink of water, and then continued. "It is easy to think of one killer out there being responsible for all three crimes, but I urge everyone to keep an open mind. It could be multiple killers. Cases like this can bring on others who want to get into the act. There may be one, or even two imitators."

"But because of the similarities that I am about to share, I think we can say for sure that Wanda and Michelle were murdered by the same person. Carmen, maybe not. Even though Carmen was found nude, this is not necessarily a difference in M.O., because we know Carmen lost her pants in the frenzied activity alongside the Western Expressway. Now for the autopsy findings."

He read on, "Carmen Colón, age 10, born February 1, 1961. Carmen was approximately 54.5" tall and weighed 70.5 lbs. She was of Puerto Rican descent and had long dark brown hair and brown eyes. Was murdered on Tuesday, November 16, 1971. Her nude body was found in the town of Riga, near the Chili border, on Thursday, November 18, 1971. A full autopsy was performed on the body. She had been raped and suffered a fracture to her skull and one of her vertebrae which took place before she had been manually strangled to death. Fingernail marks scarred her neck and much of her body. There was food in her stomach that had been digested not long before her death, food which can be assumed had been given to her by the killer and not necessarily a meal eaten at home. The autopsy also revealed traces of semen. There was also light-colored cat fur found on her clothing.

"Wanda Walkowicz, age 11, born August 4, 1961. She was 48" tall and weighed 65 lbs. She had a fair, freckled complexion, red hair, blue eyes. Was murdered on Monday, April 2, 1973. Her fully clothed body was found in the town of Webster on Tuesday, April 3, 1973. A full autopsy was performed on the body. She had been sexually assaulted, then strangled from behind with a ligature, most likely a belt. Several defensive wounds indicated Walkowicz had evidently fought her murderer. There was custard found in her stomach. In addition, her body had been re-dressed after death. The autopsy also revealed traces of semen and pubic hair upon the child's body. There were several strands of white cat fur found on her clothing."

He went on, "Michelle Maenza, age 11, born November 28, 1961. She was 57" tall and weighed 92 lbs. She had long brown hair, brown eyes, and a round face. Was murdered on November 26, 1973. Her body was found fully clothed in Wayne County in the town of Macedon. A full autopsy was performed on the body. She was raped before she was strangled from behind with a ligature, possibly a thin rope. There were bruises on her face and upper arms and shoulders revealing extensive blunt force trauma to her body. Semen was recovered. In her stomach was evidence she would eaten a hamburger. The autopsy also revealed traces of semen. Numerous strands of white cat fur were discovered upon her clothing. Leaf samples matching the foliage where her body was discovered were retrieved from within one of her clenched hands, indicating she had likely been strangled to death at or near the location where she was found."

"Does anyone wish to add more?" asked Detective Sanders.

"Yes, if I may," Wayne County Sheriff Tucker intervened. "I photographed the crime scenes and have copies of the sites if anyone wants to look at them."

"Yes," Detective Sanders replied. Let us take a look."

The photographs were passed around for the task force to review. Though most had seen write-ups or been at the site, they took their time reviewing the images. Then the detective summarized their findings with a case-by-case description.

It was the consensus that the crime scenes in general were the same. Carmen Colón's body was found on November 18, 1971 at around 4:30 p.m. in a ditch on Stearns Road in Riga, near Chili. It was a lonely stretch of road.

Wanda's body was found at the Bay Bridge Rest Area off Route 104 in Webster at 10:15 am April 3rd, 1973. The area was an open field with no trees to hide what the killer was doing, and her body was found in a ditch.

Michelle's body was found on Eddy Road in Macedon, 70 yards east of Mill Road at 10:30 a.m. on November 28, 1973. This was a lonely stretch of road with bushes and trees lining the area. Her body was also found in a ditch along the roadside.

The abduction of each girl was similar: Late afternoon on a school day, picked up in an urban, populated area and dumped in a barren rural area. Each girl was raped, then strangled by both a belt and hands.

It was a fact that there was little effort given to concealing the bodies.

There was a pause as the officers finished writing down the details.

One officer raised his hand. "I think the killer specifically selected his victims, and there is something to the fact that the first name and last name start with the same initial. But if they did not know the child, they would have to have access to public records. Someone who works in the social services department would be my guess. That is how they could know about the matching first name and last name initials."

"Yes, that would make sense. A case worker would know the names of the children in the family. That could also be the reason the child went willingly with her abductor."

Another member of the Task Force's hand went up. "I have my doubts about both those statements. If the children had been abducted from their homes it would make sense, but all three were abducted off the street. Think about that for a minute. And if the killer has a need to rape, why would he care about the initials? He would have to stop and have a conversation, asking the child her name before abducting her. It just does not make sense."

Several people in the room nodded, thinking it over. Detective Sanders agreed, "We need to stick to the facts we know. The similarities of the crimes lead us toward the belief that we have a serial killer in Rochester. In addition, and it seems to make sense that somebody was setting out to kill young girls of that age."

"Yes, and I think this guy believes he is too clever to be caught, which is why he does not bother to hide the bodies."

"Another thing to consider: Since all three girls were Catholic, people with religious backgrounds should be scrutinized.

Puzzled looks appeared on several faces.

"What I am saying is that maybe the murderer knew the girls from church and was able to get information about them that way. Just a thought."

The search and interview base was growing. Assignments were presented and officers assigned before they left the room. Now, as they trekked out to review the leads that had come in and to re-interview witnesses, they felt confident they were getting close.

On the same day that Michelle went missing, a woman, Terry Lockport, had reported seeing a young girl resembling Michelle in a parked car at a fast food restaurant in the Panorama Plaza in Penfield. And she had provided the best description of the suspect. With her input and verification from several other witnesses, they had the sketch of the man that they had used at the start, but later that sketch was prepared in a color rendition complete from the head to just below the shoulders. Even later, the sketch given to the investigators was a full body rendition.

The suspect had dark hair that he wore longish with the front falling forward, covering his forehead, and hanging down to his eyes. In the sketch, his eyes were penetrating with thick eyebrows above and bags below, as if he needed sleep. He had a strong nose and wore a thin mustache above his thin lips. He also had a beard that looked as if he had not had a chance to shave.

He wore a blue jean jacket with the collar up, a blue plaid shirt and blue jeans tucked into his mid-calf high boots.

During each interview, the sketch was shown and the man in the sketch was identified as having been seen with

Michelle at each location: the Ackerman Street-Webster Avenue area, the Carrols Drive-In, and the roadside of Route 350 in Macedon.

Chapter 43

The media coverage was frantic. When covering homicide, a reporter must approach the incident with caution, sensitivity, and tact, especially in this case, which was now viewed as a possible triple murder of three little girls.

It was difficult reporting because family and friends of the three young girls were in a fragile state. Even though similarities existed from one case to the next, covering the homicide required significant knowledge of all three cases to get the story right. Not only that, but it was important not to suggest that there might be a serial killer loose in the city. That could start a panic. They had been advised that serial killing is the rarest form of homicide, so not to jump to that conclusion.

Just like the police, the news media identified how their staff would gather information and what should be covered.

At the group meetings, the reporters were constantly reminded to keep in mind that the story was about three little girls being murdered, and not to look at it as just a crime statistic. They had to tell the story from a human perspective.

Details on the case were checked and double-checked. They called and verified records to find out from police as much as they could about the situation. If there was any doubt about the classification or connections between the cases, they needed to ask.

They also were aware that police records might not always be accurate. Misinformation is possible and common. They were told to always corroborate their information against other sources. The rule was not to rush to publish, especially in a breaking news moment, unless they had fully vetted the information.

The police had their sources, and the media added their own sources, going beyond the obvious. They contacted counselors, social workers, teachers, and guidance counselors, and did not stick just to those who had come in contact with the girls. They tactfully talked with family members and friends and made sure they had the proper names, positions, and spelling of the names of the people they interviewed. With so many members of the task force from different precincts, it was possible lines would cross, and information would be misquoted, unless they kept on top of it.

The stories would be complex since there were complicated family experiences to deal with. They were involved with challenging family situations, to say the least.

First there was Carmen Colón, whose relatives often did not speak English or, if they did, not well, so the reporters would need a translator to help them there.

Then there was Wanda Walkowicz, whose family was still reeling from her murder, just 239 days before the murder of Michelle Maenza.

They had been supplied with pictures of Carmen and Wanda and the verified facts put in the earlier news articles. Now, with Michelle Maenza, they discussed comparisons where they existed and obtained a picture of Michelle to run in the ad campaigns.

The most pertinent addition to the cases was that they now had a composite drawing of the man identified as possibly abducting Michelle Maenza. As soon as it was in their hands, they released it quickly. The police had informed them that he was a person of interest, and not to present him to the public as the murderer.

The media was dedicated to helping to solve the cases. So, to enhance public interest in the search for the killer, for each case the Times-Union and The Democrat and Chronicle offered a $2,500 reward for any information that would lead to the capture of the murderer.

But they were not the only ones wanting to help. Another $2,500 was put up by civic groups like the Northeast Kiwanis Club and the Italian American Civil Rights League.

The Rochester Telephone Company offered their support by placing a half-page ad in the morning paper asking for tips.

Then, following the previous patterns of gathering information, there were new hotlines set up. It became the consensus that it was important to keep the story alive and seeking the help of the public might help identify the murderer and obtain justice for the families.

Not only can police use the media to solve crimes, but they can also use it to help find missing, endangered, or distressed people. The media can also give law enforcement officers important clues as to where criminals or victims may be found.

Chapter 44

The newspapers and the police departments were flooded with calls, most of which were of little help. But that did not stop the investigators from following up each detail of the lead. They were kept busy answering the calls and checking them out. Even when the calls had tapered off, during daytime hours they still numbered close to seventy-five an hour.

The Rochester Police Department, the Monroe County Sheriff's Office, and the New York State Police, all worked endlessly on the three cases. Joining them was the Wayne County Sheriff's Department whom they welcomed with open arms.

It was important to keep everyone informed of the advancements as well as the setbacks in the case, and that included the Wayne County Crime Scene Photographer, Theo Jones. Theo was a particularly important part of the task force, as he had been the third person at the scene where Michelle's body was found, and he had photographed not only the crime scene, but also the entire autopsy.

Though no one had said it, the first and last name initials being the same was on the investigators' minds. "There is a connection among all three murders. The initials may be just a coincidence, but it may mean something. I think we need to investigate individuals in the school, social workers, etc.... those who would have been privy to the records of the girls."

The officer speaking could see the nods around the room, which encouraged him to continue. "The initials. The double initials in the names...Carmen Colón, Wanda Walkowicz, and Michelle Maenza. If that is significant, we need to know for sure. The media is calling it the 'Double Initial Murders' for a reason. We need to prove or disprove that fact."

This gave leverage for another officer to speak up. "Yes, but not only that. We have a signature move: He disposes of the bodies in similar, rural areas. Carmen Colón in Chili, Wanda Walkowicz in Webster and Michelle Maenza in Macedon." This was the first time the body dumps were perceived as also being part of the killer's MO.

The investigation was now in full force. Chief of Detectives, Alexander Ford, met with the Chief Deputy of Wayne County Sheriff's Department, Dennis Norton, to discuss strategy going forward. Plans were drawn designating areas to canvass, and individuals who should be interviewed again, starting from the first murder through the last.

Nothing was to be taken off the plate until it had been proven unrelated. They went over the facts, not eliminating the facts that all the families were Catholic, on welfare, and the fathers were not around. You never knew what might be significant until it had been investigated.

It was apparent that it would be difficult to distinguish between all three cases, what was a genuine connection and what was coincidence. This worried the Chief of Detectives, especially when it came to the initials which he believed to be merely a coincidence. In any case, the police were not wasting time working on theories based on letter combinations but concentrated on who would be suspects of interest because they knew the girls' names. The main facts that mattered right now were first, the time of day the murders happened, and second, that each girl was found alongside rural roads. It did not matter how they spelled their names.

"I do not think the guy is familiar with the girls," William Sanders said. "These murders are not premeditated crimes. We are dealing with someone who has a mental problem, and when he gets the sex urge, he strikes. There's no planning and no connection with the victims, which will make it harder to find him."

"So, that makes the idea we are dealing with a serial killer more a possibility. If that is the case, It is just a matter of time before he strikes again."

"That is not what I meant. I want us to focus on the evidence, piece together clues, and solve the crime.

"Okay, the evidence. What about the fact they got into the car?"

"Yes, what about it? I believe the girls got into their killer's car because they were enticed, not because they knew the person."

"You are saying maybe our killer had a cat and used it as a mechanism to get the girls in the car. Or, did he do it by offering to give them a treat?"

"Yes. These are little girls who can be easily persuaded when the right carrot is dangled in front of them. No matter if they are streetwise or not, they still can be persuaded."

It remained a crap shoot as they tried desperately to identify the killer without boxing themselves into a type or method. They followed the clues they had and went wherever they led; from family to friends and to individuals identified as sex-offenders.

They re-interviewed every suspect from the first murder victim. Sometimes the same detective covered the interview, but in most cases, a different member of the staff did it.

It was a great day when they believed they had two very viable suspects, but on further investigation, both were cleared when their alibis checked out.

Time was passing, and they were no further ahead. One investigator said, "We might get more leads if we stress to our contacts that we aren't necessarily looking for someone who stands out in a crowd. They may blend in, like the guy living next-door."

A list of school employees was compiled, in hopes that police might find someone who had had contact with all three girls. Investigators went to the last school and previous schools where the girls had been enrolled.

They worked the angle of Welfare workers who might have had contact with the families. They checked the files and identified names of caseworkers and set up appointments to study them as possible suspects, as well as to get as much detail as they could about the families, the girls, and their personal viewpoints.

While all this was happening, there were many reports coming in from individuals saying that their enemy was the killer, and others who reported their husbands or ex-husbands should be looked at as the possible killer.

The epidemic of callers and follow-ups was ongoing. Even when it came to those who called and said they would not tell what they knew until they were guaranteed the reward money, the police tried different methods to get them to talk. The stubborn ones would say they wanted to make sure they were getting a good chunk of the award. In some cases, the interviewer could squeeze the information out, but in others, they just had to hang up.

Unfortunately, no matter how odd or demanding the callers, they could not afford to completely ignore any of them.

Not all tips proved fruitless. There was the one on Friday, November 30, when the police interviewed Monica Wilson, the child who saw Michelle in the front seat of a tan two-door with a dent on its left side. Monica had reported seeing the car speeding down Ackerman Street where it went around the corner onto Webster, almost hitting another car that was turning onto Ackerman.

What made Monica's report credible was a corroborating witness. Terra Witherspoon, a driver, said she was turning left from Webster onto Ackerman and her car was almost hit by a vehicle speeding out of Ackerman into Webster--exactly as Monica had described. Terra stated that at least two other vehicles were forced to stop abruptly because of the near collision.

Mindful that getting information out to the public would reap more leads, none of this was held back. As a result, that news brought a call from a woman who began to tell the Gannett Rochester Newspapers' 'Secret Witness Line' operator that she was one of the motorists forced to stop because of the near collision at Ackerman and Webster. The operator got excited and waited patiently for the woman to finish her report, but the woman became nervous and hung up before completing her message.

When a second woman called in to report the same near collision, she gave information about the car Michelle was reportedly riding in, but became fearful that she was not speaking to someone directly involved in the investigation. She said she would make no further comments until her identification number was given. Frustrated, but having at least collected some information from the caller, the operators turned in whatever they had.

On November 30, an anonymous caller reported that a cashier in the Goodman Plaza vicinity told her she had heard and seen a man at the plaza's coin laundry offer Michelle a ride home, and that Michelle had accepted. The cashier had then said she saw the man and the girl, whom she believed to be Michelle, leave together.

At first, this sounded like a key piece of evidence, except the caller was not the witness, but a Goodman Plaza cashier was, and the caller had talked to her. When she was asked for the name of the cashier she replied, "I do not know her name, but if I saw her, I would recognize her."

"Would you come forward and talk with us?"

The plea was ignored as the caller hung up, so all they were left with was a possible sighting by an unidentified cashier.

The police had done numerous investigations at the Goodman Street Plaza that had involved all the stores on the strip, looking into the possibility that someone visiting the plaza had also been there on the day of the abduction. In reviewing their notes, they identified anyone who had seen any man with a girl in the coin laundry. In each case they had asked the individual to describe the girl if they did not know her name.

In the hopes that there might be more to report, they interviewed Alfred Porter, the witness who had come forward to tell them he'd seen a man in a light-colored car with the trunk up, parked on Route 350 at dusk. The car had been near Eddy Road and close to the spot where Michelle's body had been found. Porter did have a little more to add when he was asked.

"Did you remember the make of the car or the license plate number?"

"Yes. I saw the same beige vehicle I had stopped to help, but this time I was able to get a full license number.

"I do remember the chubby young girl. The man grabbed her and pushed her behind his back when he saw me."

"How close did you get to him?"

"Three or four feet in front of him."

"Remember what he was wearing?"

"Jeans, light blue jacket."

"What type of jacket?"

"Snowmobile or skiing jacket. It zipped up the front, was quilted and came down to his hips. It was open, and I could see he had on a plaid shirt. There was one collar hanging outside the jacket."

"Would you recognize him if you saw him again?"

"I think I would. I got a surprisingly good look at him. I remember the odd things about him."

"What do you mean?"

"He was dirty, disheveled and unshaven. Oh yes, he had long dirty fingernails."

The officer stopped and looked through some papers. He found what he was looking for and held it up.

"Does this look like the man?"

"Yes, just like him. I saw the first sketch in the paper after I met with that sketch artist person, but now, with the color and full body, I can say it is a good match of what I saw."

This was a promising lead. Sheriff Tucker wasted no time in tracing the license plate number given him by Alfred Porter. The search met with success, and with several other officers, Sheriff Tucker drove to the address they had been given, in Lyons, New York.

Careful not to excite the homeowner, they stood off to the side and rang the doorbell. The door was opened on the second ring. Sheriff Tucker could see a resemblance to the sketch, though this man was not wearing dirty clothes or appear disheveled. Nevertheless, they introduced themselves and asked if he would come with them to be questioned on an open case.

When the man asked, "What case? What is this about?" they did not answer him, just asked him to come with them. He did.

At that point they knew him to be a petty criminal with nothing more on record, but they started by questioning him about his whereabouts on the date of the murder of Michelle Maenza. The man nervously informed them he had been home with his family in Lyons, New York.

While keeping him in the interview room, an officer was sent out to verify his statement. He was found to be telling the truth. The man was released and taken home.

At the next task force meeting, they went over everything they had learned to add to the investigation. It had been pointed out earlier that, in the list of similarities between the crimes, the fact that the girls were killed on the day of their abduction and not held for any length of time needed to be explored further.

It was CSI Harris and CSI Patterson who presented an overview to help in the investigation.

"Let me begin by telling you that I think we are looking for a serial killer. Any time a person murders more than three people, he can be classified as a serial killer. And yours is what we call a disorganized serial killer who is usually far more impulsive, often committing his murders with a random weapon available at the moment, and usually not attempting to hide the body. He is likely to be unemployed, a loner, or both, with very few friends. This kind of killer often turns out to have a history of mental illness, and his modus operandi or lack thereof is often marked by excessive violence, and sometimes necrophilia or sexual violence. That, and the fact that he frequently has a low IQ, make it harder to make sense of what he does."

"So, in contrast, what is an organized serial killer?"

"An organized serial killer often plans the crime methodically."

"So, what about motive?"

"I believe the motive in these cases is he is a child sexual predator who kills for sex. He hunts in an area he is familiar with, in this case, low income areas. There are noticeable similarities between each murder. Not only similarities in the murder, but with the victims as well. For instance, demographic profile, appearance, gender or race."

"Any ideas on how to find him?"

"Yes, he may have done this before or been in some type of trouble."

"So, what are we looking for? At one point we thought there may be a female involved or maybe just a female committing the murders."

Lifted eyebrows appeared as the same question ran though their minds. The girls had all been sexually assaulted.

"Female serial killers are rare compared to their male counterparts, but they do exist. As for partnerships, most likely that is not a situation to consider. I think we are dealing with one murderer and he is male."

"Should we be looking at different races?"

"The racial demographics regarding serial killers are often subject to debate, but in most known cases the majority of serial killers are white males, from a lower-to-middle-class background, usually in their late 20s to early 30s."

"So why would someone go about killing little girls? What do they gain?"

"The motives of serial killers are varied, but the one you are seeking is hedonistic. His motive is sex, and it does not matter whether the victims are dead. I think with this killer his sexual gratification depends on his need to have absolute control, dominance, and power over his victims, and the infliction of torture, pain, and ultimately death is part of the attempt to fulfill his need. Another aspect to consider is, he will usually use weapons that require close contact with the victims, such as knives or hands, which in this case was strangling."

Credence was given to the idea that they needed to proceed with the investigation, knowing they were heading up a serial murder investigation. So much evidence had been generated so far, and they were careful to review and analyze it all. Not only did they thoroughly investigate each lead, they had a standardized method of documenting and distributing information.

It was not farfetched to reconsider known serial killers such as Arthur John Shawcross, also known as the Genesee River Killer, an American serial killer who had been active in Rochester, New York. Shawcross' intelligence had been tested to be sub-normal or even 'borderline retarded.' His first known murders were in 1972 when he killed a young boy and a girl in his hometown of Watertown, New York. Then there was Kenneth Bianchi, also known as 'The Hillside Strangler,' born in Rochester, New York, on May 22, 1951, to an alcoholic, prostitute mother, who gave him up for adoption at birth. Another well-known serial killer was Joseph Naso, a New York native and former photographer who lived in Rochester in the 1970s.

The search for the man witnesses identified as having been seen with Michelle Maenza was still ongoing, when on January 1, 1974, five weeks after the death of Michelle, something happened that gave the police hope that soon they would be solving the case.

IN CONCLUSION

Chapter 45

It was January 1, 1974, just five weeks after the murder of Michelle Maenza when another incident took place.

He had done it before and was confident he would get away with it again. Unaware, the 16-year-old girl walking to work on Ashwood Drive near Lyceum Street, did not see the man following her in a car until it was too late.

He was out of the car and able to grab her before she knew it was happening.

"I have a gun," he whispered in her ear.

Frightened for her life, she did not fight him as he grabbed her left arm tightly and led her at gunpoint to a garage behind a house on Ashwood Drive.

Looking out her window at just the precise time that the incident unfolded, a neighbor saw the man grab the woman and watched as he led her behind the house. She could see the frightened look on the girl's face. She immediately called the police.

"I just saw a man grab a girl off the street and take her to a garage behind a house on Ashwood Drive." She then gave them her address

Sgt. Paul Finch was daydreaming, thinking this had been the merriest of all Christmases. He could just see his girls in their pretty red flannel nightclothes in the living room where the magnificent Christmas tree stood over all the new toys and new clothes underneath. He remembered the laughter as their brother teased them, and then the sound of ripping open all the packages. Later, only after they had played with every new toy and tried on every new piece of clothing, would they finally grab their Christmas stockings and pour out their contents: oranges, apples, candy, chewing gum, and boxes of cookies.

He was just about to think about the Christmas feast when the call came, announcing a possible abduction in progress on Ashwood Drive. He quickly pulled himself together and checked the area where he was stationed. He was parked close to Ashwood Drive, so he called in to announce he was going to the scene. "Send backup," he added before climbing out of his patrol car and heading toward Ashwood.

Inside the garage, the man had wasted no time. He pulled the girl further inside. It had been careless to grab her in broad daylight, but he knew people in the area tended to keep to themselves and not mind any business that did not concern them. Nevertheless, he did not expect he had much time, so he gruffly whispered, "Take your clothes off. NOW!"

She was frightened, her hands shaking as she slowly started to unbutton her shirt. "Hurry up, or I'll kill you."

He knew that would work. It always did. He could see the girl was moving quicker now, all modest and shy, which made it even better for him. He grinned, feeling superior as he took in the girl's appearance. 'Not bad,' he was thinking, when the door to the garage swung open. Standing in the doorway was a police officer, gun drawn and aimed at him. "Drop the gun, drop the gun."

The man had only seconds to decide. He sprang into action, bolting out of the garage before Sgt. Finch knew what he was doing.

"Was he alone?" He asked the trembling girl.

"Yes."

"Okay, you stay here. Another officer is on his way."

Without waiting, he began running after the assailant. Another storm had blown in and dropped a layer of snow on the ground which, if he lost sight of his quarry, would make it easy to follow his footsteps, but he could see him as the assailant rushed ahead through the adjoining backyards.

The abductor knew it was useless. He looked over his shoulder and saw the police officer gaining on him. Again, he thought quickly, and as he approached a parked car, outside 304 Fieldwood Drive, he tried the door. Luckily for him it was unlocked, and he climbed in.

Sgt. Finch was now right on his heels. The detective slowed down, and at a snail's pace cautiously approached the car. Ice sheeting on the windows prevented full visibility as he squinted, trying to see inside. When he could make out what was happening, he drew back. The man had his gun drawn.

Sgt. Finch took a few steps away from the car door and broadcast on his portable radio, "I have the suspect in sight outside 304 Fieldwood Drive. He is in a parked car, and has his gun drawn. I need backup right away."

While he waited, he tried to get the plate number, even though he was quite sure this was not the assailant's car. He could make out the first three numbers and wrote them down, reciting them as he did so, "nine-seven-two." The rest of the plate was covered with snow. He thought about moving in closer to brush the snow off, but just as he was about to make his approach, he heard the very, very sharp, and loud sound of gunfire coming from the car.

Immediately he stopped moving and raised his own firearm in anticipation. Sgt. Finch was trying to see through the side window of the car, but just as he started to move forward again, his backup arrived, touched his shoulder and together they moved forward with guns drawn.

There was no reaction coming from the car so keeping only their sides towards the car, they leaned in. Sgt. Finch felt the weight of his pistol as he took in the scene inside the car. He turned to his partner, allowing him to get a good view, and together they replaced their guns in their holsters.

Inside the car blood splattered the driver's side window, but the two police officers were still cautious as they forced open the door. It was then that they had a clear vision of the suspect slumped over the wheel of the car, with a gunshot wound in his right temple. On the seat beside him was a .45 automatic colt pistol.

When his backup moved, Sgt. Finch took in the scene. He saw the .45 pistol and the hole in the man's right temple. Temple shots are one of the deadliest places to get hit. A .45 acp is one of the worst handgun rounds to be hit in the head with, but he was cautious still, knowing it was possible, though unlikely, the man was alive. These are big heavy bullets that carry a great deal of kinetic energy and are not likely to be deflected at all. So, if the bullet had gone in one temple and out the other, in all probability the man was dead. Even if he were still breathing, he certainly could no longer function.

Finch went to the opposite side of the car. The window was impossible to see through, so cautiously he opened the door. He wanted to see the trajectory the bullet had taken. The most likely scenario for survival is if the bullet was angled in some way and exited quickly, for example, out the forehead. This path would destroy fewer vital areas. But there was no exit wound on the man's forehead.

Studying the man, Finch could make out that the bullet angled from his temple to the back of his skull. He was sure the man was quite dead.

Sgt. Finch made the call for an ambulance, while his partner taped off the crime scene area so that it was secure. Soon the CSI unit arrived and began documenting what had taken place, and, as soon as they were done, they released the officers.

Sgt. Finch made sure to point out that the assailant probably did not own the car. He also gave the details of the call, where the incident started, and the path they had taken from that location to where they were now. He gave them the address of the caller, and the address where he had seen someone looking out the window earlier. When he was sure they had noted all the details that he had, he left the scene, giving his name and badge number to be contacted when they knew the name of the assailant.

The CSI team assigned men to scour the area for evidence, while other investigators interviewed the caller and the 16-year-old girl.

The Monroe County Medical Examiner ruled the death was a suicide and that released the body. In the meantime, details coming in spiked Detective Alex Ford's interest.

Soon they had a name. The dead man was Dennis Termini, and he had served as a volunteer firefighter.

Detective Ford dug deeper into the story. What he learned was that years earlier Termini had raped another teenager in a garage. While both victims were older than the three girls whose murders they were trying to solve, the more he searched, the more he felt that Termini looked like a prime suspect. Not only did his car match the description of cars seen during the abductions, he had a map in his car folded in a way that highlighted Wayne County.

In the profile that had been developed on the cases, it had been assumed that only an authority figure could have lured the girls into the vehicles without a fight. Termini had kept his firefighter uniform in the car.

Detective Ford was excited now as he pored through the life of Dennis Termini. Alex put in a call to New York State Police Investigator, Winston James.

"Hey, Will, what do you know about Dennis Termini?"

"Hold on. I pulled his file when we heard that the man who shot himself when your guys were trying to apprehend him was Dennis. He is not a good guy."

They had indeed done their homework, and soon Alex learned that Dennis Termini was a 25-year-old Rochester firefighter. Their investigation had been ongoing, but they were sure he was the man responsible for no less than fourteen rapes of teenage girls and young women. The man was a serial killer. He was labeled the 'Garage Rapist,' since he would take his chosen victim to a garage to rape her.

"Stop, stop. I think he must be our man. Can you send me a copy of the file?"

"Sure."

The next day Alex had the Termini file in his hands. This man was being looked at for murders committed between 1971 and 1973, the same span as the murder of the three girls. The more he read, the more excited he became. Termini was known to have owned a beige vehicle like the vehicle observed by several eyewitnesses to the abductions.

He lived at 139 Bock Street, which was close to the area where Michelle Maenza had last been seen alive.

Alex stretched and then bent over the file once again. Termini had been identified as having attempted to abduct another teenage girl at gunpoint but had fled the scene when the teenager refused to stop screaming.

Alex left his office and looked around the room until he saw the man he was seeking. "Detective Barnes, can you come in here?"

Peter Barnes got up from his desk and gingerly walked towards his boss's office.

"What is it?"

"Follow me." Alex went back to his office and ripped off a piece of paper. He wrote the name, address, and phone number of the teenage girl down for the other man. Peter followed him, took the proffered paper, and looked at it. Then he looked questioningly at his boss.

"I want you to contact this girl and see if you can bring her in for an interview, but first, show her the drawing of the suspect we have in our file in the case of the three girls."

"You got it, Boss."

"And, Peter, call me immediately if she identifies the guy in the drawing as the one who tried to rape her."

Five weeks had passed since the death of Michelle Maenza on November 26, 1973, and the team felt confident they had found the murderer. A subsequent forensic examination of Termini's vehicle did reveal traces of white cat fur on the upholstery, making him the prime suspect in the case.

Unfortunately, doubt would soon seep in. The teenage girl who had escaped was shown the sketch made by Amanda as she interviewed the witness Theresa Lockport. It was the only description they had of the suspect in the murders of Carmen Colón, Wanda Walkowicz and Michelle Maenza. She studied it and then told them this was not the guy who had tried to rape her. That was disappointing.

They had a picture of Dennis Termini and decided to show that to witnesses to see if anyone would identify him as the murderer of the three girls. No one could identify him. Alex had hoped, since Dennis Termini had wielded a gun during the attempted rape of the teenage girl who got away, maybe he was not the rapist known as the 'Garage Rapist,' since that rapist was known to use a knife. That had given him hope that he could be their guy.

While both victims were older than the girls in their case, he could not let the idea go, and he put Termini at the top of the suspect list.

In the record of the investigators who had gone to interview the Rochester city schools, it had been noted that all children in fourth through sixth grade were required to watch a movie called Stranger Beware. Michelle had watched it. She knew not to willingly get in a car or walk off with a stranger. Would Michelle and the other girls have ignored the advice? The investigators were re-thinking everything now that every suspect had proved to have iron-clad alibis.

Dennis Termini made sense as a suspect for the November 1971, murder of Carmen Colón, ten, the April 1973, murder of Wanda Walkowicz, eleven, and the November 1973, killing of Michelle Maenza, eleven.

It had been conjectured that the three girls might have been lured into a car by an authority figure who had convinced them he was safe. Termini, as a firefighter, fit the bill.

But they had to move on. Exhausted, but refusing to give up, the task force questioned more than 800 suspects.

Chapter *46*

Four police agencies — State Police, Monroe County Sheriff's Office, Wayne County Sheriff's Office, and Rochester Police — worked closely, chasing down every lead. The team of investigators met frequently, comparing notes, and dredging up new information and suspects to pursue.

There were many similarities between the murders and the girls themselves. The three young girls had first names and surnames starting with the same letter, and all three were less than a year apart in age. They were each from practicing Catholic families, and in school they struggled to keep up with their classmates. Finally, the girls all came from homes where they lived with one parent.

What was puzzling was that the three girls were running errands for their parents when they were abducted. This meant they were not at their homes, so the abductor would not immediately know who they were. That made moot the idea of him picking them out because of their first and last names.

Another idea of how they may have been lured into the car might be that he called them by a name, any name he could think of now. A child of that age might stop and experience at least a moment of uncertainty, and instinctively correct him.

The circumstances of the deaths of Wanda Walkowicz, in April 1973 and Carmen Colón, in November 1971, were almost identical to those of Michelle Maenza. But although they saw them as being the work of one suspect, the police continued to investigate them as separate incidents.

In the 1970s, the FBI's Behavioral Sciences Unit developed the practice of profiling. The infamous Ted Bundy had been one of the first serial killers to be profiled. They began by taking information gleaned from past serial murders and using that to recreate characteristics to identify the individual. That, along with the crime-scene information and witness statements, helped to paint a picture of the criminal.

In the case of Carmen, Wanda, and Michelle, they were three Caucasians, which generally meant that the killer would be Caucasian too. The crime scenes in all three cases were not the result of careful planning, so the killer was not intelligent and was probably young. The girls were strangled in part by hands which meant that he was probably disorganized and acted quickly.

Profiles are not one hundred percent accurate, but they are usually found to be very close.

The task force did not relent, never surrendering to the knowledge that there are times when, no matter how long the investigation lasts or how hard the investigators work, a suspect cannot be found. That there are cases where there is a lack of evidence for the police either to find a suspect or to make an arrest. For the investigators, solving this case had become a mission. But even with all their dedication to solving the cases, these three went cold.

The Alphabet Murders (also known as the Double Initial Murders) became the catchphrase for the cold case. No stone was left unturned in the search for who had murdered the three little girls whose surnames began with the same letter as their first names. A hotline continued for tips in the case and hundreds of calls were fielded. But sadly, no arrests were ever made.

When next the investigators met, they were taking what they knew and working backwards, then forwards. What may have been on everyone's minds was now a focus of the investigation. They needed to identify the serial killer.

First, they analyzed how the killer picked these three girls. As they brainstormed the situation they came up with a new set of similarities in the cases. There was the availability of each of the three girls because of their lifestyles. Then there was the fact they were vulnerable at the time of their abduction. Finally, the killer desired young females. This gave them a platform to go from.

So now the question was, how does one spot a person who murders three or more strangers and does it after a significant period has passed?

The answer might be to establish a pattern in the time period. One that came to mind was the choice of April and November for the murders. Weak, but at least this was something.

Slowly they developed a mental sketch of a person who could commit such cold-blooded murders repeatedly.

Was the killer a power junkie like Ian Brady, known as the 'Moors Murderer', who, with his accomplice Myra Hindley, killed five children between 1963 and 1965? At one point they had thought there might be a woman involved in the murders. The girls were strangled. Strangling is an act of power over the victim.

Just as easily, the killer might be just a clever manipulator. He saw his victims in a position where he could effectively press the right buttons to encourage them to come with him. This led the investigators toward thinking the killer could be in some type of role that the girls respected. Of course, at the age of the victims, that could have meant a firefighter or a teacher.

The team studied what was known about serial killers, and taking that information, they applied it to the cases. Then they began interviewing. The confusion and counter productiveness created by changing the structure of a task force mid-investigation was not lost on them, but they had established a new game plan.

In the case of Carmen Colón, there were two prime suspects. They were Miguel Colón and James Barber. Both were in the Bull's Head neighborhood at the time of Carmen's abduction and both ultimately demonstrated a violent nature. They both had fled the area immediately following Carmen's death. But if the investigation were now focused on a possible serial killer, could these men be considered for the other murders?

The more they learned, the more it became a possibility that the Carmen Colón case might be an isolated one, and not connected to those of Michelle Maenza and Wanda Walkowicz.

The records showed that police also had an interest in an individual by the name of James Barber, a known sex-offender. They had questioned him in the Carmen Colón murder, but nothing had come of this lead. Soon thereafter he left Rochester and was gone before the Wanda Walkowicz murder took place.

Following the normal investigative pattern, relatives were considered suspects. Carmen's uncle, Miguel Colón, who lived with her mother after Carmen's biological father, Justiniano, left, had been high on the suspect list. Miguel Colón was unable to provide a credible alibi for the date of his niece's murder, and no one could vouch for his whereabouts. But the police had only circumstantial evidence, but no physical evidence. There was nothing found at the crime scene, nor, when they searched his vehicle, did they find anything connecting him to the murder.

Though some on the task force thought that Carmen's killer might be someone different from the killer of the other two girls, no one doubted that, in Wanda's and Michelle's cases, they were looking for the same killer.

They turned to their identified and most promising suspect, Dennis Termini. He lived near where Michelle Maenza was last seen. As they dug deeper, they found evidence that supported Termini being the killer in the other cases. Termini had stalked the neighborhoods where Carmen Colón, Wanda Walkowicz, and Michelle Maenza lived. His history showed that he stalked his victims on foot and by car and had abducted several girls whom he had driven to secluded locations and raped. On the other side of the coin, the girls that Termini raped were older than these three, and after he had raped them, he had left them alive. For a serial killer that would be a major change to the pattern

Not to be overlooked was another obvious suspect, Kenneth Bianchi. What they knew about him was that he was born to a young alcoholic prostitute in Rochester on May 22, 1951 and adopted by Frances and Nicholas Bianchi. He was raised in Rochester and attended Holy Family Catholic School. He married, but his wife walked out on him in the same year Carmen Colón was abducted and murdered.

In the 1970s, Bianchi stood behind a counter selling soft drinks and ice cream at a soda fountain in Rochester. During the investigation into the murders, they found out that all three victims had eaten, and that they had been fed by their killer. In at least two of the cases the food appeared to be from a fast-food facility. Further investigation into Bianchi uncovered the fact that he also worked as an ambulance driver, supporting the theory that the girls went with an individual who looked official. He might have been wearing his uniform. Bianchi had no criminal record, but he owned a two-tone Cadillac that was dark on the bottom and white on top, the same color and type of car as the one witnesses had glimpsed on the expressway during Carmen's attempted escape from her killer.

The investigation continued, uncovering another possible suspect, Joseph Naso, a New York native who lived in Rochester during the early 1970s. Naso was born in Rochester, and people who knew him thought he was a suspicious character. This lead was not substantiated by any evidence, but they kept his name in the active file.

By now the files were thick with evidence and suspects. Investigators look at the MO, or modus operandi, of the crime. The MO reflects what the killer had to do to commit the crime. This includes everything from luring and restraining his victim to the way that he murders her. The problem was, as time went on, the serial killer's MO could change as he learns from past mistakes.

The other problem was, if they were dealing with a serial killer, he would keep killing until he was caught, he died, he killed himself or he just burned out. So, if they wanted to solve the cases, they needed to catch him as soon as possible. But how could they figure this out? And how are serial killers caught?

Chapter 47

The slayings, which took place between 1971 and 1973, were dubbed the "double initial" killings and the "alphabet killings" because each child had matching initials. They shattered any sense of safety for the residents of the neighborhood and several areas around it.

The three victims — Carmen Colón, 10, Wanda Walkowicz, 11, and Michelle Maenza, 11 — were abducted during the day, sexually assaulted, strangled, and dumped outside the city of Rochester, expanding the area of tension. Carmen was found in the Chili/Riga area, Wanda was dumped in Webster and Michelle was in Macedon, a town in Wayne County.

Rochester residents had every reason to fear for the safety of their families. How can three little girls vanish in broad daylight without anybody seeing a thing?

Once the profile was completed, investigators looked at the existing list of suspects to determine which one was most likely to have committed the crime. They then determined how best to capture him.

But not all serial killers are caught. With the case going cold, if the culprit were in fact a serial killer he might be arrested or picked up for another crime, and evidence might be found that could lead investigators to the murders. That scenario was something to hope for.

Some murders stick in our minds. Some lives are extinguished in such strange and horrifying ways that they haunt us for years. They become those famous murders that dominate headlines and airwaves around the world and haunt our dreams. The well-documented murders of Carmen Colón, Wanda Walkowicz and Michelle Maenza comprised one of those cases.

www.ingramcontent.com/pod-product-compliance
Lightning Source LLC
Chambersburg PA
CBHW022329280326
41934CB00006B/583